GUIDE TO PASSING THE
PSI
REAL ESTATE EXAM

3RD EDITION

LAWRENCE SAGER

Real Estate Education Company®
a division of Dearborn Financial Publishing, Inc.

This publication is designed to provide accurate and authoritative information in regard to the subject matter covered. It is sold with the understanding that the publisher is not engaged in rendering legal, accounting or other professional service. If legal advice or other expert assistance is required, the services of a competent professional person should be sought.

Publisher: Carol Luitjens
Acquisitions and Development Editor: Diana Faulhaber
Managing Editor: Ronald J. Liszkowski

Published by Real Estate Education Company,®/Chicago,
a division of Dearborn Financial Publishing, Inc.®
155 North Wacker Drive
Chicago, Illinois 60606-1719
(312) 836-4400
http://www.real-estate-ed.com

Printed in the United States of America

98   99   10   9   8   7   6   5   4   3

Library of Congress Cataloging-in-Publication Data

Sager, Lawrence.
    Guide to passing the PSI real estate exam / Lawrence Sager.—3rd
ed.
       p. cm.
    ISBN 0-7931-2253-8
    1. Real estate business—United States—States—Examinations,
questions, etc. I. Title.
HD1381.5.U5S24 1997   96-45449
333.33′0973—dc21   CIP

CONTENTS

PREFACE

The growing complexity of the real estate business has been accompanied by an increased emphasis on real estate education. Evidence for this emphasis is the trend toward state requirements for both prelicense and continuing education. Accordingly, many states currently employ professional testing organizations to aid them in the development and administration of licensing examinations. One of these organizations is PSI Real Estate Licensing Examination Services, Glendale, California, which has developed widely used licensing exams for real estate professionals.

The focus of this study guide is preparation for PSI's licensing examinations. Of the existing books devoted to preparing for real estate licensing exams, this is the first study guide geared specifically to the PSI examination. The PSI exam is distinctive and challenging. As such, it warrants the specialized focus of *Guide to Passing the PSI Real Estate Exam*.

This book is intended to guide prospective licensees in their preparation for the exam. It is intended to *direct* effort. The study aids presented will help the student make the best use of his or her preparation time. It is hoped that this study guide will enable the prospective salesperson or broker to achieve success not only on the licensing exam but ultimately in the dynamic field of real estate.

My thanks to all those who participated in the preparation of this text. I am especially grateful for the comments and advice of the reviewers: Leona Busby, Paul F. Wilkinson, CRS, Long & Foster Institute of Real Estate, J. Michael Smith, First School of Real Estate and Maurice Boren.

My thanks also to the Real Estate Education Company staff, Carol Luitjens, Diana Faulhaber and Ron Liszkowski.

This book is dedicated to my wonderful wife, Adrienne, for all of her support and encouragement.

ABOUT THE AUTHOR

Lawrence Sager is a licensed real estate broker, certified residential appraiser and REALTOR®, holds a master's degree in urban land economics from the University of Illinois and is Real Estate Coordinator at the Madison Area Technical College. His writings have appeared in numerous publications on real estate and related fields.

Sager has acted as research consultant for Madison Area Technical College, the University of Wisconsin and other public and private organizations. He is a Certified Fair-Housing trainer and has served as president of the Community Reinvestment Alliance, in Madison, Wisconsin. He has worked with the Wisconsin Real Estate Examining Board as a course writer and as the assistant executive secretary in the certification of educational programs for real estate licensure. He is a member of the Professional Standards Committee of the Greater Madison Board of REALTORS® as well as the Appraiser Application Advisory Committee of the Wisconsin Department of Regulation and Licensing and the Advisory Committee on Continuing Assessor Education of the Wisconsin Department of Revenue. He is the author of *Guide to Passing the Real Estate Exam (ACT)*, the *Wisconsin Supplement for Modern Real Estate Practice* and the 1980 and 1983 editions of the *Wisconsin Real Estate Manual*.

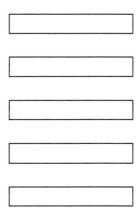

PART 1 / USE OF THE MANUAL

The aim of this manual is to prepare you on as many levels as possible to pass the real estate licensing examination compiled by the PSI Real Estate Licensing Examination Service, in Glendale, California. The *Guide* addresses two primary aspects of test taking:

1. the structure and format of the exam and

2. the content of the exam.

The organization of the *Guide* follows these two basic concerns. In addition to suggesting the most efficient use of this manual, Part 1 provides specific information about the PSI organization, testing procedures and the test itself. Part 2, "Examination Strategies," is intended to familiarize you with the *format* of the questions in the PSI exam and suggests a strategy for optimizing test scores. Several studies have shown that given two examinees of equal ability and subject knowledge, the one who is more familiar with the form and style of the test will consistently score better than the other. Accordingly, Part 2 discusses the mechanics and the strategies of a test. It explains, for example, the parts of a question and how a typical question is developed. It illustrates how to analyze a question for clues to the right answer and how to determine what skills the question is intended to measure. Particular attention is given to the types of questions used by PSI in its real estate licensing examinations.

Exam content receives the foremost emphasis in the remaining parts of the *Guide*. Part 3 presents a strategy for optimizing test results by using the diagnostic exams and formats of concepts presented in Parts 4 to 7 and 9 to 12. Part 8 is a test of real estate mathematics.

Finally, Part 13, "Salesperson Examination," and Part 14, "Broker Examination," afford an opportunity to take a sample 100-question exam to measure your knowledge and the test-taking skills you have gained. The Glossary is a handy reference list of real estate terms and definitions.

EXAMINATION INFORMATION AND BACKGROUND

PSI's Real Estate Licensing Examination is prepared by a committee of test-development specialists, outstanding educators in real estate and representatives from U.S. licensing jurisdictions. This committee has devised the national and, in some cases, the state portions of both the broker and the salesperson licensing exams.

The most important step in building the PSI examination is preparing the blueprint for the exam. Committee members define the test outline in detail: what subject matter should be covered, how many questions should be devoted to each topic, what abilities should be tested, how difficult or easy the questions should be. Using the completed test specifications as a guide, PSI item writers in the field submit a first draft of questions, which is reviewed and revised by other panels of experts for legal and factual accuracy. Their revision then is reviewed by additional panels of real estate practitioners to assess the difficulty of questions as part of an additional validation process.

Alternative forms of the salesperson and broker examinations are compiled. To protect exam security, the questions and their presentation in each section differ from one alternate test to another. Because the examinations cover the same content and are equally difficult, the system is fair to all examinees.

The salesperson exam contains from 110 to 150 multiple-choice questions. Ample time is allowed to complete the test.

The exam has two parts. The first part is a 100-question test that measures your understanding of real estate practices and principles common to all the participating jurisdictions. Discussions in Part 2 of the *Guide* provide a breakdown of the divisions of the national test and their relative importance in the exam.

The second part of each exam (30 to 50 questions) is the state test. The questions focus on real estate regulations and practices and state statutes that are unique to each jurisdiction. More information on the content of this part of the exam can be obtained from your real estate commission.

All questions on the salesperson examinations are multiple choice, with four alternatives. (Formats are discussed in detail in Part 2, "Examination Strategies.") Objective or multiple-choice questions are advantageous because they can accurately test several different levels of an applicant's knowledge in a limited amount of time and can be scored quickly.

Each correct answer counts as one point; no credit is given for wrong answers, but neither are penalties given. This means that it will benefit you to answer all the questions on the exam as best you can. The answer sheet should be free of all marks except filled-in ovals and identifying information; marking more than one answer to a question counts as a wrong answer. The example below illustrates the correct way to fill in an answer:

* How many alternatives does a PSI exam question have?

    1. Three   Sample Answer Spaces
    2. Four
    3. Five   (1) (2) (3) (4)
    4. Six

You must pass both the national section and the state section of the test. The required percentage of correct answers varies from one licensing commission to another; this information is available from your local jurisdiction. PSI policy is to send all examinees their score reports. Each of these reports indicates the examinee's scores on each of the two major sections of the exam (national and state), as well as on the various content areas in each major section. The scores represent the examinee's performance on a scale of 0–100. At present, PSI does not allow an applicant to review her or his examination.

On the day of your real estate exam, take your test center admission ticket, personal identification, several number-two pencils, an eraser and a watch to the testing center. Many jurisdictions allow examinees to use silent, battery-powered calculators although these calculators cannot have alphabetic keypads or paper tape. Slide rules also are allowed, but you should be able to work the math problems without such aids. No other paper or aids should be taken to the test site.

Standard instructions and procedures are part of the written exam booklet and probably will be read to you by a test supervisor before you begin the exam. When you get your test booklet, read the directions completely. When you receive your answer sheet from the test supervisor, be sure to enter your identifying information on it properly. Otherwise, the report of your score could be delayed or lost.

Approximately half of the states using PSI currently are having their examinees take the exam by computer. Taking the PSI examination by computer is simple; neither computer experience nor typing skills are required for taking the test, which requires you to use fewer than 12 keys. Upon being seated at the computer terminal, you will be prompted to confirm your name, identification number and the examination for which you are registered.

An introduction to the computer and keyboard will appear on the screen prior to your starting the exam. The time allowed for this introduction will not count as part of your exam time.

The introduction includes a sample screen display telling you to press one, two, three or four to select your answer or to press ? to mark for a later review. You then press "enter" to record your answer before moving on to the next question. You may change your answer as often as you like before pressing enter. Note that during the examination, the time remaining for your examination will be displayed at the top of the screen and updated as you record your answers. After you have answered every question in the examination, if you have time remaining you will be given the opportunity to review all of the questions in the examination. You also will have the choice of reviewing only those questions that you marked for review or ending your examination and seeing your results. You may change your answers during the review options. You may repeat the review options as time allows.

SALESPERSON EXAMINATION

The content order in Parts 4 through 11 of this text follows the organization of the basic areas of PSI's national salesperson test:

1. Property ownership
2. Laws of agency
3. Contracts
4. Federal laws and regulations
5. Real estate mathematics review
6. Valuation and real estate economics
7. Finance
8. Land-use controls and regulations

Parts 4 to 7 and 9 to 11 begin with a brief examination of the topic covered in each section. These pretests, called "diagnostic tests," will help you determine your particular strengths ıs indicate which section of the examination needs additional review. pecific real estate concept, terminology or application that you do not answers for each pretest are keyed to an outline of the information hat subsection. The concepts-to-understand outlines that immediately l pretests are useful as a general review. In addition, in conjunction an help you identify your problem topics quickly and accurately. The ure for using these sections is to take the pretests, then check your ıswer key provided at the end of the pretest. If your evaluation of your ıtes that you misunderstand the topic, review the outline that follows. If necessary, cᴏₙₛᵤₗₜ her texts for additional clarification. If your evaluation on the pretest indicates that you understand the concept but missed the question because of its structure, then reread Part 2, "Examination Strategies." If the math is a problem, check Part 8 for a basic real estate mathematics review.

As a final check on your knowledge, read the "Study and Review Checklist" in Part 3. When you feel sufficiently prepared, turn to the 100-question sample exam in Part 13 (for salesperson) or Part 14 (for broker). These exams closely approximate an actual PSI exam in content and format. They offer an opportunity to thoroughly test your knowledge and test-taking skills. The answer key and its explanations will help you identify your problem topics, based on the results of your diagnostic pretests and the sample exam. Consider consulting real estate principles and practice texts if you missed a significant number of questions that relate to a specific topic.

PSI Test Specifications for Salespeople

In the national portion of the real estate licensing examination for salespersons, PSI has defined its testing priorities as follows:

- **Property Ownership** composes 12 percent of the test, that is, 12 questions. This segment of the exam covers general topics such as classes of property, land characteristics, encumbrances, types of ownership, deeds and title insurance.

- **Laws of Agency** makes up 20 percent of the test. This category covers topics such as representation and disclosure, agent for seller, agent for buyer, subagency and dual agent.

- **Contracts** is 16 percent of the test and covers topics such as listing contracts, purchase agreements, counteroffers, amendments, cancellation agreements, leasing agreements, options, land contracts for deed and legal descriptions.

- **Federal Laws and Regulations** composes 15 percent of the test. This segment covers compliance with fair-housing regulations, truth-in-lending laws, the Real Estate Settlement Procedures Act (RESPA), selected Internal Revenue Service (IRS) regulations and antitrust laws.

- **Real Estate Mathematics** makes up 10 percent of the test. This category tests the ability to calculate land and building areas, real estate commissions and mortgage payments, and your understanding of and ability to work with percentages.

- **Valuation and Real Estate Economics** is 10 percent of the test. This segment covers the methods used to estimate value as well as how economic and financial conditions affect real estate values.

- **Finance** makes up 10 percent of the test and covers a knowledge of financing alternatives and practices of financial institutions.

- **Land-Use Controls and Regulations** is 7 percent of the test. This segment covers the kinds of restrictions that can be put on property use, including public restrictions such as zoning ordinances and building and housing codes and private restrictions such as those identified in deed restrictions.

BROKER EXAMINATION

The broker exam comprises 125 to 150 questions (100 in the national test and, usually, 25 to 50 in the state test) and lasts up to five hours. In the *Guide*, Part 14, "Broker Examination," contains a discussion of the broker exam and a 100-question sample exam. The answer key that follows includes discussions of the answers and references to the outline sections that cover the topics.

The "Study and Review Checklist" in Part 3, the diagnostic tests and concepts-to-understand outlines in Parts 4 to 7 and 9 to 12, the math review in Part 8 and the sample exams in Parts 13 and 14 should be of considerable study value to the prospective broker in preparing for the exam.

PSI Test Specifications for Brokers

In the national portion of the real estate licensing examination for brokers, PSI includes the same categories covered in the salesperson exam. The difference between the two national tests is the proportion of questions in each category. The distribution in the broker exam is as follows:

- **Property Ownership** (10 percent or 10 questions)

- **Laws of Agency** (18 percent or 18 questions)

- **Contracts** (14 percent or 14 questions)

- **Federal Laws and Regulations** (13 percent or 13 questions)

- **Real Estate Mathematics** (9 percent or 9 questions)

- **Valuation and Real Estate Economics** (9 percent or 9 questions)

- **Finance** (10 percent or 10 questions)

- **Land-Use Controls and Regulations** (7 percent or 7 questions)

- **Brokerage Management** (10 percent, or 10 questions). This is covered only on the broker exam. This section covers types of ownership, sales associate relationships, risk management and trust accounts.

The state supplement exam for brokers contains approximately 25 to 50 questions and is based on a state's statutes, rules and contractual forms. Some of the states develop their own broker exams, in cooperation with PSI.

PART 2 / EXAMINATION STRATEGIES

The PSI real estate examinations are achievement tests that candidates must pass before they can work as salespeople or brokers in their states. An achievement test measures an individual's proficiency in a given field. The ultimate objective of the license exam is to maintain the standards of the industry and to protect the public from persons not qualified to practice real estate sales and brokerage. The exam, therefore, tests

- the knowledge applicants have gathered through license-preparation courses and individual study and

- the ability of the applicants to use that knowledge in real estate applications.

GUIDELINES FOR PREPARING FOR THE EXAM

Mental and Physical Preparation

Multiple-choice tests demand a special type of mental preparation. While memorizing definitions, terms and formulas, keep in mind that some questions also will require you to apply your knowledge to novel situations. Concentrate on real estate principles as you study, and try to *apply the principles and facts to real-life situations*.

An excellent method of preparing for an exam is to take similar tests prior to the actual exam. You can gain important percentage points simply by being an experienced test taker. The more similar to the actual exam the practice test is in content and format, the more you will benefit. This is the strategy behind the presentation of the diagnostic tests and the salesperson and broker exams in this manual. Taking the sample tests under actual test conditions (see Part 1 for details) will improve both your knowledge of the subject and your psychological readiness.

You will earn a better score if you are in top physical and mental shape the day of the test. It is a good idea to review your notes within the 48 hours before the exam. Get your normal amount of rest the night before the exam; it *is not* wise to stay up all night in a panic-stricken effort to cram. Eat normally, but do not have a heavy meal before going to the test.

Your *attitude* is at least as important as your metabolic state. You should be prepared, determined and positive. A small amount of anxiety is natural—it can even help you do your best—but too much anxiety is a handicap. Try to remain calm before and during the exam—do not worry about results at this point. Panic is irrational and self-defeating; it only will decrease your score.

Build your confidence by finding out ahead of time how to get to the test location and by arriving a few minutes early. Bring all the appropriate materials. Find a seat at the front of the room, if possible, so you can hear the instructions clearly. Identify the test supervisors in case you have a question or problem later.

Do not *anticipate* the difficulty of the exam. There are bound to be some test candidates working themselves into a panic with last-minute cramming. Do not let their behavior affect you.

Following Directions

One of the major causes of incorrect answers is carelessness. Listen attentively to the test supervisor's instructions. Try not to let your eagerness to start the test make you miss the general rules.

Remember, if you are using an answer sheet, the scorer only registers pencil marks; it cannot tell the difference between a stray mark and an intended answer. An answer will not be counted unless the pencil mark is fairly dark and in the correct place. Keep your responses within the oval, but fill the space entirely. Do not write your answers on scratch paper and then transfer them to the answer sheet all at one time. This procedure invites errors and wastes valuable test-taking time.

Read all written directions carefully, then follow them *exactly*. A sample worked-out problem usually is provided. Even if you think you are familiar with that type of problem, *never* skip the instructions. If you are using an answer sheet, place the answer sheet to the right of the exam booklet if you are right-handed, to the left if you are left-handed. When you actually begin the exam, read carefully, not quickly. Be sure that you understand each question completely before answering.

A major cause of test errors is simply failure to think. Many tests measure judgment and reasoning, as well as factual knowledge. Always try to choose the *best* answer to a question; more than one alternative may be partially correct. Do not look for trick questions; choose the most logical answer to the premise of each question.

Words used in the questions will have their standard meanings unless they are special real estate terms. It sometimes helps to rephrase a question if you are not sure of the answer. For example, you may suspect that **4** is true in the following item:

> *   In holding a deposit on an offer, which of the following would be the best place to put the money, provided you had no instructions to the contrary?
>
> 1.   In your office safe
> 2.   In a neutral depository in the buyer's name
> 3.   In your checking account
> 4.   In a neutral depository

By rephrasing mentally "The best place to put a deposit on an offer would be in a neutral depository," you can clarify your thoughts about **4** being the correct answer. Be careful, though, not to change the meaning of the question when you rephrase it.

Pacing

Work through the exam at a comfortable rate. You are allowed ample time to finish the 140- to 150-question exam; however, you should work as rapidly as you can without sacrificing accuracy. Budget your time before you begin the exam. If you are not taking the test on a computer, keep a watch handy. Plan on having more than half the questions answered before half the exam time has elapsed. *NOTE:* With the computer you do not have to waste time shading-in your answers—and your results are immediate. In Iowa, for example, you have $2^1/2$ hours to take the test.

You may want to take a short break halfway through the exam. If you are ahead of schedule, you can afford to look up from your paper; take several deep, slow breaths; stretch your legs; relax in your seat; and rest for a minute or two. This breaks physical and mental tension and helps prevent mistakes.

As you work through the exam, answer the easy questions first—they are worth the same number of points as the hard ones, and they will build your confidence. Mark difficult items and time-consuming calculation problems and return to them later. You may find clues in later questions; or, if time runs out, you will have all the sure points. Do not give hurried answers just because you are intimidated by the number of questions. Most objective items are not very time-consuming. Do not become discouraged if the exam seems difficult. No one is expected to get a perfect score.

DEVELOPING TEST QUESTIONS

The PSI exams are the result of a collaboration by real estate experts and educators. How the tests for salespeople and brokers are organized and how many questions are associated with each topic of the exam were covered in Part 1, "Use of the Manual." This section discusses the mechanics of test building.

Both the broker and the salesperson exams are completely multiple choice. Each test usually includes two types of questions. The first type tests your knowledge of general real estate, and the second tests your ability to apply this knowledge to specific real estate situations. The parts of a typical multiple-choice question are diagrammed on the example below:

> *   When a claim is settled by a title-insurance company, the company acquires all rights and claims of the insured against any person who is responsible for the loss. This is called
>
> 1.   escrow.   3.   certificate of title.
> 2.   abstract of title.   4.   subrogation.

The Stem

The first step in developing a question is to write the *stem,* or *lead.* The stem provides all the information necessary to determine the correct response. It usually does not include irrelevant or extraneous information; the exceptions generally are items dealing with mathematics.

The stem can be an incomplete statement, as in the preceding example, or a question.

* A lease provides a minimum rent of $250 per month plus 5 percent of annual gross income over $100,000. If the tenant did $145,000 in business last year, what total rent was paid?

1.	$3,000	3.	$4,500
3.	$5,250	4.	$7,250

The correct answer is **3**. Although the direct question lead tends to be somewhat less ambiguous than the incomplete statement, it usually is slightly longer and contains fewer clues to the correct response.

The Alternatives

The alternatives then are written, with the correct, keyed response embedded among the choices. In the PSI exam, the alternatives are presented in a multiple-choice format. The multiple-choice format, as illustrated in the preceding example, supplies four separate alternative answers. In this format, you are asked to consider four possible answers, alone and in combination. Study the following example:

* Listing agreements include which of the following?

1. An open listing only
2. An exclusive-right-to-sell listing only
3. An open listing and an exclusive-right-to-sell listing
4. A contract for deed

The correct answer is **3**. The purpose of distractors is to differentiate between well-prepared examinees and those who do not know the subject. Test developers often use popular misconceptions or even true statements that do not apply to the stem as distractors. Questions that do use true statements as distractors test not only your knowledge but also your judgment concerning the relevance of that knowledge. The difficulty of a question depends on the quality, or plausibility, of the distractors. In the worst case, where you have no idea which answer may be correct, the chance of answering it correctly is 25 percent because, theoretically, one out of four questions could be answered correctly just by guessing. The question is much easier, and the odds of guessing correctly much higher, if one or two responses can be immediately eliminated.

SAMPLE QUESTIONS

The questions on the exam are not set up to trick you. You will, however, encounter several exam questions on the broker's exam that are more complex than the majority of the questions. Such questions are usually in a situational (story) format. You will need to read each question carefully to know exactly what is being asked before you begin to formulate your answer.

Examples of questions that seem to be the most difficult for examinees are illustrated in this section. These include questions involving superfluous facts, reading comprehension, multistep math, value judgments and best answer.

Superfluous Facts

Exam questions frequently contain superfluous facts that are not needed to answer the questions. For example:

* A family paid $50,000 for their home five years ago, making a $10,000 down payment. Their monthly payment, including interest at $7^3/4$ percent, is $286. The interest portion of their last payment was $225.27. What was the approximate loan balance before their last payment?

   1. $29,480.64   3. $44,283.87
   2. $34,880.52   4. None of the above

The only facts needed to answer this question are the amount of the last interest payment and the rate of interest. To solve, simply multiply the amount of the monthly interest, $225.27, by 12. Then divide the result by the interest rate, 0.0775, to get the approximate loan balance, $34,880.52.

Reading Comprehension

Another type of question you may find on the test requires that you read each word extremely carefully for comprehension. For example:

* Closing of a transaction for a residential property is set for April 19, 1996. The seller has a three-year insurance policy that expires June 25, 1997. The seller has prepaid a three-year premium of $555. The buyer is to take over the policy as of the date of closing. The amount credited to the buyer at closing is

   1. $185.00.   3. $231.25.
   2. $202.99.   4. none of the above.

The answer is **4**, because the prorated amount of the prepaid insurance would be *debited* to the buyer.

Multistep Math

A type of question that frequently appears on PSI exams involves mathematics problems that require several steps. For example:

* A woman bought a house at exactly the appraised value. She negotiated a loan through a savings-and-loan association at 75 percent of the appraised value. The interest rate was 9 percent. The first month's interest was $405. What was the approximate selling price of the property?

   1. $54,000   3. $72,000
   2. $60,000   4. None of the above

To answer this question, first multiply $405 by 12 to get the approximate annual interest ($4,860). Then divide $4,860 by the interest rate, 0.09, to get the amount of the loan ($54,000). Finally, divide $54,000 by 0.75 to find the appraised value ($72,000), which is the same as the purchase price. Sometimes, a candidate who understands the mathematical process can use the answer key and work backward. In this case, for example, choose **3**, $72,000.

$$\$72,000 \times 75\% \ (0.75) = \$54,000 \times 9\% \ (0.09) = \$4,860 \div 12 \text{ months} = \$405.$$

Value Judgments

A few questions on the exam may require you to make value judgments. For example:

* A broker listed a small house for $86,000, obtaining an executed sales contract on it within six weeks at $85,000. The broker learned there was an existing $75,000 first mortgage and a $5,000 second mortgage on the property. The broker knew the real estate could be refinanced on a new $70,000 first-mortgage loan. The holder of the second mortgage told the broker he was willing to discount his $5,000 note, selling it for $4,500. The buyer has $20,000 cash and qualifies for a new $70,000 first-mortgage loan. The broker should

    1. say nothing to the seller about refinancing and allow the transaction to close.
    2. tell the seller the second mortgage can be paid off at a $500 discount.
    3. tell the holder of the second mortgage the property is sold and, therefore, he or she should demand the full amount of $5,000.
    4. buy the second mortgage himself at the $500 discount.

The answer, of course, is **2.** As an agent of the seller, the broker must act in the seller's best interest. Furthermore, alternative **4** would be illegal, for the broker would become a principal in the transaction without informing anyone.

Best Answer

You frequently will be asked to choose the best answer from alternatives when the ideal answer is not present. For example:

* A broker listed a beachfront home at $263,000. Three weeks later, the broker was fortunate to obtain a full-price offer on the beach house. Stopping by the house after the sales contract was executed and in force, the broker was appalled to see a large foundation crack. Two days later the broker noticed the crack had been carefully repaired. The broker knew that the seller was unaware of the crack because she had extremely poor eyesight. The broker suspected that the crack had been fixed by the seller's son-in-law, a building contractor. The broker should

    1. disclose the fact of the crack to the buyer.
    2. immediately cancel the sales contract.
    3. keep quiet about the crack because it has been repaired.
    4. confront the son-in-law with his suspicions and threaten to sue.

The best alternative available here is **1**. It would be best of all to inform the seller of the crack, requesting permission to inform the buyer, but that alternative does not appear here. Note that this question also asks you to make a value judgment.

HOW TO ANALYZE A QUESTION

Apparent Content

In general, the PSI exams are designed to measure your real estate knowledge and skills. Multiple-choice questions can test much more than your recall of specific facts. The PSI exam will, in fact, test how well you understand a given concept; whether you can apply rules to real-life situations; and how well you can analyze, synthesize and evaluate information and then arrive at a correct conclusion. If you can determine what ability the question is trying to measure, it will help you become a more effective test taker. The levels of skill the PSI exam seeks to measure are illustrated by the following examples:

Example 1

* How many acres are there in a section?

    1. 16   3. 200
    2. 36   4. 640

The answer is **4**. This is an example of *recall*, or recognition. The point of the question is to find out if you know this fact about sections—logic does not help much in determining the answer. The *factual question* is the easiest type to recognize.

Example 2

* Brokers owe their primary fiduciary duty to which of the following?

    1. The principal   3. The public
    2. The lender   4. The real estate commission

The answer is **1**. This type of question seeks to measure your understanding of the concept of fiduciary duty—and who it involves. *Comprehension questions* such as this often require you to identify real estate principles, laws or practices.

Example 3

* An investor leases a 20-unit apartment building for a net monthly rental of $5,000. If this figure represents a 7.5 percent return on investment, what is the original cost of the property?

    1. $80,000   3. $800,000
    2. $200,000   4. None of the above

The answer is **3**. Multiply the monthly rental by 12 to get the rental income ($60,000). Then divide $60,000 by 7.5 percent (0.075) to get the investment cost ($800,000). *Application questions* such as this are one level higher than comprehension questions. They ask you to use recall or understanding to solve a new real estate–related problem. Knowledge of real estate laws, regulations, principles and practices must be applied to concrete situations encountered on the job. Math problems are usually of this type.

Example 4

* Which of the following types of financing would be the most appropriate for a young veteran who has just used most of his savings to complete his degree in engineering and now would like to buy a house for his family?

   1. A conventional mortgage
   2. An installment contract
   3. A VA mortgage
   4. An FHA mortgage

The correct answer is **3**. At this point you are being tested not only on the concept of financing but also on your ability to weigh each of the options and come up with the best answer. *Analysis items* gauge your ability to identify parts of a whole, understand the relationships among the parts or identify the way that these elements are organized. You may have to differentiate between reasons and conclusions or indicate the relative importance of causes or factors. This question involves more than recall, for all of the options are true. You must take your thinking one step further.

Example 5

* Which of the following types of listing agreements affords the broker the most protection?

   1. An open listing
   2. An exclusive-agency listing
   3. A net listing
   4. An exclusive-right-to-selling listing

The correct answer is **4**. *Evaluation questions* such as this one test your ability to determine the best solution or to judge value in some manner. Often you must use recall, comprehension, analysis *and* synthesis to arrive at the answer.

Studies show that items testing the lower levels of cognition (recall or recognition) are easier than application, comprehension and higher-level questions. However, items testing the higher cognitive functions often can be solved by using general intelligence rather than specific real estate knowledge. Your score can be improved simply by exercising logic. You can turn this to your advantage by reasoning through difficult problems using the following seven steps:

1. Read the items carefully to determine the general subject the item is testing and exactly what is asked.

2. Reread the question for essential facts and qualifiers.

3. Eliminate answers that you know are incorrect.

4. Rephrase the problem (often helpful).

5. Determine what principles or formulas are necessary and how to solve the problem.

6. Apply relevant information to arrive at a solution.

7. Reread the question and check the answer.

Try this item for practice:

*   If an offer to purchase is received under certain terms and the seller makes a counteroffer, what is the prospective purchasers' legal position?

    1.   They are bound by the original offer.
    2.   They must accept the counteroffer.
    3.   They are relieved of the original offer.
    4.   They must split the difference with the seller.

The answer is **3**. How do you use the seven steps to arrive at that answer? In step 1, you determine that the subject is whether an offer is binding under certain circumstances. Now perform step 2: Reread the question to determine that the prospective purchasers make an offer and the seller makes a counteroffer. In step 3 you eliminate any obviously incorrect answers—in this case, response **4**. Step 4 suggests rephrasing the problem: "If the buyers make an offer under certain terms and the seller makes a counteroffer, the buyers. . . ." Step 5 is performed so automatically for this type of question that you may not be conscious that you are doing it. You need to know that an offer is not binding on the prospective purchasers once a counteroffer has been made. In step 6 you determine that alternative **3** is correct. Step 7 ensures that you have understood the question and have marked the right answer.

Although this logical process may seem long or complicated, your mind will accomplish it automatically within a few seconds once you train yourself to *think or reason through questions.*

Functional Content

There are two basic approaches to answering test questions. So far in this section, we have concentrated on one approach—determining the *apparent content* of the item, that is, the real estate facts being tested. To answer questions with the apparent content approach, you must draw on your knowledge of real estate and follow the logical problem-solving processes described earlier. You will answer most of the questions on the PSI license exam on the basis of their apparent content.

There may be a few questions, however, whose answers you will be unsure of based on the apparent content. Questions also can be analyzed on the basis of their *functional content.* The functional content of a test item consists of clues and cues that are inadvertently built in by the test developer and tend to lead you to the correct answer. Making a *psychological* as well as a *logical* analysis can lead you to the correct answer to a question, or at least can improve the guessing odds. These subtle clues and cues are called *specific determiners,* which are signs unrelated to actual subject-matter knowledge that lead you to infer that a particular answer is correct or incorrect. This section discusses 11 different types of specific determiners and illustrates common functional content patterns. (An asterisk indicates the correct answer.)

1.   *Length of alternative responses*—There is a tendency for item writers to express the correct response more carefully and in greater detail than the distractors. Therefore, the correct answer often is longer than the other alternatives. For example:

*   If property is held by two or more owners as tenants in common, one owner's interest would pass on his or her death to which of the following?

        1.   The remaining owners
*   2.   The heirs or whoever is designated in the decedent's will as the devisee
        3.   The surviving owner and/or her or his heirs
        4.   The state

2.   *Grammatical clues* — The correct response sometimes is more consistent grammatically or semantically with the stem, although test developers try to avoid this. The following items point out some clues of which to be aware.

*   A man agrees to buy the seller's land for $30,000. The buyer deposits the purchase price with a third party and the seller deposits the deed with the third party. The third party is instructed to record the deed when the seller shows good title to the land. The third party is to pay the seller $30,000 less agreed tax proration when the buyer has good title. This procedure is called an

        1.   provisional sale.
        2.   sale upon condition.
        3.   power of attorney.
*   4.   escrow.

A or *an* in the stem can indicate whether the correct answer starts with a consonant or with a vowel.

*   Who are the parties involved in a warranty deed?

        1.   Mortgagor
        2.   Exchangor
        3.   Exchangee
*   4.   Grantor and grantee

As shown in the above question, the stem may imply a singular or a plural response, thus helping you narrow the range of possible answers. Awkward phrasing of one or more alternatives suggests that they are distractors.

3.   *Qualifiers and absolute words* — Alternative responses often contain qualifying words and phrases that are clues to their correctness or incorrectness. Qualifiers that lessen the strength of the statement usually are found in true or correct statements. Such qualifiers include *generally, may, often, should, tend to* and *usually.* Absolute words usually are found in incorrect responses. These include *absolute, absolutely, all, alone, always, completely, doubtless, entirely, forever, indefinitely, indisputable, infallible, infinite, irrefutably, must, never, no, none, only, positive, quite, shall, sole, totally, unchangeable, undeniable, undoubtedly, unequivocal, unquestionable, wholly* and *without exception.* Study the following example.

*   A real estate broker acting as the agent of the seller

*   1.   should render faithful services to the seller.
        2.   can always make a profit, if possible, in addition to commission.
        3.   must agree to a change in price without the seller's approval.
        4.   can accept a commission from the buyer without the seller's approval.

4. *Repetition of phrases or word matching*—An obvious specific determiner is the repetition of a key phrase in both the stem and the correct answer. In some cases, synonyms for key words in the stem will appear in the correct answer.

* Which of the following represents a failure to perform or fulfill a contract?
    1. Defect
    2. Delinquency
    3. Subordination
  * 4. Breach of contract

More subtle cues are provided by verbal associations (word matching) that you make naturally and must recognize consciously.

* Which of the following is a capitalization rate?
  * 1. A factor used to estimate a property's value from its annual net income
    2. A percentage of gross annual income
    3. Income from an investment property
    4. The amortization of an investment

You can eliminate all answers except **1** and **2** simply by realizing that a *rate* can be a factor (**1**) or a percentage (**2**) but cannot be a dollar amount (**3**) or a concept (**4**).

5. *Homogeneity of alternatives*—Questions usually are designed so that the four responses are homogeneous; that is, they share similar features. If one answer strikes you as odd or dissimilar, study it carefully. It may be the correct choice.

* Which of the following would *not* be a party to a trust deed transaction?
    1. Beneficiary
  * 2. Mortgagor
    3. Trustor
    3. Trustee

6. *Generality of responses*—Sometimes the correct response is more general and inclusive than any distractor. Such "soft" statements almost have to be true because they are so general.

* Licensed real estate salespeople are expected to be expert in which of the following?
    1. Appraisal
    2. Investment
  * 3. Basic real estate principles
    4. Construction

7. *All of the above and none of the above*—Any question that offers "all of the above" as an option has a useful functioning content pattern. If you know that at least two of the other responses are correct, you can deduce that "all of the above" is the right answer, even if you are unfamiliar with the remaining responses. Conversely, if you know that one of the options is incorrect, you can eliminate both that option and "all of the above," improving your odds of guessing. "None of the above" is rarely a correct response, except occasionally in math problems. PSI tends to use "none of the above"

in its math problems, so that they cannot be calculated backward from the answers. PSI also tends to avoid "all of the above" in exam questions.

8. *Synonymous distractors* — Whenever you read two alternatives that have the same meaning, you know that neither is correct. Synonymous distractors are a trap that test developers fall into when they are hard-pressed for a fourth alternative.

> *   An owner had a wet bar installed in a home. This is considered
>
> 1.   an improvement.
> * 2.   a fixture.
> 3.   a chattel.
> 4.   personal property.

Answers **3** and **4** have the same meaning; neither is correct.

9. *Opposite alternatives* — After writing the keyed response, a test developer may include its opposite as a distractor. Therefore, if opposites appear among the alternatives, one may be the correct answer. Study responses **1** and **2** below.

> *   Who usually bears the cost of the sales commission?
>
> 1.   The buyer
> * 2.   The seller
> 3.   The broker
> 4.   The mortgage lender

In some cases, responses that exclude each other will cover the entire range of possibilities. You then can be even more certain that one of the pair is correct.

10. *Overlapping answers* — When one response to a question with a single correct answer includes or overlaps another response, you should realize that either both are correct or both are incorrect. This narrows your choices significantly.

> *   The duties of a broker to her principal include
>
> 1.   care.
> * 2.   care and obedience.
> 3.   appraisal.
> 4.   notice.

In questions asking for the best answer, one of the overlapping alternatives usually is correct.

11. *Vague pronouns* — Because test developers write the correct response first, they always use the correct noun in it. Later, when they write the distractors, they may unthinkingly use pronouns with the correct response as the antecedent rather than the question stem. A simple example follows:

> *   A woman lists with a broker for $50,000. A minority group member makes an offer of $45,000, but the broker does not present the offer. Which of the following is true?
>
> * 1.   She is a victim under the Federal Fair Housing Act of 1968.
> 2.   The fact that the offer was not presented is a violation of RESPA.

3.   The offer was so low that there was no need to present it to the seller.
4.   An offer does not always have to be presented to the seller.

If you encounter an item like this, the correct answer will be the one that has a proper pronoun referent or that contains the noun itself.

The benefit of specific determiners is not that they help you pass the exam without knowing the material or that they lead you to the correct answer every time. Their value is that they help you focus on likely responses and eliminate other answers. Mental alertness should supplement your real estate knowledge. Multiple-choice tests are intended to test your knowledge of what is not correct as well as what is correct, so do not hesitate to reason your way through difficult items using elimination.

Rational guessing is related more to problem solving and judgment than to luck. The PSI real estate licensing exam is designed to reward correct responses, not to penalize examinees for incorrect guesses. Make sure, therefore, that you have answered every question before turning in the exam.

EXAM STRATEGY

Many people study diligently and simply show up at the examination site without having given any thought to a strategy for taking the test. To maintain your confidence, poise and positive mental attitude, you should start the examination with a game plan for taking the test.

We suggest that you develop your own strategy for completing the test. An example of an exam strategy follows:

Unless testing is computer-generated, start with the state examination. It is the shorter test, comprising 40 to 50 questions. Read each question once to determine the particular subject matter of the question. Carefully underline key words. Read the question a second time, and concentrate on determining the correct response. If you are uncertain of the correct answer, eliminate obviously incorrect responses. If you still are uncertain of the single best answer, circle the question number in the test booklet or ask the computer to record the number for future review of the choice selected and move on to the next question. The entire state exam should be completed in this fashion even if, hypothetically, you have answered only 8 of 40 questions. Then move to the national exam, again answering the questions you know and skipping the questions you are uncertain about. By doing this, you divide the test into two parts:

1.   the part you know, which you answer quickly and efficiently and remove from further consideration, and

2.   the part you do not know but have managed to isolate, to which you can devote the remainder of your test time.

If math is your strength, you should next complete the math. There will be approximately ten math questions on the exam. After completing the math (on a mental high), your strategy is to go back to the state portion, then the national portion, and make a second pass through the exam. Do this until both tests have been completed.

Multiple-choice items often test not only your knowledge of specific points but also your ability to relate other information to the point. Many important topics have more than one question allotted to them. The correct answer to one question often can be found in some portion of another, so jot down the numbers of the questions that you think contain clues. This will help you in rechecking answers or answering questions you skipped.

If math is not your strength, do not let yourself be intimidated by the calculation problems. A good approach to math questions is to estimate the answer before actually working the problem. Figure neatly and carefully—this reduces error; then compare your answer with your original estimate. If they are different, you may have misplaced a decimal or used the wrong equation. If you cannot tell from the problem what equation to use, make up a simple, similar problem and determine the equation from that. If you cannot solve a problem, or if you obtain an answer that is not one of the options, check to see if you used all the figures given in your calculations. If you cannot solve a math problem in the usual way, you sometimes can find the correct solution by working backward from the given answers.

Math problems often use varying units that must be converted. You may have to change income per month to income per year before applying a formula, or you may have to convert square feet to acres before proceeding with a calculation.

If you really have no idea how to solve a math problem and must guess blindly, eliminate the two most extreme numerical answers and mark one of the remaining choices. This tactic is not always correct, but the odds favor it.

After completing every question on the exam, proofread your answer sheet if you are taking the exam with an answer key. Make sure that your answers are next to the correct numbers, that you did not misread any of the questions and that you marked the answer you intended for each item. By using extra time to correct any careless mistakes, you may boost your score significantly. *Do not change an answer unless you are sure the new one is correct. Studies show that an examinee's first response usually is correct and that changes will decrease the score.*

By developing an exam strategy similar to this, you will be in command of the exam rather than the exam being in command of you.

PART 3 / A STRATEGY FOR STUDYING

This chapter gives you a strategy for studying, incorporating the diagnostic tests and outlines of concepts to understand that follow in Parts 4 through 12. Next is the "Study and Review Checklist," which you can use as an easy reference to see if you are familiar with the subjects covered on the PSI examination.

Parts 4 through 11 correspond to testing areas on the PSI exam for salespersons: "Property Ownership," "Laws of Agency," "Contracts," "Federal Laws and Regulations," "Real Estate Mathematics Review," "Valuation and Real Estate Economics," "Finance," and "Land-Use Controls and Regulations." Part 12, "Brokerage Management," is for those taking the broker exam. Each part begins with an "Outline of Concepts to Understand" for the subject area. The "Outline of Concepts" is followed by a "Review List" of items you should be familiar with for the subject area. Each part ends with the "Diagnostic Test," its "Answer Key" and a test score box. Take the pretest and analyze your results before reviewing the content outline. If your progress score suggests that you need improvement, use the test results to establish your priority areas for study.

Keep in mind that the outline format of the concepts is primarily designed to organize your real estate knowledge in a concise fashion. If you are having difficulty with a particular topic, consult real estate practice and theory texts for a comprehensive explanation of the topic. *Modern Real Estate Practice* (published by Real Estate Education Company) provides a solid core of information.

HOW TO USE THE PROGRESS SCORE

After completing and correcting the diagnostic test, count the number of questions missed and enter that number in the box under "Your Score" after "Total Wrong." Then subtract the number of incorrectly answered questions from the total points. Finally, analyze your results by finding where your score of correct answers falls in the "Range" column; the rate corresponding to your score describes your progress. Your score will fall under "GOOD," "FAIR" or "NEEDS IMPROVEMENT."

For example:

PROPERTY OWNERSHIP

Rating	Test Score Range	Your Score	
GOOD = 80% to 100%	32–40	Total number	40
FAIR = 70% to 79%	28–31	Total wrong	– 6
NEEDS IMPROVEMENT = Below 70%	23 or less	Total right	34

Passing requirement— 28 or better

If your score on a diagnostic test is rated "GOOD," this area is one of your strengths. However, we suggest that a student should strive for a 90-percent-correct score before taking the actual exam. A rating of "FAIR" or "NEEDS IMPROVEMENT" in a subject suggests that this is an area you need to concentrate on.

DEVELOPING A STRATEGY FOR STUDYING

After you have pinpointed the areas that need particular study, you can begin studying the material in the concepts-to-understand outline. To increase the effectiveness of your study time, we suggest that you follow these three easy rules.

Organize Your Study Time. Educators suggest that regular short study periods are better than lengthy cram sessions. You should study when you are at your best mentally and physically; this may be early in the morning. The following chart will help you organize your study time in relation to the specific areas on the examination.

Scheduled Hours for Study

NATIONAL EXAM	M	T	W	Th	F	Sa	Su	TOTAL
Property Ownership								
Laws of Agency								
Contracts								
Federal Laws and Regulations								
Real Estate Mathematics Review								
Valuation and Real Estate Economics								
Finance								
Land Use Controls and Regulations								

STATE EXAM	M	T	W	Th	F	Sa	Su	TOTAL
Real Estate Law								
Rules and Regulations								
Special State Considerations								

Study in Depth. It is important to realize that you cannot simply read the text in preparing to successfully complete the exam. You must arrive at a thorough understanding of the subject matter. This can be easily achieved by writing a sample test question to yourself about the paragraph you have just read. It is a good practice to outline the thoughts of the paragraph in your own words or develop relationships between items. In other words, create mental images that will help you recall difficult concepts. Acronyms are useful when memorizing a series of items. For example, the five duties that an agent owes to a principal are COALD: care, obedience, accounting, loyalty and disclosure. During this stage, you should work alone.

Regularly Review Material Studied. In many cases, this can be accomplished by having a study partner assist you in reviewing your knowledge of vocabulary words, concepts and relationships. This also can be achieved by taking regular exams on the subject matter. Other tips include the following:

- Make flash cards with terms on the front and definitions on the back.

- Tape-record terms: term . . . pause . . . definition.

- Encourage group or one-on-one discussion.

A study and review checklist follows for your use in preparing for the PSI exam.

STUDY AND REVIEW CHECKLIST

National Exam

I.   Property ownership

    A.   Classes of property

        1. Real
        2. Personal
        3. Fixtures

    B.   Land characteristics

        1. Physical
        2. Economic
        3. Legal description

    C.   Encumbrances

        1. Liens
        2. Encroachments
        3. Easements

    D.   Type of ownership—freehold and nonfreehold

        1. Estates
        2. Tenancies
        3. Common ownership areas (condominiums, cooperatives and time-shares)
        4. Leasehold

    E.   Deeds

    F.   Escrow process (duties and responsibilities of escrow)

G.   Title insurance/preliminary title report

II.   Laws of agency

A.   Representation and disclosure

1.   Agent for seller
2.   Agent for buyer
3.   Dual agent

III.   Contracts

A.   Listing contracts

B.   Buyer/broker contracts

C.   Offers to purchase

D.   Counteroffers

E.   Amendments

F.   Land contracts for deed

G.   Cancellation agreements

H.   Leasing agreements

I.   Options

J.   Addenda

IV.   Federal laws and regulations

A.   Compliance with fair-housing regulations

B.   Truth-in-lending (Regulation Z)

C.   Real Estate Settlement Procedures Act (RESPA)

D.   Foreign Investment and Real Property Tax Act (IRC Section 1445)

E.   IRS regulations (Independent Contractor and Employee, 1099 forms, Declaration of Value, Imputed Interest, 1031 Tax-Deferred Exchange)

F.   Antitrust law

V.   Real estate mathematics

A.   Listing

B.   Selling

C.   Settlement

VI.   Valuation and real estate economics

A.   Methods of estimating value

1.   Market approach
2.   Cost approach
3.   Income approach
4.   Reconciliation process

 B. Elements of value

  1. Utility

  2. Supply and demand

  3. Market cycles, patterns and trends

 C. Depreciation

 D. Capitalization rate

 E. Difference between comparative market analysis and appraisal, gross-rent multiplier and gross-income multiplier

VII. Financing

 A. Mortgage insurance

 B. Secondary market

 C. Government/conventional loans

 D. Seller financing

 E. Discount points

 F. Closing statements

 G. Notes and mortgages or trust deeds

 H. Assumptions/assignments

 I. Lender fees

 J. Estimating costs for buyer or seller

 K. Interest on contracts

 L. Imputed interest

VIII. Land-use controls and regulations

 A. Planning and zoning

 B. Property taxation

 C. Floodplain, wetlands and shoreline regulations

 D. Health and safety codes

 E. Environmental concerns

 F. Deed restrictions

IX. Brokerage management

 A. Types of ownership

 B. Sales associate relationships

 C. Risk management

 D. Trust accounts

X.   Specialty Areas

State Exam

XI.   General topics

    A.   State statutes

    B.   State license laws, rules and regulations

    C.   Responsibilities of broker and salesperson

    D.   Contractual forms

XII.   Specific topics

    A.   Listing agreement

    B.   Sales contract

    C.   Closing

    D.   Land descriptions

    E.   Title and method of transfer

    F.   Deeds, land contract, contract for deed, trust

    G.   Financing, mortgages and usury

    H.   Interests in real estate

    I.   Forms of ownership

    J.   Leases and landlord-tenant law

    K.   Land-use controls, such as zoning

    L.   Taxation

    M.   Consumer-protection laws

    N.   Equal-opportunity laws

    O.   Condominiums, cooperatives and time-shares

    P.   Transfer fees

    Q.   Mortgage foreclosure and redemption

    R.   Disclosure requirements

    S.   Real estate education

    T.   Professional organizations

    U.   Trust accounts

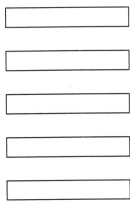

PART 4 / PROPERTY OWNERSHIP

OUTLINE OF CONCEPTS TO UNDERSTAND

I. Property ownership

   A. Classes of property

      1. Real property—the land and anything permanently affixed to it; includes the interests, benefits and rights inherent in the ownership of real estate

      2. Personal property—movable objects (chattels) that do not fit into the definition of real property; conveyed by bill of sale

      3. Fixture—an item of personal property that has been converted to real property by being permanently affixed to the land or building

         a. A fixture that is detached from the land or the building would revert to personal property.

      4. Trade fixture—an item installed by a tenant according to the terms of a lease and removable by the tenant before the expiration of the lease—personal property

         a. If not removed, the trade fixture becomes real property of the building owner by accession.

II. Land characteristics

   A. Physical

      1. Immobile—the geographic location of a parcel of land is fixed; can never be changed.

      2. Indestructible—the long-term nature of improvements plus permanence of land tends to create stability in land development.

      3. Unique or nonhomogeneous—all parcels differ geographically and each parcel has its own location.

   B. Economic

      1. Scarcity—although there is a substantial amount of unused land, supply in a given location or of a specific quality can be limited.

      2. Improvements—placement of an improvement on a parcel of land affects value and use of neighboring parcels of land.

3. Permanence of investment—improvements represent a large fixed investment; some, such as drainage and sewerage, cannot be dismantled or removed economically.

4. Area preference, or situs—this refers to people's choices and desires for a given area.

C. Legal descriptions

1. Metes and bounds

   a. Begins at a specific point and proceeds around boundaries of parcel by reference to linear measurements and directions

   b. Boundaries established on basis of actual distance between monuments (fixed objects)

   c. A boundary must return to the point of beginning so that the land described is fully enclosed.

2. Rectangular (government) survey

   a. Based on measurements from base lines and principal meridians

   b. Base lines run east and west; principal meridians run north and south.

   c. Designed to set up checkerboard pattern of identical squares over specific area

      1) Parallel lines six miles apart divide land into rows, east and west of the principal meridian, that are referred to as *ranges*.

      2) Parallel lines six miles apart divide land into rows north and south of the baseline that are referred to as *tiers*.

      3) The grid that divides the land into *townships* is formed by superimposing these two sets of lines.

         a) A township is six miles square (36 square miles).

         b) A township contains 36 sections; each section is a square mile and contains 640 acres (one acre = 43,560 square feet).

         c) Sections are numbered from the northeast corner; the first row of six sections runs east to west, the second row west to east, and so on, with section 36 being located in the southeast corner of the township.

   d. The land description is based on references to either a section or some portion of a section, such as one quarter-section (160 acres) or one half-section (320 acres).

   e. A typical description: the NE$\frac{1}{4}$ of the SW$\frac{1}{4}$ of Section 4, Township 3 North, Range 2 east of the Principal Meridian

3. Subdivision plats

   a. Location of an individual parcel is indicated on a map of the subdivision, which is divided into numbered blocks and lots.

   b. Each parcel is referred to a lot, block, subdivision name, city and state.

4. Street address: an informal reference too inaccurate for a legal description

III. Encumbrances

A. A charge, claim or liability that attaches to and is binding on real estate

B. General classifications of encumbrances

1. Liens—affect the title

a.   A lien is a charge against property that provides security for a debt or obligation of the property owner.

b.   If the debt is not repaid, the lienholder has the right to have it paid out of the debtor's property, generally from the proceeds of a court or foreclosure sale.

c.   A specific lien relates to specific property; a general lien, such as a judgment or court decree, applies to all the debtor's property.

d.   Possible specific liens against an owner's real estate include real estate taxes, mortgages and mechanics' liens.

e.   Real estate taxes and special assessments usually take priority over all other liens, regardless of date.

f.   In some states, mechanics' liens may be given priority over previously recorded liens because mechanics' liens go back to when the work was started, not to when the lien was recorded.

2. Encumbrances that affect the physical condition of the property include encroachment, easements, and restrictions.

a.   Use restriction—a deed restriction or covenant is a private agreement placed in the public record that affects the use of the land.

b.   Easement—a right acquired by one party to use the land of another party for a special purpose.

   1)   Easement appurtenant

     a)   An easement annexed to ownership for the benefit of another's parcel of land

     b)   Requires that there be two tracts of land, either contiguous or noncontiguous, owned by different parties

     c)   The tract over which the easement runs is known as the *servient tenement*; the tract that benefits from the easement is known as the *dominant tenement*.

     d)   Appurtenant easements "run with the land" and are not terminated by the sale of either the servient or dominant tenement.

   2)   Easement in gross—a mere personal interest in or right to use the land of another, such as the right of way for a pipeline; there is no dominant tenement, just a servient tenement

   3)   Easement by necessity—arises when there is no other access to a street or public way

   4)   Easement by prescription

     a)   Acquired when the claimant has made use of another's land for the prescriptive period, generally from 5 to 20 years

     b)   Claimant's use must have been continuous, without the owner's approval, visible, open and notorious.

   5)   License

     a)   Permission to enter the land of another for a specific purpose, such as permission to park in a neighbor's driveway or to go hunting on another's property

     b)   Differs from easement in that it can be canceled or terminated by licensor

   6)   Encroachments—illegal extension of a building or some other improvement, such as a wall or fence, beyond the land of its owner and onto the land of an adjoining owner

IV.   Types of ownership—freehold and nonfreehold

    A.   Interests in real estate—feudal versus allodial rights

        1.   Feudal—system of land ownership in which the king or government held title to the land; the individual was merely a tenant who held rights of use and occupancy at the sufferance of the overlord

        2.   Allodial—system in which an individual can hold land free and clear of any rent or service due the government; system under which land is held in the United States

    B.   Limitations on ownerships—individuals' ownership rights subject to certain rights of government:

        1.   Police power—power of the state to establish legislation to protect public health and safety and promote general welfare

        2.   Eminent domain—right of government to acquire private property for public use while paying just compensation to the owner

        3.   Escheat—reversion of real estate ownership to the state, as provided by state law, when an owner dies and leaves no heirs or no will disposing of the real estate or when the property is abandoned

        4.   Taxation—charge on real estate to raise funds to meet the public needs of the government

    C.   Estates in land

        1.   Refers to degree, quantity and nature of interest that a person has in real property for a lifetime (life estate) or forever (inheritable freehold)

        2.   Freehold estates—estates of indeterminable length, such as those existing for a lifetime or forever

        3.   Fee simple
            a.   Highest type of interest in real estate recognized by law
            b.   Holder entitled to all rights incident to property
            c.   Continues for indefinite period and is inheritable by heirs of owner

        4.   Defeasible fee (qualified, conditional, determinable or base fee)
            a.   Continues for an indefinite period; may be inherited
            b.   Estate extinguished on the occurrence of a designated event, the time of such occurrence being uncertain
            c.   May be based on either certain or uncertain event

    D.   Life estate

        1.   Limited in duration to life of life tenant or life or lives of some other designated person or persons

        2.   Not an estate of inheritance, because estate terminates at the death of the life tenant or the designated person

        3.   May be created for the life of another person (estate pur autre vie)

        4.   Future interests in the property after the death of the life estate owner
            a.   Remainder interest—if the deed or the will names a third party to whom title will pass on the death of the life estate owner, then such party is said to own remainder interest.
            b.   Reversionary interest—if the deed does not convey remainder interest to a third party, then on the death of the life estate owner, full ownership reverts to the original fee simple owner or, if he or she is deceased, to heirs.

        5.   Limited to the lifetime of the owner of the life estate (life tenant)

    E.   Life tenant

        1.   Interest in real property is time-ownership interest.
        2.   Generally not answerable to the holder of future interest (remainderman)
        3.   Has limited rights, that is, can enjoy the rights of the land but cannot encroach upon the rights of the remainderman
        4.   May not commit waste (permanently injure the land or property)
        5.   Entitled to possession of the property and to all income and profits arising from property during the term of ownership
        6.   Life interest may be sold, leased, mortgaged or gifted but may be of little value because all interest must be forfeited at the death of the life tenant; remainder interest cannot be encumbered by the life tenant.

    F.   Legal life estates

        1.   Curtesy—husband's life estate in all inheritable real estate of the deceased wife
        2.   Dower—wife's life estate in all inheritable real estate of the deceased husband
        3.   Many states have abolished curtesy and dower in favor of the laws of descent and distribution, by which the surviving spouse is frequently allowed to take a specific portion of the estate in fee rather than life estate.
        4.   Inchoate—a right not yet perfected. An estate waiting to happen upon the death of one's spouse

    G.   Homestead

        1.   Tract of land owned and occupied as the family home
        2.   In states with homestead-exemption laws, a portion of the area or value of land is exempted, or protected, from judgment for unsecured debts.

V.   Freehold estates—leasehold estates

    A.   Ownership by natural persons

        1.   In severalty—one owner
        2.   In co-ownership—two or more owners
            a.   Tenancy in common
               1)   Each owner holds an individual interest in severalty.
               2)   Each owner can sell, convey, mortgage or transfer his or her interest without the consent of the other co-owners.
               3)   Upon the death of a co-owner, the individual interest of the deceased passes to heirs or devisees according to the will; there is no right of survivorship.
               4)   Tenants in common may partition the land.
           b.   Joint tenancy
               1)   Owners have the right of survivorship.
               2)   Four unities—title, time, interest and possession—are required to create a valid joint tenancy.
               3)   Termination results from the destruction of any of the four unities.
               4)   Joint tenants may partition the land.
           c.   Tenancy by the entirety
               1)   Owners must be husband and wife.
               2)   Owners have the right of survivorship.

      3) Title may be conveyed or encumbered only by the deed signed by both parties (one party cannot convey a one-half interest).

      4) Usually no right of partition

  d. Community property (marital property)

      1) Husband and wife may have sole ownership of the separate or individual property if it was owned solely by either spouse before the marriage or was acquired by gift or inheritance after marriage.

      2) Husband and wife are equal partners in the community or marital property (property acquired during the marriage).

      3) Upon the death of one spouse, the survivor automatically owns one-half of the community property, with the other half being distributed according to the deceased's will.

      4) Antenuptial agreements are contracts (prior to marriage) that preserve separate property ownership.

3. In trust—by a third person for the benefit of another

4. Ownership by a business organization

5. Partnerships

  a. Association of two or more persons to carry on business as co-owners and share in the profits and losses of that business

  b. Types of partnerships

      1) General—all partners participate in the operation of the business and may be held personally liable for business losses and obligations.

      2) Limited

         a) Includes general as well as limited, or silent, partners

         b) General partner runs the business

         c) Although limited partners do not participate, they may be held liable for business losses, but only to the extent of their investment.

6. Corporations

  a. Ownership in severalty—corporations are considered by law to be a single entity.

  b. Each stockholder's liability for losses generally is limited to the amount of investment.

7. Syndicates—joining together of two or more parties to create and operate a real estate investment

8. Cooperatives

  a. Title to the land and the building held by the corporation

  b. Each purchaser becomes a stockholder and receives a proprietary lease; each purchaser holds a personal property interest.

  c. Taxes and the mortgage are liens against the corporation which are generally given to the shareholders.

  d. Owner-occupants may be forced to pay for the shareholders who are unable to pay, to prevent foreclosure on the entire building.

9. Condominiums

  a. Generally created under a horizontal property act

  b. The owner holds fee-simple title to one unit and a specified share in the common elements.

  c. Default in payment of taxes, mortgage payments or monthly assessments by one unit owner may result in a foreclosure sale of

that owner's unit; this does not affect the titles of the remaining owners.
10. Time-shared ownership
   a. Allows multiple buyers to buy interests in real estate with each buyer receiving the right to use the facilities for a specified period of time
   b. Owners' use and occupancy is limited to the contractual period that was purchased.
   c. The owner is assessed for common expenses and maintenance based on the ratio of the ownership period to the total number of ownership periods in the property.
   d. Time-share estate includes a fee-simple interest in condominium ownership or perhaps a leasehold estate.
   e. Time-share use is a contractual right under which the developer owns the real estate.

B. Leasehold estate—less-than-freehold estate involving the tenant's right to occupy the real estate during the term of the lease; usually considered personal property (nonfreehold)

   1. Estate for years—lease for a definite period of time; terminates automatically without notice by either party
   2. Periodic estate (estate from year to year)—lease for an indefinite period of time without a specific expiration date; notice must be given to terminate
   3. Tenancy at will—lease that gives the tenant the right to possess with the consent of the landlord for an indefinite period of time; terminated by giving notice or by the death of either the landlord or the tenant.
   4. Tenancy at sufferance—tenant continues to hold possession without the consent of the landlord

VI. Types of leases

A. Gross lease—tenant pays a fixed rent, while landlord pays all taxes, insurance, etc.

B. Net lease—tenant pays rent plus all or part of property charges

C. Percentage lease—usually provides for minimum fixed rent plus a percentage of that portion of tenant's business income that exceeds a stated minimum

D. Graduated lease—provides for rent increases at set future dates

E. Index lease—allows rent to be increased or decreased periodically based on changes in the government cost-of-living index

VII. Deeds—transfers of title

A. By descent

   1. Every state has a law known as the statute of descent and distribution.
   2. When a person dies intestate, the decedent's real estate and personal property pass to her or his heirs according to statute.

B. By will

   1. A will takes effect only after the death of the testator; until that time any property covered by the will can be conveyed by the owner.

2. State laws usually require that on the death of a testator, his or her will must be filed with the court and probated to pass title to the devisees.

C. By involuntary alienation—transferred without owner's consent

1. Escheat—when a person dies intestate and leaves no heirs or abandons the property, title to her or his real estate passes to the state.
2. Eminent domain—the government may take the private property for public use through a suit for condemnation; the owner must be given just compensation.
3. To satisfy debts—debt is foreclosed, the property sold and the proceeds of the sale applied to pay off the debt
4. Natural forces
    a. Accretion—slow accumulation of soil, rock and so on deposited by the movement of water on the owner's property
    b. Erosion—gradual wearing away of the land by the action of natural forces
    c. Avulsion—sudden tearing away of the land by the action of water or earthquake
    d. Reliction—new land is acquired as water recedes
5. Adverse possession—actual, visible, hostile, notorious, exclusive and continuous possession of another's land under a claim of title; periods of time may be tacked on by successive owners/tenants

D. Voluntary alienation—either gift or sale; to transfer title during his or her lifetime, an owner must use some form of deed of conveyance

1. Deeds—written instruments of conveyance from the owners (grantors) to the recipients (grantees)
    a. General warranty deed—contains promises or covenants
        1) Provides the greatest protection of any deed
        2) Covenant of seisin—the grantor has the title and possession and has the right to convey.
        3) Covenant against encumbrances—the grantor warrants that the property is free from any liens or encumbrances except those specifically stated in the deed.
        4) Covenant of quiet enjoyment—the grantor guarantees that the title is good against a third party.
        5) Covenant of further assurance—the grantor promises to obtain and deliver any instrument required to make the title good against third parties.
        6) Covenant of warranty forever—the grantor guarantees that if the title fails, the grantee will be compensated for the loss sustained.
    b. Special warranty deeds—the grantor warrants only that the property was not encumbered during the time that the title was held, except as noted in the deed.
    c. Bargain and sale deed—contains only an implied warranty that the grantor holds the title and possession of the property
    d. Quitclaim deed—contains warranties and conveys only such interest, if any, that the grantor may have when the deed is delivered but conveys that interest completely; often used to cure a defect in title

VIII. Escrow process

    A. Means by which the parties to a contract carry out the terms of their agreement

    B. Parties appoint a third party to act as an escrowee, or escrow agent.

    C. In the sale of real estate, the seller's deed and the buyer's money are deposited with an escrow agent under an escrow agreement that sets forth conditions to be met before the sale will be consummated.

    D. The escrow agent holds the deed and when the title conditions and the other requirements of the escrow agreement have been met, records the deed; the title passes and the sale is completed.

IX. Title insurance/abstracts

    A. Requirements for a valid conveyance

        1. Grantor—must have legal existence, be of legal age and be legally competent to convey the title

        2. Grantee—must be named in the deed in such a way that he or she can be identified

        3. Consideration—must be acknowledged by the grantor; in most states, consideration must be stated in dollars

        4. Granting clause—must contain words that state the grantor's intention to convey the property

        5. Habendum clause—follows granting clause when necessary to define the terms of ownership to be enjoyed by grantee

        6. Description of real estate—must use a legal description that is understood by the parties

        7. Signature of grantor—must be signed by all the grantors named in the deed; a seal sometimes is required

        8. Acknowledgment—provides evidence that the signature is voluntary and genuine; not essential to the validity of the deed unless required by state statutes

        9. Delivery and acceptance—actual delivery of the deed by the grantor and either actual or implied acceptance by the grantee

      10. Exceptions and reservations ("subject-to" clauses)—should specifically note encumbrances, reservations or limitations that affect the title being conveyed, such as liens and easements

    B. Recording of deeds and conveyance of title

        1. The title generally passes to the grantee when the executed deed is delivered and accepted.

        2. Exceptions:

           a. Torrens property—the title transfers when the deed has been examined and accepted for registration.

           b. Closing in escrow—the date of delivery is generally the date that it was deposited with the escrow agent; if the escrow does not close, no title passes.

        3. Recording a deed or taking possession of a property give constructive notice to the world that one has rights in the property.

        4. An unrecorded deed is valid between the parties to a transaction.

C. Types of proof of title
1. Abstract of title and lawyer's opinion
a. Abstract of title—condensed history of all instruments on record affecting the title to the property
b. Attorney's opinion of title—the buyer's attorney examines the abstract for flaws and prepares a written opinion of the condition of ownership.
2. Torrens system
a. A certificate of title accompanied by the owner's signature is filed with the registrar's office and used to verify future transfers.
b. Title to Torrens—registered property never can be acquired through adverse possession.
3. Certificate of title—prepared by an attorney without preparation of an abstract; attorney provides an opinion on the ownership of title; is not a title insurance policy

D. Title insurance
1. Protects insured against loss resulting from certain defects in the title, such as a forgery or defect in the public record, other than those exceptions listed in the policy
2. Most standard coverage policies will not cover situations arising from questions of survey, defects of which the policyholder has knowledge or unrecorded documents.
3. Extended coverage policies will cover additional risks that may be discovered only by inspection of the property, including unrecorded rights of persons in possession, or by examination of an accurate survey.

X. Other important terms
A. Accession—acquiring the title to additions or improvements to real property as a result of accretion of alluvium or annexation of fixtures (including accession of trade fixtures not removed by the tenant prior to lease termination)

B. Accretion—increase in land resulting from soil being deposited by the natural force of water

C. Alluvion—actual soil increase resulting from accretion

D. Appurtenances—rights belonging to land

E. Assignment—transfer of rights and/or duties under a contract
1. Rights can be assigned, unless the contract expressly forbids assigning them.
2. Obligations often can be assigned, but the original party is secondarily liable for them.

F. Benchmark—permanent metal marker embedded in cement, used as a reference to measure the elevation above sea level

G. Cloud on title—any claim that may impair the title to a property

H. Cul-de-sac—street open at only one end and generally with a circular turnaround at the other end

I. Datum—horizontal plane from which elevations are measured

J.   Erosion—washing away of land caused by flowing water

K.   Estovers—legally allowed necessities, such as the right of a tenant to use timber on leased property to support a minimum need for fuel or repairs

L.   Fixtures—personal property that has been affixed to and becomes part of the real property

M.   Good consideration—love and affection with no monetary measure of value

N.   Inchoate right—incomplete right, such as a wife's dower interest in her husband's property during his life

O.   Incorporeal right—nonpossessory right in property, such as an easement

P.   Laches—court doctrine that bars a legal claim because of undue delay to assert the claim

Q.   Lis pendens (Latin term for *action pending*)—recorded document that creates constructive notice that an action relating to a specific property has been filed in court

R.   Novation—also a transfer of rights and/or duties under a contract

    1.   Original contract canceled
    2.   New contract negotiated and drawn, with the same parties or a new second party
    3.   Original party, if replaced, not liable

S.   Parol-evidence rule—law that states that no prior or contemporary oral or extraneously written agreement can change the terms of a contract

T.   Partition—legal alternative for the dissolution by the court of co-ownership when the co-owners do not voluntarily agree to the termination

U.   Quiet-title action—court action to establish the title to a specific property, for example, where there is a cloud on the title

V.   Statute of frauds—law that requires that certain contracts be in writing before they can be enforced; contracts for the sale of land and leases of more than one year are generally required to be in writing and signed by all parties

W.   Statute of limitations—law that refers to the length of time within which a party may sue

X.   Valuable consideration—consideration with a monetary measure of value

Y.   Waste—tenant abuse that results in permanent injury to the land or property

Z.   Writ of attachment—writ filed during a lawsuit that prevents the debtor from transferring the property involved in the suit

REVIEW LIST

The student should have an understanding of the following areas of property ownership:

1. Classes of property

    a. Real
    b. Personal
    c. Fixtures

2. Land characteristics

    a. Physical
    b. Economic
    c. Legal description

3. Encumbrances

    a. Liens
    b. Easements
    c. Encroachments

4. Types of ownership—freehold and nonfreehold

    a. Estates
    b. Tenancies
    c. Common ownership areas
    d. Leasehold

5. Deeds

6. Escrow process

7. Title insurance

8. Other important terms

DIAGNOSTIC TEST

1. The term situs refers to

    1. uniqueness.
    2. area preference.
    3. immobility.
    4. scarcity.

2. Which of the following is a physical characteristic of land?

    1. Indestructibility
    2. Scarcity
    3. Permanence of investment
    4. Situs

3. The owner of a life estate in property

    1. does not pay real estate taxes.
    2. is entitled to possession of the property.
    3. may not receive income from the property.
    4. is not responsible for all repairs on the property.

4. Three women own a motel as tenants in common. One of the women decides to sell all of her assets. She may legally

   1. sell, because a tenant in common may sell her portion of the assets if a majority of the co-owners also agree to sell.
   2. not sell, because a tenant in common's interest always remains encumbered.
   3. sell, because a tenant in common has a separate legal title to the undivided interest.
   4. not sell, because there is a right of survivorship.

5. Which of the following statements is FALSE?

   1. Fixtures that are purchased, paid for and installed after the execution of a mortgage are subject to liens of the mortgage.
   2. When a landowner tears down a fence, with the intention that it be permanently removed, and piles the material on the land, such material is real property.
   3. Generally, trade fixtures that were installed by the tenant are personal property.
   4. A hot-water heater installed on the property becomes a fixture.

6. A man signed a lease for six months. This is an example of

1. an estate for years.	3. a tenancy at will.
2. a periodic estate.	4. a tenancy at sufferance.

7. Specific liens would NOT include which of the following?

1. Mortgage liens	3. Real estate taxes
2. Judgments	4. Mechanics' liens

8. A farmer purchased land with no access to a street or public way. After an unsuccessful attempt to gain access through negotiation, he was able to gain access through an

1. easement appurtenant.	3. easement by necessity.
2. easement in gross.	4. easement by prescription.

9. A woman built a fence that extended beyond the boundary of her property onto her neighbor's property. This is an example of

1. laches.	3. encroachment.
2. easement by necessity.	4. easement appurtenant.

10. A grandmother owned a life estate measured by her own life in residence. She leased the property for five years using a standard lease contract. Shortly thereafter, she died. The lease was

    1. valid only as long as she was alive.
    2. valid for five years.
    3. invalid because she, as an owner of a life estate, cannot lease the property.
    4. valid for up to one year after her death.

11. An electrician did some rewiring in a home, for which he has not yet been paid. One month after the work was completed, the electrician drove by the home to discover a For Sale sign on the property. The electrician should

    1. file a mechanic's lien.
    2. offer to purchase the house.
    3. obtain injunctive relief.
    4. sue the listing broker.

12. You have purchased the right to live in an apartment in a resort during the 32nd complete week of each calendar year for the next 30 years. The type of interest you have is called a

    1. joint tenancy.
    2. time-share estate.
    3. tenancy in common.
    4. estate for years.

13. An owner in a condominium project does NOT

    1. hold a fee simple title to his or her unit.
    2. have an undivided proportionate interest in the common elements.
    3. have to pay mortgages, taxes and assessments that are liens against other units in the project.
    4. have a real property interest.

14. Which of the following statements does NOT correctly describe a cooperative development?

    1. Title to the land and building is owned by a corporation.
    2. Mortgage and taxes are liens against the corporation.
    3. Each buyer of an apartment becomes a shareholder in the corporation.
    4. The owner holds a real property interest.

15. A tenant failed to remove her trade fixtures prior to the expiration of her lease, which resulted in the landlord's acquiring title to the trade fixtures. Acquiring property in this way is known as

    1. accession.
    2. novation.
    3. laches.
    4. partition.

16. Included among the features of taking title to real property as tenants in common is that

    1. ownership interests must be equal.
    2. each co-owner's interest may be conveyed separately.
    3. a co-owner cannot will his interest in a property.
    4. the last survivor owns the property in severalty.

17. A homeowner employed a contractor to build a swimming pool on his property. Upon completion of the swimming pool, the contractor filed a lien to receive payment of the contract fee. Such filing could be considered any of the following **EXCEPT**

    1. a specific lien.
    2. an encumbrance.
    3. a general lien.
    4. a mechanic's lien.

18. A family bought a 40-year-old house, and the broker told them the garage was built 30 years ago. Because the buildings were located on a ''postage-stamp-sized'' lot, the family hired a surveyor who told them the garage extended six inches onto a neighbor's lot. Because the husband had taken a real estate course, he realized that this could be a prescriptive easement and was similar to

1. a dominant easement.
2. a license.
3. a servient easement.
4. adverse possession.

19. The deed that provides the buyer with the greatest protection is the

1. bargain and sale deed.
2. warranty deed.
3. quitclaim deed.
4. special warranty deed.

20. A warranty deed generally will transfer title to the grantee when it is

1. acknowledged.
2. signed by the grantee.
3. signed by the grantor.
4. delivered and accepted.

21. A man has a claim affecting the title to another man's property. The owner has been trying to sell the property, and the man with the claim is concerned about the possibility of a bona fide purchaser buying it before he obtains a judgment to protect himself during the course of the court action. To protect himself, the man with the claim should

1. file a lis pendens or notice of intent.
2. publish a notice in the newspaper.
3. bring a quick summary proceeding.
4. notify the owner that any attempt to sell the property will be considered fraud.

22. X and Y own adjoining parcels of real estate. X has granted Y an easement over his property for ingress and egress. If Y decides to sell his land to Z, which of the following would be true?

1. The status of the dominant and servient tenements would not change.
2. The easement would be terminated, for Y no longer would be the owner of the property.
3. X may sell the easement to the new owner Z.
4. To be valid, the deed of conveyance from Y to Z must specifically mention the easement.

23. Legal seizure of property to be held for payment of money pending the outcome of a suit to enforce collection is

1. a lis pendens.
2. an attachment.
3. a writ of execution.
4. an abstract of judgment.

24. Two women bought a building and took title as joint tenants. One of the owners died testate. The remaining owner now owns the building

1. as a joint tenant with rights of survivorship.
2. in severalty.
3. in absolute ownership under the law of descent.
4. subject to the terms of the deceased owner's will.

25. Which of the following would be an example of voluntary alienation?

    1. Sale   3. Escheat
    2. Eminent domain   4. Adverse possession

26. A grantee has received an executed, notarized deed. The grantee takes possession of the property, but does not record the deed. The conveyance is

    1. invalid between the parties and valid as to third parties with constructive notice.
    2. valid as between the parties and valid as to subsequent recorded interests.
    3. valid as between the parties and invalid as to subsequent recorded interests without notice.
    4. invalid as between the parties.

27. A man takes possession of an owner's land after obtaining the owner's permission. The man's possession continues for 26 years. Thereafter the man attempts to get title to the property. Will the man succeed?

    1. The man will be successful because he possessed the property for 26 straight years.
    2. The man will be successful because he satisfied all the requirements of eminent domain.
    3. The man will be unsuccessful because he cannot obtain title to property through possession for a prescriptive period.
    4. The man will be unsuccessful because not all the requirements of adverse possession have been satisfied.

28. A husband and wife own property as tenants in the entireties. The husband dies and his will names their son to inherit the property. Which of the following statements is correct?

    1. The son and his mother own the property as tenants in common.
    2. The son owns the property in severalty.
    3. The son and his mother own the property as joint tenants.
    4. The son has no interest in the property.

29. Two brothers could take title to income property in unequal shares under which of the following?

    1. Severalty   3. Joint tenants
    2. Tenants by the entirety   4. Tenants in common

30. Which of the following statements does NOT correctly describe a properly executed will?

    1. It takes effect only after the death of the devisee.
    2. It specifies who will inherit the owner's property.
    3. It must conform to the state statute.
    4. It cannot supersede state laws of dower and curtesy.

31. Generally, title insurance coverage extends to

    1. defects known to the buyer.
    2. liens listed in the policy.
    3. defects listed in the policy.
    4. defects not found in public records.

32. A contractor builds an addition to a house for a contract price of $52,000 and records his mechanic's lien notice. Before making any payment, the owner has the house jacked up and put on a platform prior to moving it to another location. The contractor should

    1. have his attorney prepare and record a covenant.
    2. file an encroachment notice.
    3. record an attachment.
    4. have his attorney prepare and record a notice of lis pendens.

33. What do the following situations have in common?

    I.   A man's property is taken by the city and used for a new highway.
    II. A woman's land gradually is wearing away because of wind.
    III. A developer's property is sold at a foreclosure sale.

    1. They will require the use of a warranty deed to transfer title.
    2. They are all examples of voluntary alienation of title.
    3. They are all examples of eminent domain.
    4. They are all examples of involuntary alienation.

34. Legal descriptions may NOT be based on

    1. the government survey.
    2. metes and bounds.
    3. an informal street address.
    4. a subdivision plat.

35. A land description that begins at a specific point and proceeds around the boundaries of a parcel by reference to linear measurements and directions is based on

    1. metes and bounds.
    2. the rectangular survey.
    3. a subdivision plat.
    4. a survey.

36. In the government survey method

    1. base lines run east and west.
    2. principal meridians run east and west.
    3. base lines run north and south.
    4. a township contains 26 sections.

37. A section contains

    1. 43,560 square feet.
    2. 640 acres.
    3. 160 square rods.
    4. 320 square rods.

38. You and your sister own a house. Your sister would like to sell her interest in the house to her cousin. You and your sister own the house under which of the following?

    1. Tenancy by the entirety
    2. Tenancy at will
    3. Tenancy in common
    4. Estate for years

39. A plumber sells his home, in which he has installed washerless faucets. After the contract has been executed, he decides to replace the faucets with standard faucets. Which of the following is true?

    1. The plumber may remove the faucets at any time.
    2. Standard faucets are a good replacement.
    3. The plumber can be held liable for removing the faucets because they are fixtures that were in place before the contract was signed.
    4. This question should be decided by the broker who took the listing.

40. A deed must be signed by the

    1. grantor.   3. grantee.
    2. vendee.   4. vendor.

ANSWER KEY

Question	Answer	Outline Reference	Question	Answer	Outline Reference
1.	2	II	21.	1	IX
2.	1	II	22.	1	III
3.	2	IV	23.	2	IX
4.	3	IV	24.	2	IV
5.	2	I	25.	1	VI
6.	1	IV	26.	2	VIII
7.	2	III	27.	4	VI
8.	3	III	28.	4	V
9.	3	III	29.	4	V
10.	1	IV	30.	1	VI
11.	1	III	31.	4	VIII
12.	2	V	32.	3	IX
13.	3	V	33.	4	VI
14.	4	V	34.	3	II
15.	1	IX	35.	1	II
16.	2	IV	36.	1	II
17.	3	III	37.	2	II
18.	4	VI	38.	3	V
19.	2	VI	39.	3	I
20.	4	VIII	40.	1	V

PROPERTY OWNERSHIP

Rating	Test Score Range	Your Score	
GOOD = 80% to 100%	32–40	Total number	40
FAIR = 70% to 79%	28–31	Total wrong	–__
NEEDS IMPROVEMENT = Below 70%	23 or less	Total right	__

**Passing requirement—
28 or better**

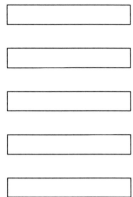

PART 5 / LAWS OF AGENCY

OUTLINE OF CONCEPTS TO UNDERSTAND

I.   Laws of agency

    A.   The brokerage business is one of agency; the broker is hired by the principal to become her or his agent.

        1.   The agent is a broker who consents to represent the interest of another person and is authorized to act accordingly.
        2.   The principal is the buyer or seller who employs and delegates to the agent the responsiblity of representing the principal's interests.
        3.   *Agency* refers to the fiduciary relationship between the agent and the principal.
        4.   *Fiduciary* means the relationship of trust and confidence that the agent has with the principal.
        5.   The client is the principal to whom the agent gives counsel and advice.
        6.   The customer is the third party for whom a service is provided.
        7.   The principal is obligated to compensate the agent as well as cooperate with and not hinder the agent's ability to fulfill the fiduciary obligations.
        8.   Simple agency involves a broker representing either the seller or buyer in a transaction; limitation avoids conflicts and results in loyalty and client-based service to just one client.
        9.   Subagency is brought about when one broker, generally the seller's agent, appoints other brokers (with authorization of the seller) to assist in carrying out client-based functions on behalf of the principal; cooperating brokers have the same fiduciary responsibilities to the seller as the listing broker.

    B.   The broker owes a fiduciary duty to the principal, who may be the seller, buyer, lessor or lessee of property; the broker must perform duties of care, obedience, accounting, loyalty and disclosure for the principal (COALD).

    C.   The broker owes a fiduciary duty to the principal, but the broker is obligated to disclose to the customer material facts relating to a property; in addition, the seller usually is responsible for revealing any latent defects to the buyer.

    D.   General agent versus special agent

1. A general agent is one authorized by another to negotiate contracts for that person in a given range of matters.
2. A general agent, for example, a property manager, is authorized to represent the principal in all matters concerning one area of the principal's interest.
3. A special agent is authorized to represent the principal in one specific transaction; a real estate broker is a special agent.
4. A broker is a special agent employed by a seller to find a buyer for the seller's property or employed by a buyer to assist in the buying process.
5. As a special agent, the real estate broker is not authorized to sell property or to bind the principal to any contract.

E. To be entitled to a brokerage commission, a broker must

1. Be a licensed broker
2. Be the procuring cause of the sale/purchase
3. Be employed by the principal
4. Act according to the laws of agency

F. When a broker is employed by a seller and finds a buyer who is "ready, willing and able" to purchase on the terms and conditions of the listing or on any terms acceptable to the seller, the broker then is entitled to the commission even if

1. The sale is not completed because of the principal's default.
2. The buyer cancels because of the seller's fraud, of which the broker had no knowledge.

G. Real estate brokers may share a commission only with their own salespeople or with other licensed brokers.

H. Real estate brokers may not offer legal advice; only a licensed attorney may do so.

I. Dual agency—the broker is prohibited from representing both the seller and the buyer in the transaction without their prior, mutual knowledge and consent.

J. The broker must exercise reasonable care when representing the principal.

K. The broker is obligated to act in good faith and conform with the principal's legal instructions and authority.

L. The broker may not act as both the agent and the party to a transaction without prior knowledge and consent of all the parties.

M. All offers must be presented by the broker to the principal promptly when received.

N. A fixed place of business must be maintained by the broker.

O. The broker may be required to deposit all the funds entrusted to her or him in a trust account or do what all parties agree should be done with the funds and may not commingle such funds with operating funds.

P. The broker generally is prohibited from placing blind ads—those that do not identify the broker as the advertiser.

Q. The broker's commission is negotiable between the seller and the broker, usually is specified in the listing agreement and is computed as a percentage of the total amount of money involved, but may be expressed as a flat fee; net listings generally are not allowed in most states.

R. Buyer agency—the broker may be hired by a potential buyer; the broker and the buyer usually draw up a buyer agency agreement. The buyer/broker must

1. Be fair and honest to the seller, but owes greater responsibility to the buyer, including duties of skill and care to promote and safeguard the buyer's best interest
2. Disclose to the buyer pertinent facts (which he or she might not be able to disclose if a subagent of the seller) such as the seller is near bankruptcy or the property is overpriced
3. Use negotiating strategy and bargaining talents in the buyer's best interest

S. Transactional broker (nonagent or facilitator) is not an agent of either party. The transactional broker

1. Assists the buyer and seller with formalities and necessary paperwork required for transferring ownership of real property
2. Is expected to treat all parties honestly and competently and is equally responsible to both
3. May not disclose confidential information to either party and may not negotiate for either the seller or buyer

T. Broker Protection Clause—this states that the property owner will pay the listing broker a commission if, within a specified number of days after the listing expires, the owner transfers the property to someone the broker originally introduced to the owner.

U. Cooperative brokers, generally selling brokers, who work with the listing broker to bring the seller and buyer together

II. Salespersons

A. Salespersons are responsible only to the brokers under whom they are licensed and can carry out only those responsibilities assigned by their brokers.

B. Salespersons have no authority to make contracts or receive compensation directly from the principals.

C. All salespersons' activities must be carried out in the name of their supervising brokers.

D. Salespersons may work under brokers as either independent contractors or employees.

E. Salespersons are compensated on the basis of agreements between themselves and their brokers.

F. Salespersons may not place ads without identifying their associated brokers.

G. Salespersons are agents of their brokers and subagents of the party represented, which may be a buyer or a seller.

III. Broker's ethics

A. Fraud

1. Fraud versus puffing

a.   Fraud is a misrepresentation of facts known to be false, made with the intent to deceive and relied on by the injured party to his or her detriment; it also includes nondisclosure of pertinent facts by silence.

b.   Puffing is an opinion not made as a representation of fact.

2. Fraudulent acts not only are unethical but can result in the revocation or suspension of a broker's license.

B.   Code of Ethics—standards of ethical conduct subscribed to by members of the National Association of REALTORS® or other real estate trade organizations. Sections of the REALTOR® code have been made a part of the rules and regulations governing the conduct of real estate licensees in many states.

REVIEW LIST

The student should have an understanding of the following areas of the laws of agency:

1. Representation and disclosure

    a. Agent for seller
    b. Agent for buyer
    c. Dual agent

DIAGNOSTIC TEST

1. *A* agrees to buy *B's* real estate for $123,000. *A* signs a sales contract and deposits $12,300 earnest money with *B's* broker, *C*. *B* is unable to show good title, and *A* demands the return of his earnest money from *C*, as provided in the contract. What should *C* do?

    1. Deduct the commission and return the balance to *A*.
    2. Deduct the commission and pay the balance to *B*.
    3. Return the entire amount of earnest money to *A*.
    4. Pay the entire amount to *B* to dispose of as *B* sees fit.

2. A broker employs several salespeople at her office. Early one day one member of the sales staff submitted a written offer with an earnest money deposit on a house listed with the broker. Later the same day another salesperson submitted a higher written offer on the same property, also including an earnest money deposit. The broker, in accordance with the policy of her office, does not submit a second offer unless the first has been presented *and rejected* by the seller. In this case the seller accepted the first offer, so the seller was not informed of the second offer. In this situation, the broker's actions are

    1. permissible, provided the commission is split between the two salespeople.
    2. permissible, if such arrangement is written into the salespeople's employment contracts.
    3. not permissible, because the broker must submit all offers to the seller.
    4. not permissible, because the broker must notify the second buyer of the existence of the first offer.

3. An owner lists her home for $98,000, and the broker tells the prospective buyer to submit a low offer because the seller is desperate. The buyer offers $96,000 and the seller accepts. In this situation

    1. the broker was unethical, but because no one was hurt, the broker's conduct is not improper.
    2. the broker violated the agency relationship.
    3. the broker's action was proper in obtaining a quick offer.
    4. any broker is authorized to encourage bidders.

4. A salesperson can advertise a property for sale if she

   1. holds an active real estate license.
   2. includes her name in the ad.
   3. pays for the ad.
   4. includes her broker's name in her ad.

5. A doctor listed his home with a broker under an exclusive-right-to-sell agreement. The listing salesperson and his broker signed the listing contract. All of the following statements correctly describe the relationship among the parties **EXCEPT**

   1. the broker has a fiduciary relationship with the seller.
   2. the salesperson has a fiduciary relationship with the broker.
   3. if the salesperson dies, the listing contract will be terminated.
   4. if the broker dies, the listing contract will be terminated.

6. A real estate broker is usually

   1. a special agent.   3. a general agent.
   2. a universal agent.   4. an ostensible agent.

7. All of the following are true concerning a real estate broker **EXCEPT**

   1. all offers must be presented by the broker to the principal.
   2. brokers may place blind ads.
   3. a fixed place of business must be maintained by the broker.
   4. the broker's commission usually is specified in the listing agreement.

8. All of the following are true concerning a real estate salesperson **EXCEPT**

   1. the salesperson is responsible to the broker under whom she or he is licensed.
   2. all of a salesperson's activities must be carried out in the name of his or her principal broker.
   3. the salesperson must work under the broker as an independent contractor.
   4. a salesperson is compensated on the basis of an agreement between herself or himself and the broker.

9. You are a broker who has listed a home for a neighbor. Which of the following terms describe your relationship with the seller?

   1. You are a subagent of the seller.   3. The seller is your customer.
   2. The seller is your client.   4. The seller is your agent.

10. A man who owned a single-family house had his unlicensed son-in-law do the electrical work in preparing his home for sale. The man did not disclose this to the broker at the time of executing the listing. After completion of the sale, the new owner suffered a financial loss because of the faulty electrical wiring done by the owner's son-in-law. The broker

    1. could be reprimanded for not forewarning the purchaser.
    2. is innocent of any wrongful act.
    3. will be held liable for monetary damages suffered by the purchaser.
    4. should have arranged for a proper electrical inspection prior to the sale.

11. A home is listed for $100,000 and sells for $90,000. The broker's commission is 7 percent of the selling price. The commission is

    1. $630.
    2. $700.
    3. $6,300.
    4. $7,000.

12. You are acting as a facilitator in the sale of a house without being an agent of either party. You are a (an)

    1. buyer's broker.
    2. cooperative broker.
    3. listing broker.
    4. transactional broker.

13. The responsibilities of a broker in an agency relationship include

    1. managing the property.
    2. providing financing.
    3. accountability for funds received.
    4. accepting an offer for the seller.

14. The listing broker owes fiduciary duty to the

    1. buyer.
    2. lender.
    3. seller.
    4. buyer's attorney.

15. A broker lists an accountant's property. The broker may

    1. reject an offer for the seller's property.
    2. bind the seller to a contract.
    3. advertise the seller's property.
    4. offer legal advice to the seller.

16. A broker has received several offers for a property he has listed. The broker must present each offer to the seller

    1. promptly on receipt.
    2. individually.
    3. as soon as the seller has decided on any previous offer.
    4. prior to the seller's deciding on any previous offer.

17. A salesperson sells a property listed by her broker. The salesperson may accept her share of the commission from

    1. the seller.
    2. her broker.
    3. the buyer.
    4. the buyer's attorney.

18. Which of the following is a violation of the broker's fiduciary relationship with a seller?

    1. The broker charges no commission.
    2. The broker charges a 40 percent commission.
    3. The broker tells a prospective buyer the lowest price the seller will accept.
    4. The broker tells a prospective buyer the highest price the seller will accept.

19. All of the following statements correctly describe a fiduciary **EXCEPT** a

    1. Fiduciary owes loyalty to the principal.
    2. Fiduciary must conform to the principal's legal instructions.
    3. Fiduciary is an agent.
    4. Fiduciary is a neutral third party.

20. A salesperson is working under a broker. The salesperson may

    1. work under the broker as an independent contractor.
    2. place an ad without identifying the broker.
    3. receive a commission directly from a seller.
    4. receive a commission directly from another broker.

21. A special agent could best be described as someone who

    1. has power of attorney.
    2. has authority to sell a property.
    3. has authority to represent a principal in a specific transaction.
    4. has authority to represent a principal in all matters concerning an area of the principal's interest.

22. A broker presents a seller with a written offer to purchase. The broker is responsible for

    1. explaining the advantages or disadvantages of the offer to the seller.
    2. explaining the legal implications of accepting the offer.
    3. binding the seller to the offer.
    4. preparing the title search once the offer is accepted.

23. A broker is listing her neighbor's home. The commission should be determined by

    1. the size of the broker's firm.
    2. rates approved by the Real Estate Commission.
    3. rates approved by the local Board of REALTORS®.
    4. negotiation with her neighbor.

24. A broker recently has listed a home under an exclusive-right-to-sell listing contract. The broker generally will earn his commission when

    1. he submits an offer to purchase to the seller.
    2. the seller signs an offer to purchase.
    3. he finds a buyer "ready, willing and able" to buy on the terms of the listing.
    4. the closing has taken place.

25. A broker has earned a commission on the sale of her listing by another broker. The listing broker may pay part of her commission to

    1. the selling broker.
    2. the selling salesperson.
    3. the out-of-state salesperson who referred the seller to her.
    4. the buyer's attorney.

26. A broker has just received an earnest money payment on an offer to purchase. The broker must place the earnest money in his

   1. trust account.
   2. business account.
   3. personal checking account.
   4. savings account.

27. A salesperson working for a broker has just written an offer to purchase on her broker's listing in which the buyer has written a check for earnest money and stated that the broker hold the funds. Which of the following statements describes how the earnest money payment should be handled?

   1. The salesperson should place the earnest money in her checking account and await the closing of the transaction.
   2. The salesperson should give the earnest money check to the seller's attorney.
   3. The salesperson should place the earnest money check in a safe deposit box until the transaction is concluded.
   4. The salesperson should give the earnest money check to her broker for deposit in the broker's trust account.

28. A licensed real estate broker who engages the services of a licensed salesperson on the basis that the broker can direct what the salesperson can do but not how it is done has

   1. engaged an independent contractor.
   2. discriminated illegally.
   3. practiced steering.
   4. established an employer-employee relationship.

29. A broker's license can be revoked if he or she

   1. advertises property for sale without including the salesperson's name in the ad.
   2. negotiates a commission based on what the broker says is the rate set by the local board of REALTORS® but that exceeds the customary rate.
   3. pays a commission that exceeds the customary rate.
   4. advertises free market analysis as a means of obtaining listings.

30. What is the listing broker's legal responsibility to a prospective purchaser?

   1. The broker must not use fraud or deceit.
   2. The broker must help the buyer get the lowest price possible.
   3. The broker is only a middleman. Neither the buyer nor the seller can charge her or him with avoiding a legal duty.
   4. There is none at all.

ANSWER KEY

Question	Answer	Outline Reference		Question	Answer	Outline Reference
1.	3	I		16.	1	I
2.	3	I		17.	2	II
3.	2	I		18.	3	I
4.	4	II		19.	4	I
5.	3	III		20.	1	II
6.	1	I		21.	3	I
7.	2	I		22.	1	I
8.	3	II		23.	4	I
9.	2	I		24.	3	I
10.	2	I		25.	1	I
11.	3	Part 8		26.	1	I
12.	4	I		27.	4	I
13.	3	I		28.	1	I
14.	3	I		29.	2	I
15.	3	I		30.	1	I

LAWS OF AGENCY

Rating	Test Score Range	Your Score	
GOOD = 80% to 100%	24–30	Total number	30
FAIR = 70% to 79%	21–23	Total wrong	–__
NEEDS IMPROVEMENT = Below 70%	20 or less	Total right	__

Passing requirement— 21 or better

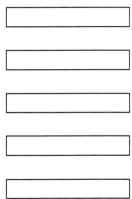

PART 6 / CONTRACTS

OUTLINE OF CONCEPTS TO UNDERSTAND

I.   Voluntary agreement between legally competent parties to do or refrain from doing some legal act, supported by legal consideration

II. Essential elements of a valid contract

    A.   Competent parties—must be of legal age and mentally competent

    B.   Offer and acceptance (mutual assent)—must be a "meeting of the minds"

        1.   Any offer or counteroffer may be withdrawn at any time prior to acceptance by the offeree.

    C.   Legality of object—purpose must be legal

    D.   Consideration—an act of forbearance, or the promise thereof, given by one party in exchange for something from the other. Forbearance is a promise not to do something

    E.   Description of real estate—must be accurate

    F.   Written and signed—generally required by the statute of frauds for most real estate contracts.

III. Contract classifications

    A.   Expressed—parties state terms and show intentions in words; may be either oral or written.

    B.   Implied—agreement demonstrated by acts and conduct.

    C.   Bilateral—both parties promise to do something; one promise is given in exchange for another.

    D.   Unilateral—only one party makes a promise; if the second party complies, the first party is obligated to keep the promise, such as an option or open listing.

    E.   Executed—both parties have fulfilled their promises and thus performed the contract.

F.   Executory—something remains to be done by one or both parties.

IV.   Legal effect of a contract

A.   Valid—complies with all essentials of a contract; binding and enforceable on both parties

B.   Void—lacks an essential element of a valid contract; has no legal effect

C.   Voidable—appears to be valid on its surface but may be disaffirmed because one of the parties signed when a minor, when under duress or as a result of fraud or misrepresentation

D.   Unenforceable—appears to be valid, but neither party may sue the other to force performance; for example, an oral agreement to pay a commission

V.   Discharge of contract

A.   Performance—all terms carried out

B.   Substantial performance—party remains liable because the contract was not completed exactly as required

C.   Mutual agreement—parties agree to cancel

D.   Operation of law—voided by minor or because of fraud or the expiration of the statute of limitations

VI.   Default/breach of contract

A.   Buyer recourse if seller defaults

1.   Rescind, or terminate, the contract and recover the earnest money.
2.   Sue for specific performance.
3.   Sue the seller for damages.

B.   Seller recourse if buyer defaults

1.   Declare the contract forfeited.
2.   Rescind the contract and keep the deposit as liquidated damages.
3.   Sue for specific performance.
4.   Sue for damages.

VII.   Types of listing agreements

A.   Open listing

1.   The seller may employ any number of brokers.
2.   The seller is obligated to pay a commission only to the broker who produces a buyer (procuring cause).
3.   If the seller personally sells the property without the aid of any broker, the seller is not obligated to pay the commission.

B.   Exclusive-agency listing

1.   Only one broker is authorized to act as the exclusive agent of the principal.
2.   The seller retains the right to sell the property without obligation to the broker.

C. Exclusive-right-to-sell listing

1. One broker is given the exclusive right to sell the property.
2. The seller gives up the right to sell the property without paying the broker's commission.
3. The broker receives the commission regardless of who sells the property.

D. Net listing

1. The list price is based on the amount of money the seller will receive if the property is sold, plus the commission.
2. If the property is sold, the seller receives only the net amount for which the property was listed, and the broker retains the remainder.
3. Prohibited or discouraged in many states.

E. All listings are agreements between the broker and the seller, not the salesperson.

F. Types of buyer agency agreements

1. Exclusive right agreements—the buyer must compensate her agent whenever she purchases a property of the type described within the period described.
2. Exclusive agreement—the buyer's agent is assured of buyer loyalty relative to any other agents. The buyer may, however, purchase property on his own without the assistance of an agent and thus without any compensation being due to the buyer's agent.
3. Open agreement—the buyer can work with more than one buyer's agent at the same time but owes compensation only if she uses the services of a buyer's broker.
4. Situations where it is appropriate for a buyer to enter into a relationship with buyer broker.
    a. A family business relationship or friendship exists, which makes it difficult for broker to be completely loyal to the seller.
    b. Working with former seller clients as buyer customers.
    c. The buyer prefers to have the agent as her advocate.
    d. The broker is buying for himself; he must disclose he is a licensed agent and representing himself and not a seller.

G. Ways in which buyer's broker can be compensated

1. Retainer fee.
2. Gives buyer incentive to perform contract.
3. Fee may be refundable or nonrefundable.

H. Flat or fixed fee

1. Can calculate a straight fixed fee
2. The fee can be paid by the buyer or as a co-op fee by the seller.
3. The hourly fee should reflect the market as well as what other professionals are receiving.
4. Percentage fee
    a. It can be a percentage of the sales price or MLS (mulitple listing service) co-op fee.
    b. Creates a disincentive for buyer's broker to get a lower price for buyer.

VIII.   Termination of listings or buyer agency agreements

    A.   Operation of law

        1.   Contracting with an individual while she or he is in a state of diminished capacity
        2.   Death or incapacity of either party
        3.   Destruction of the property or change in the property use because of an outside force
        4.   Bankruptcy of either party

    B.   Acts of the parties

        1.   Mutual consent
        2.   Completion of the objective
        3.   Expiration
        4.   Revocation by the principal
        5.   Renunciation by the agent
            a.   Subject to liability for damages caused by revoking or renouncing the agreement

IX.   Contract for the sale of real estate

    A.   Required by the statute of frauds to be in writing to be enforceable.

    B.   Sets forth all details of the agreement between the buyer and the seller for the purchase and sale of real estate.

    C.   When the contract has been prepared and signed by the purchaser, it is an offer to purchase the subject real estate.

    D.   An offer becomes a contract when accepted and binding when it is communicated to the buyer.

    E.   More detailed than the deed itself because the contract in effect dictates the contents of the deed and all other terms and conditions.

    F.   After both the buyer and the seller have executed the sales contract, the buyer acquires the interest in the land, known as *equitable title.*

    G.   A "time is of the essence" contract must be performed in the time specified; any party who does not perform on time is guilty of breach of contract.

X.   Earnest money deposits—not required for a legal contract

    A.   Generally give evidence of intention to carry out the terms of contract

        1.   Usually must be held by the broker in a special trust, or escrow, account
        2.   Cannot be commingled, mixed with a broker's operating funds or converted to a broker's own use
        3.   The amount is generally determined by negotiation between the buyer and seller.
        4.   A deposit is not legally required to create a valid contract.

XI.   Options

    A.   Contract by which the optionor (owner) gives the optionee (prospective buyer) the right to buy at a fixed price within a stated period of time.

B. The optionee pays the fee for the option right and assumes no obligation to make any other payment until the optionee decides, within a specified time, to either exercise the option right or allow the option to expire.

XII. Installment contract/contract for deed/land contract

A. Means of financing a purchase: the buyer gives the seller a nominal down payment and regular periodic payments over a number of years, including interest.

B. Legal title to real estate remains in the vendor's (seller's) name during the term of contract.

C. The vendee (purchaser) takes possession when the contract is executed.

D. The vendee will not receive the deed to the property until the entire purchase price has been paid.

E. The vendee has the equitable title during the life of the contract.

XIII. Other real estate contracts

A. Counteroffer—new offer made in response to an offer received; original offer is, in effect, rejected and cannot be accepted thereafter unless revived by the offeror

B. Amendments—licensees in many states are required to fill out amendment forms to change the language in either the listing contract or the offer to purchase.

C. Cancellation agreements—forms used to terminate a transaction; used in some states by a broker to get a written release from both the buyer and the seller to authorize the refund of earnest money

D. Leasing agreement—written or oral contracts between the tenant (lessee) and the landlord (lessor); transfers the right to exclusive possession and the use of the landlord's real property to the lessee for a stated consideration (rent) and for a specified period of time; the statute of frauds requires that the lease for more than one year be in writing to be enforceable

E. Addendum—adds additional terms and conditions to the approved forms, thus incorporating them into the legal document; may or may not require preparation by an attorney

REVIEW LIST

The student should have an understanding of the following types of contracts:

1.   Listing contracts

2.   Buyer/broker contracts

3.   Offers to purchase

4.   Counteroffers

5.   Amendments

6.   Cancellation agreements

7.   Leasing agreements

8.   Options

9.   Addenda

DIAGNOSTIC TEST

1.   A contract in which the intentions of the parties are shown by their actions is

   1.   an expressed contract.
   2.   an implied contract.
   3.   an executory contract.
   4.   a bilateral contract.

2.   All of the following are essential elements to a contract **EXCEPT**

   1.   patent of parties.
   2.   legality of object.
   3.   offer and acceptance (mutual assent).
   4.   competent parties.

3.   The lessee in a leasing agreement is the

   1.   tenant.
   2.   property manager.
   3.   landlord.
   4.   rental agent.

4.   A lease that is signed by a person who is 17 years of age is

   1.   unilateral.
   2.   void.
   3.   illegal.
   4.   voidable.

5.   Contracts for sale of real estate must be in writing to be enforceable, according to the

   1.   statute of limitations.
   2.   parol evidence rule.
   3.   statute of frauds.
   4.   real estate commission.

6. A broker lists a home for $80,000. The broker brings an offer to the seller for $78,000, which is rejected by the seller. The broker obtains another offer, for $80,000, for the seller. Before he can deliver the offer, however, the offeror withdraws it by calling the broker at the seller's home. There is

   1.   an implied contract.
   2.   a unilateral contract.
   3.   an executory contract.
   4.   no contract.

7. You have entered into an option contract with an optionee who has 30 days to exercise his option. Your option could be called a (an)

   1.   voidable contract.
   2.   unilateral contract.
   3.   unenforceable contract.
   4.   bilateral contract.

8. Which of the following contracts generally is prohibited or discouraged in many states?

   1.   Option
   2.   Land contract
   3.   Open listing
   4.   Net listing

9. You order dinner in a restaurant. You are required to pay for the dinner through what kind of contract?

   1.   Bilateral
   2.   Express
   3.   Voidable
   4.   Implied

10. A broker and a seller have signed an open listing contract. This agreement is an example of

   1.   a unilateral contract.
   2.   an executed contract.
   3.   a bilateral contract.
   4.   an unenforceable contract.

11. Which of the following correctly describes an open listing?

   1.   The seller may employ any number of brokers.
   2.   Only one broker is authorized to act as agent for the seller.
   3.   The broker is entitled to a commission regardless of who sells the property.
   4.   The broker's commission is based on the excess over the sales price stated in the listing.

12. A salesperson obtains a written offer to purchase a home that she has listed for sale. The seller accepts the offer, and the salesperson promptly telephones the purchaser to notify him of the acceptance. Because the purchaser lives in a nearby town, the salesperson informs him that she will deliver a copy of the contract in three days. The salesperson has an enforceable contract when

   1.   the seller signs the acceptance.
   2.   the offer to purchase is presented to the seller.
   3.   the acceptance has been telephoned to the salesperson who is representing the purchaser.
   4.   a copy of the contract is delivered to the purchaser in three days.

13. A contract that has no legal effect because it does not contain all essential requirements of a contract is

   1. voidable.
   2. unenforceable.
   3. void.
   4. canceled.

14. All of the following might legally terminate a listing with a broker **EXCEPT**

   1. bankruptcy of the client.
   2. insanity of the broker.
   3. inability of the broker to find a buyer within a reasonable amount of time.
   4. an economic depression.

15. *A* gave an option on her property for 90 days to *B* and received a cash consideration of $100. *B* later assigned the option to *C* for a valuable consideration. Before expiration of the option, *A* stated that she no longer wanted to sell the property. Which of the following is correct?

   1. The option is void, for an option cannot be assigned.
   2. The option is not binding on *A,* for $100 is not sufficient consideration.
   3. *C* would have a good chance in court to compel *A* to sell to him, if he exercises the option before its expiration date.
   4. *A* can refuse to sell, for the consideration paid by *C* was not in cash.

16. Both the buyer and the seller agree to wait until the broker's exclusive-right-to-sell listing has expired. They then have a third party buy the home. After a short while, the third party conveys ownership to the interested buyer, who was introduced to the owner by the listing broker. In this case,

   1. the broker is not entitled to a commission because the listing expired.
   2. if the listing broker can prove collusion, he can collect full commission.
   3. the broker may sue both the buyer and the seller for the commission.
   4. the broker is entitled to his commission because he performed the task for which he was hired.

17. Procuring cause would not be required for a broker to receive a commission in a (an)

   1. open listing.
   2. exclusive-right-to-sell listing.
   3. net listing.
   4. exclusive agency listing.

18. When a broker sold a property, the sales contract contained the following statement: "Buyer to accept property in an 'as is' condition." Both the seller and the broker knew the plumbing was in a major state of disrepair but did not tell the buyer. Would an action for damages against the broker, based on fraud, be successful?

   1. No. The "as is" provision in the contract is evidence of a meeting of the minds.
   2. No. The contract specifically stated that the property was being sold "as is."
   3. Yes. The duty to disclose a material fact cannot be avoided by an "as is" provision.
   4. Yes. "As is" refers only to exterior defects.

19. A broker brings a seller an offer-to-purchase contract for the listed price of $114,500, with the stipulation that the seller must furnish a title insurance policy to prove marketable title. The seller refuses the offer. The broker

   1. can collect full commission because sellers must always provide title insurance.
   2. can collect one-half of the commission.
   3. can collect nothing.
   4. can collect one-half of the first month's mortgage payment.

20. A seller listed her home with a broker. Shortly thereafter, the seller telephoned the broker and withdrew the exclusive-right-to-sell listing. A week later, she sold the home to her neighbor for a higher price than the price on the listing. In this situation, which of the following is true?

   1. The owner has the right to terminate the listing at any time without being liable for damages.
   2. Under an exclusive right-to-sell listing, the broker is not entitled to damages.
   3. The broker is not entitled to a commission because the seller obtained a better price than she would have received through the broker's efforts.
   4. If the owner withdrew the listing after the broker spent money on it, the owner may be liable to the broker for damages.

21. A salesperson for a broker listed an owner's home under an exclusive-right-to-sell listing contract. Which of the following statements correctly describes this situation?

   1. The listing belongs to the salesperson.
   2. If the principal sells his own house, he will not have to pay a commission.
   3. The listing belongs to the broker.
   4. The listing belongs to both the salesperson and the broker.

22. An owner gives an exclusive-right-to-sell listing to a broker for a six-month period. During the exclusive period, the owner also gives an open listing to another broker who produces a buyer. What is the owner's liability for payment of a commission?

   1. Only one commission must be paid, which both brokers share on a 50/50 basis.
   2. The owner is liable only to the first broker for the payment of a commission.
   3. The owner is liable for payment of a commission to both brokers.
   4. The owner is liable only to the second broker for the payment of a commission.

23. A buyer has contracted with a seller to purchase property. The contract was ratified on January 10. The closing was on March 31. What is the status of the contract on April 1?

   1. Void
   2. Anticipatory
   3. Executed
   4. Executory

24. A listing contract

   1. is a conveyance.
   2. is a contract of employment.
   3. is a unilateral contract.
   4. is terminated on the death of the listing salesperson.

25. A salesperson

    1.   may receive a commission directly from a principal.
    2.   can carry out activities in his or her own name.
    3.   is responsible primarily to the broker under whom she or he is licensed.
    4.   may place a blind ad.

ANSWER KEY

Question	Answer	Outline Reference	Question	Answer	Outline Reference
1.	2	III	14.	4	VIII
2.	1	II	15.	3	XI
3.	1	XIII	16.	2	VII
4.	4	IV	17.	2	VII
5.	3	II	18.	3	IX
6.	4	II	19.	3	IX
7.	2	III	20.	4	VIII
8.	4	VII	21.	3	VII
9.	4	II	22.	3	VII
10.	1	VII	23.	3	III
11.	1	IX	24.	2	VII
12.	4	IX	25.	3	VII
13.	3	IV			

CONTRACTS

Rating	Test Score Range	Your Score	
GOOD = 80% to 100%	20–25	Total number	25
FAIR = 60% to 80%	15–19	Total wrong	–__
NEEDS IMPROVEMENT = Below 60%	14 or less	Total right	__

Passing requirement— 20 or better

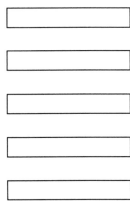

PART 7 / FEDERAL LAWS AND REGULATIONS

OUTLINE OF CONCEPTS TO UNDERSTAND

I. Federal Fair Housing Laws

   A. Civil Rights Act of 1866—prohibits racial discrimination in the buying, renting, selling, holding or conveying of real and personal property

   B. Federal Fair Housing Act of 1968—provides that it is unlawful to discriminate on the basis of race, color, religion, or national origin when selling or leasing residential property

      1. In 1974, the Housing and Community Development Act added sex.

   C. An amendment to the federal fair housing law went into effect in March 1989 adding handicap and familial status to the list of protected classes and giving the U.S. Department of Housing and Urban Development (HUD) more enforcement authority.

      1. The new amendment defines *familial status* as one or more individuals who have not reached the age of 18 being domiciled with a parent or another person who has or is seeking legal custody.
         a. A person who is pregnant also is included in the definition of *familial status.*
         b. All properties must be made available under the same terms and conditions as available to all other persons unless a property meets the standards for exemption as "housing for older persons."
      2. The new amendment defines *disability* as a physical or mental impairment that substantially limits one or more of a person's major life activities.
         a. A definition of *disability* does not include the current illegal use of or addiction to a controlled substance.
         b. Persons who have AIDS also are protected under the handicap classification as are persons in an addiction recovery program.
         c. Persons renting a dwelling are required to permit handicapped persons to make modifications of existing premises at their own

expense if these modifications are necessary to afford full enjoyment of the premises.
    d. In a rental-property situation, a landlord may condition the agreement to allow modifications upon an agreement to restore the interior of the premises to the premodification condition.
    e. There are a number of accessibility and usability requirements covering certain types of newly constructed residential buildings that must be met under federal law; access is required for common-use and public areas of the building as well as adaptive and accessible design for the interior of the dwelling units.
3. Types of illegal activity under familial status include
    a. Charging higher security deposits.
    b. Segregating families within buildings.
    c. Segregating families in certain buildings.
    d. Maintaining "adults-only" complexes that do not constitute housing for older adults, which will be defined shortly
4. Types of illegal activity under handicapped include
    a. Refusal to permit reasonable modifications that are necessary for the full enjoyment at the renter's expense
    b. Refusal to make reasonable accommodations in rules, policies, practices or services
    c. Failure to design and construct for first occupancy, as of March 1991, an accessible route into and through a dwelling
5. The 1988 amendments also provide that certain properties may be restricted for occupancy by the elderly.
    a. The amendments provide an exemption from the familial-status protection for housing intended for or occupied solely by persons 62 years of age or older or housing intended for or occupied by at least one person 55 years of age or older per unit.
    b. Properties complying with the "55-or-older" exemption must provide significant facilities and services to meet the physical and social needs of older persons, and at least 80 percent of the units must be occupied by individuals who are 55 years of age or older.
    c. Exemption properties also must publish policies and procedures that demonstrate the intent to provide housing for these individuals.
6. The 1988 amendments do not require that housing be made available to
    a. Individuals whose tenancy would constitute a direct threat to the health or safety of other individuals or that would result in substantial physical damage to the property of others
    b. Individuals who have been convicted of the illegal manufacture or distribution of controlled substances
7. The 1988 amendments also made significant changes to the enforcement mechanisms under the Fair Housing Act of 1965, including
    a. Authorizing administrative law judges to award both economic and noneconomic damages, injunctive relief and reasonable attorney fees and to impose civil penalties against violators of the act
    b. Expanding the statute of limitations for initiating administrative proceedings from 180 days to one year after the alleged discriminatory housing practice

    c.   Authorizing administrative law judges within HUD to hold contested case hearings

    d.   Requiring HUD to proceed with cases on behalf of any person alleging that she or he has been the victim of housing discrimination, regardless of whether the alleged victim provides his or her own legal counsel

8. Remedies under the new amendments include

    a.   A civil penalty against the respondent, not exceeding $10,000 for the first offense

    b.   A penalty not exceeding $25,000 if another offense was committed within the past five years

    c.   A penalty not exceeding $50,000 if two or more discriminatory practices have been found in the past seven years

    d.   An order for "appropriate" relief that may include actual damages, injunctive relief and "other equitable relief"

    e.   A recommendation for disciplinary action against a named respondent whose licensure by a governmental agency is related to the complaint (including license suspension or revocation)

9. Other prohibited discriminatory acts include

    a.   Refusing to sell, rent or negotiate with any person as a means of discrimination

    b.   Changing terms for different individuals as a means of discrimination

    c.   Making discriminatory advertising statements

    d.   Representing that a property is unavailable as a means of discrimination

    e.   Blockbusting—making a profit by inducing owners to sell because of the prospective entry of minorities into the neighborhood

    f.   Redlining—discriminatory denial of loans or insurance to people in selected areas, regardless of their qualifications

    g.   Steering—leading prospective homebuyers to specific areas or avoiding specific areas either to maintain or to change the character of an area

    h.   Denying membership in a multiple-listing service (MLS) or related groups as a means of discrimination

10. Exemptions from the law

    a.   Sale or rental of a single-family home if the home is owned by a person who does not own more than three such homes at one time and if certain conditions exist

        1)   A broker is not used.

        2)   Discriminatory advertising is not used.

        3)   If the owner is not currently living in the home or was not the most recent occupant, only one such exempt sale has been made within any two-year period.

    b.   Rental, if rooms or units are in an owner-occupied one-family to four-family dwelling

    c.   Dwelling units owned by religious organizations may be restricted to persons of the same religion if membership is not restricted on the basis of race, color, sex (or gender), national origin, disability or familial status.

    d.   Lodgings of a private club may be restricted to members as long as the lodgings are not operated commercially.

D.   Equal Housing Poster—the 1974 amendment to the 1968 Federal Fair Housing Act requires that the Equal Housing Opportunity logo (poster) be posted with the agent's license.

E.   Federal Equal Credit Opportunity Act—prohibits discrimination against credit applicants on the basis of race, color, religion, national origin, sex, marital status, age (if the applicant is of legal age) or dependency on public assistance; requires that all rejected credit applicants be informed, in writing, of the reasons for credit denial.

II.   Americans with Disabilities Act (ADA)

A.   This 1990 law affects real estate licensees because it addresses the rights of individuals with disabilities in employment and public accommodations.

B.   The ADA provides for the employment of qualified job applicants regardless of their disabilities.

C.   Any employer with 15 or more employees as of July 26, 1994, must adopt nondiscriminatory employment procedures and make reasonable accommodations to enable an individual with a disability to perform in her or his employment.

D.   The ADA (Title III) states that individuals with disabilities have the right to full and equal access to businesses and public services; thus, building owners and managers must be sure that obstacles restricting those rights are eliminated.

E.   The ADA also provides comprehensive guidance for making public facilities accessible.

F.   The law seeks to protect property owners from incurring burdensome expense to extensively retrofit an existing building by recommending reasonable achievable accommodations that will accomplish the purpose of providing access to the facility and services.

G.   Because it costs less to incorporate accessible features in the design than to retrofit, new construction, including remodeling, must meet higher standards, being readily accessible and usable.

H.   Types of alterations that might be made to public facilities and services include

    1. Attaching grab bars to a restroom stall
    2. Providing automatic-entry doors
    3. Adjusting the height of a pay telephone to make it accessible to a person in a wheelchair
    4. Converting information on real estate listings to large print or audio format

I.   The ADA provides for enforcement by allowing several remedies for a person who is discriminated against, including

    1. A temporary or permanent injunction
    2. The court may grant any equitable relief that the court considers appropriate.
    3. A civil penalty of up to $50,000 may be assessed for a first violation of the law, and a penalty of up to $100,000 may be assessed for any subsequent violation.

III. Truth-in-Lending Law

   A. Regulation Z

      1. Disclosure requirements
         a. Requires disclosure of cost in credit transactions.
         b. Customer has the right to rescind in some types of credit transactions under certain conditions, for example, a second mortgage

      2. Coverage of Regulation Z
         a. Loans to individuals covered for all real estate credit transactions for personal, family and household purposes, regardless of the amount involved
         b. Loans to individuals covered for non–real estate credit transactions for personal, family and household purposes up to $25,000

      3. Agreements not covered
         a. Personal property credit transactions for amounts of more than $25,000
         b. Real estate purchase agreements
         c. Business or commercial loans
         d. Loans with four or fewer installments
         e. Loans made without interest charges
         f. Loans to government agencies
         g. Assumptions with no change in terms
         h. Agricultural loans for amounts of more than $25,000

      4. Requirements of Regulation Z regarding finance charges
         a. All finance charges as well as the true annual interest rate must be disclosed to the customer before the transaction is completed.
         b. Finance charges must include interest, loan fees, points, service charges, finder's fees, credit fees and property and credit insurance.
         c. The finance charge must be stated as the annual percentage rate.

      5. Requirements of Regulation Z regarding liens on residences
         a. A "cooling off" period is required when liens will be placed on a principal residence; the borrower has the right to rescind the transaction up to midnight of the third business day following the transaction or until delivery of the disclosure statement, whichever is later.
         b. The right to rescind does not apply to loans to finance the purchase or initial construction of a house.

      6. Advertising
         a. Regulation Z does not require brokers to advertise credit terms; if lenders advertise some credit details, however, they must fully disclose the terms.
         b. Full disclosure of terms
            1) Amount of down payment
            2) Amount of loan or cash price
            3) Finance charges as annual percentage rate
            4) Number, amount and due dates of payments
            5) Total of all payments except where advertisement relates to first mortgage

7. Regulation Z is administered by the Federal Trade Commission (FTC) and promulgated by the Federal Reserve System (FRS).
8. Penalties for noncompliance
   a. Violation of an administration order enforcing Regulation Z is $10,000 for each day the violation continues.
   b. Engaging in an unfair or deceptive practice may result in the imposition of a fine of up to $10,000.
   c. A creditor may be liable to a consumer for twice the amount of the finance charge, from a minimum of $100 to a maximum of $1,000, plus court costs, attorney's fees and any actual damages.
   d. Willful violation constitutes a misdemeanor and is punishable by a fine of up to $5,000 or one year's imprisonment or both.

IV.   Real Estate Settlement Procedures Act (RESPA)

A.   Created to ensure that the buyer and the seller have knowledge of all the settlement costs before closing

B.   Requirements

1. Lenders must give a copy of the special information booklet, *Settlement Costs and You,* to each loan applicant.
2. The borrower must be provided with a good-faith estimate of the settlement costs by the lender no later than three business days after the receipt of the loan application.
3. The loan closing must be prepared on a Uniform Settlement Statement (HUD Form 1).
4. RESPA explicitly prohibits the payment of kickbacks and prohibits referral fees when no services are actually rendered.

C.   RESPA regulations apply only to transactions involving new first-mortgage referral loans for one-family to four-family family dwellings generally financed by the federally related mortgage loan.

V.   Foreign Investment and Real Property Tax Act (IRC Section 1445)

A.   A federal law aimed at ensuring that nonresident aliens and foreign corporations pay U.S. income tax based on gains from the disposition of U.S. real property interest

1. In real property located in the United States
2. In any domestic corporation that was a U.S. real property holding corporation during the period that the taxpayer held the interest after June 18, 1980, or at any time during the five-year period ending on the date of the disposition of the property, if earlier

B.   Generally, a transferee of any U.S. real property interest is required to withhold a tax equal to 10 percent of the amount realized by the foreign transferor on the disposition of the property.

C.   If a transferor's or transferee's agent fails to furnish the notice required, the agent, for example, a broker, is required to withhold in the same manner as would be required of the transferee, except that the agent's liability is limited to the amount of compensation that he or she derives from the transaction.

D. A buyer or other transferee of a U.S. real property interest and any corporation, partnership or fiduciary required to withhold tax must file an IRS Form 8288 to report and transmit the amount withheld.

E. Buyers or other transferees of a U.S. real property interest also must file an IRS Form 8288-A to show the amount withheld.

F. Generally, the amount required to be withheld with respect to any disposition of a U.S. real property interest cannot exceed the amount of the transferor's maximum tax liability.

G. Brokers involved in listing or selling a U.S. real property interest for nonresident aliens or foreign corporations should contact the IRS to establish the appropriate procedures.

VI. IRS regulations

A. Generally do not apply to purchases where the property will be used as a residence and the sale price is under $300,000

B. Independent Contractor and Employee—under the "qualified real estate agent" category in the Internal Revenue Code, meeting three requirements can establish independent-contractor status.

1. The individual must have a current real estate license.
2. The individual must have a written contract with the broker that contains the following clause: "The salesperson will not be treated as an employee with respect to the services performed by such salesperson as a real estate agent for federal tax purposes."
3. Ninety percent or more of the individual's income as a licensee must be based on sales production, not on the number of hours worked.
4. The broker should have a standardized agreement drafted or reviewed by an attorney.

C. 1099 forms

1. IRS rules require closing agents to report details of closing to the IRS using IRS Form 1099 S.
2. Reports must be submitted for sales or exchanges of residences with four or fewer units.
3. Commissions paid to salespeople by brokers also must be reported on IRS Form 1099 MISC.

D. Declarations of value

1. Documents or statements of value that accompany every deed or contract to be recorded in the registrar of deeds office
2. Statements of value are used by local and state tax officials for assessment purposes.

E. Imputed interest

1. The IRS will impute, or assign, interest at a prescribed rate, computed monthly, on an installment contract that fails to include an interest rate or states an unreasonably low rate.
2. Although no interest is paid, buyers may deduct for tax purposes imputed interest per annum on unpaid balances.

        3. Rate for determining whether interest should be imputed and the amount of interest that should be imputed is based on the applicable federal rate (AFR).

        4. AFR is one of three rates, depending on whether the debt instrument is
- a. Short term—not more than three years
- b. Midterm—more than three years but not more than nine years
- c. Long term—more than nine years

        5. The IRS issues alternative AFRs on a monthly basis.

        6. Installment sales less than $3,000 are not covered by the imputed-interest law.

F.   1031 tax-deferred exchange

        1. Under Section 1031 of the IRC, real estate investors can defer taxation of capital gains by making a property exchange.

        2. A property owner may exchange her or his property for another property and have tax liability on the sale only if additional capital or property is received.

        3. Tax on an exchange is deferred rather than eliminated.

        4. Properties involved in the exchange must be of like kind.

        5. *Like kind* refers to any real property to be held for income purposes or investment; it excludes dealer property and residences.

        6. Additional capital or personal property included in a transaction to even out the exchange is considered boot; the party receiving boot is taxed at the time of the exchange.

VII. Antitrust law

A.   Antitrust law prohibitions

        1. Allocation of customers or markets—agreement among brokers to divide their markets and refrain from competing for each other's business; division may take place on a geographic basis or on a certain price range of homes

        2. Price fixing—conspiracy among brokers to set prices for their services, rather than negotiate such fees

        3. Boycotting—two or more businesses conspire against other businesses to reduce competition

        4. People violating the Sherman Antitrust Act may be found guilty of a felony punishable by a maximum $100,000 fine and three years in prison.

        5. In a civil suit a broker found guilty of a violation of the Sherman Antitrust Act will be liable for three times the actual damages plus attorney's fees and costs.

REVIEW LIST

The student should have an understanding of the following areas of federal laws and regulations:

1.   Compliance with federal fair-housing laws

2.   Americans with Disabilities Act

3.   Truth-in-Lending Law (Regulation Z)

4.   Real Estate Settlement Procedures Act (RESPA)

5.   Foreign Investment and Real Estate Property Tax Act (IRC Section 1445)

6.   IRS regulations (Independent Contractor and Employee, 1099 forms, declarations of value, imputed interest, 1031 tax-deferred exchange)

7.   Antitrust laws

DIAGNOSTIC TEST

1.   All of the following are stipulations of RESPA **EXCEPT**

   1.   Lenders must give a copy of a special information booklet to each loan applicant.
   2.   The lender must provide a borrower with a good-faith estimate of settlement costs.
   3.   Paying a kickback is permitted.
   4.   The loan closing must be prepared on a Uniform Settlement Statement.

2.   The federal fair housing laws prohibit discrimination on the basis of

   1.   sexual orientation.
   2.   political beliefs.
   3.   marital status.
   4.   sex.

3.   Persuading someone to sell by telling her or him that minorities are moving into the neighborhood is illegal and is called

   1.   redlining.
   2.   blockbusting.
   3.   testing.
   4.   steering.

4.   Which of the following is exempted from the federal fair housing laws?

   1.   Rental of rooms in an owner-occupied five-family dwelling
   2.   Rental of an owner-occupied, five-family dwelling
   3.   Rental of a single-family home when a broker is used
   4.   Lodgings of a private club when the lodgings are not operated commercially

5. The practice of channeling potential buyers of one race into one area and potential buyers of another race into another area is known as

   1. canvassing.   3. redlining.
   2. blockbusting.   4. steering.

6. A real estate broker may

   1. refuse to rent to a qualified minority person.
   2. solicit listings in a residential neighborhood.
   3. refuse to negotiate with a minority person.
   4. change the terms of sale for a minority person.

7. The federal fair housing laws prohibit which of the following types of private housing?

   1. A Lutheran organization giving preference to its members in renting
   2. A Norwegian advertising his house for "Norwegians only"
   3. The Elks Club operating a rooming house on a nonprofit basis
   4. A Masonic Lodge operating a rooming house when the lodgings are not operated commercially

8. Which of the following categories is NOT protected against discrimination under the federal fair housing laws?

   1. Religion   3. Disabled status
   2. Parental status   4. Lawful source of income

9. The denial of a loan by a lender would be a violation of federal fair housing laws if it were based on

   1. lack of income.   3. age.
   2. sex.   4. marital status.

10. The need for a loan closing to be prepared on a Uniform Settlement Statement is a requirement of

    1. Regulation Z.
    2. the federal fair housing laws.
    3. Government National Mortgage Association (Ginnie Mae) (GNMA).
    4. RESPA.

11. The requirement that a lender give each loan applicant a copy of *Settlement Costs and You* is created under

    1. Federal Home Loan Mortgage Corporation (Freddie Mac) (FHLMC).
    2. Federal Housing Administration (FHA).
    3. RESPA.
    4. Regulation Z.

12. Which of the following is NOT a requirement for establishing independent-contractor status for a salesperson?

    1. The individual must have a current real estate license.
    2. Ninety percent or more of the individual's income as a licensee must be based on sales production.
    3. The individual's income must be based on the number of hours worked.
    4. The individual must not be included in company hospitalization and retirement programs.

13. Which of the following would be a violation of antitrust law?

    1. One broker refuses to cooperate with another broker who is charging sellers a "flat-rate" commission.
    2. A broker decides to stop advertising in the local newspaper until the ad rates are lowered.
    3. Two brokers agree to refuse to cooperate with another broker who is charging sellers a "flat-rate" commission.
    4. A broker decides to charge a seller an 8 percent commission on all listings for a given period of time.

14. The applicable federal rate for imputed interests is computed

1.	weekly.	3.	every six months.
2.	monthly.	4.	annually.

15. Which of the following laws provides comprehensive guidance for making public facilities accessible?

1.	RESPA	3.	Federal fair housing laws
2.	Regulation Z	4.	Americans with Diabilities Act (ADA)

16. The Internal Revenue Service (IRS) law on imputed interest does not cover installment sales less than

1.	$1,000.	3.	$3,000.
2.	$2,000.	4.	$5,000.

17. The person conducting the closing must report details of closings to the IRS on

1.	IRS form 1099.	3.	IRS form 1099 MISC.
2.	IRS form 1099 S.	4.	IRS form 1099 R.

18. Section 1031 of the Internal Revenue Code allows real estate investors to do which of the following when making a property exchange?

    1. Avoid the capital-gains tax only if the exchange is of like kind.
    2. Phase out the capital-gains tax.
    3. Defer the capital-gains tax.
    4. Avoid the capital-gains tax even if the exchange is not of like kind.

19. Salespersons working for brokers generally are classified as

    1. employees.
    2. branch managers.
    3. cobrokers.
    4. independent contractors.

20. Which of the following activities would be legal under the familial status category of the federal fair housing laws?

    1. Charging higher rents for people with pets
    2. Charging higher security deposits for families with children
    3. Segregating families within buildings
    4. Segregating families in certain buildings

ANSWER KEY

Question	Answer	Outline Reference		Question	Answer	Outline Reference
1.	3	IV		11.	3	IV
2.	4	I		12.	3	VII
3.	2	I		13.	3	VI
4.	4	I		14.	2	VI
5.	4	I		15.	4	II
6.	2	I		16.	3	VI
7.	2	I		17.	2	VI
8.	4	I		18.	3	VI
9.	2	IV		19.	4	VI
10.	4	IV		20.	1	I

FEDERAL LAWS AND REGULATIONS

Rating	Test Score Range	Your Score	
GOOD = 80% to 100%	16–20	Total number	20
FAIR = 70% to 79%	12–15	Total wrong	–__
NEEDS IMPROVEMENT = Below 70%	13 or less	Total right	__

Passing requirement—
14 or better

PART 8 / REAL ESTATE MATHEMATICS REVIEW

This review is designed to familiarize you with some basic mathematical formulas that are used most frequently in the computations required on state licensing examinations. These same computations also are important in day-to-day real estate transactions. If you feel you need additional help in working these problems, you may want to order a copy of *Mastering Real Estate Mathematics,* 5th edition, by Ventolo, Allaway and Irby (Chicago: Real Estate Education Company, 1989).

PERCENTAGES

Many real estate computations are based on the calculations of percentages. A percentage expresses a portion of a whole (or total) that is expressed as 100. For example, 50 percent means 50 parts of the 100 parts constituting the whole. Percentages greater than 100 percent contain more than one whole unit. Thus, 163 percent is one whole plus 63 parts of another whole. Remember that a whole is always thought of as equaling 100 percent.

$$60\% = 0.6 \qquad 7\% = 0.07 \qquad 175\% = 1.75$$

To express a percentage as a fraction, place the percentage over 100. For example:

$$50\% = \frac{50}{100}$$

These fractions then may be reduced to make working the problem easier. To reduce a fraction, determine the highest number that will divide both the numerator and denominator evenly (that is, with no remainder); divide each of them by that number. For example:

$$25/100 = {}^1/_4 \text{ (both numbers are divided by 25)}$$

$$49/63 = {}^7/_9 \text{ (both numbers are divided by 7)}$$

* A broker is to receive a 7 percent commission on the sale of a $50,000 house. What will the broker's commission be?

$$0.07 \times \$50,000 = \$3,500 \text{ broker's commission}$$

Percentage problems contain three elements: *percentage, total* and *part.* To *determine a specific percentage of a total,* multiply the percentage by the whole. This is illustrated by the following formula:

$$\text{percent} \times \text{total} = \text{part}$$

$$5\% \times 200 = 10$$

This formula is used in calculating mortgage loan interests, brokers' commissions, loan origination fees, discount points, the amount of earnest money deposits and income on capital investment.

A variation or inversion on the percentage formula is used to *find the total amount when the part and percentage are known.* Therefore:

$$\text{total} = \frac{\text{part}}{\text{percentage}}$$

*   A broker received a $3,600 commission for the sale of a house. The broker's commission was 6 percent of the total sales price. What was the total sales price of this house?

$$\text{total sales price} = \frac{\$3,600}{0.06} = \$60,000$$

This formula is used in computing the total mortgage loan principal still due if the monthly payment and interest rate are known. It also is used to calculate (1) the total sales price when the amount and percentage of commission or earnest money deposit is known, (2) the interest due if the monthly payment and interest rate are known and (3) the market value of property if the assessed value and the ratio (percentage) of assessed value to market value are known.

To determine the percent when the amounts of the part and the total are known:

$$\text{percent} = \frac{\text{part}}{\text{total}}$$

This formula may be used to determine the tax rate when the taxes and assessed value are known or the commission rate if the sales price and commission amount are known.

An easy way to remember the *formula,* or part, percent and total, is with the diagram in Figure 8.1. First draw the circle and divide it in half; then divide the bottom half in half. Put the term *part* in the top half of the circle and the other two terms in the two bottom portions.

Next, substitute the known amounts for the words that represent those amounts. The word that remains represents the element you are solving for. If the terms for which you have figures are below the line that divides the entire circle in half, multiply them to find the third element; if one figure is above the other, divide the top term by the bottom one.

Figure 8.1

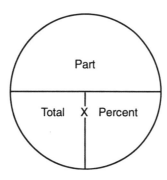

RATES

Property taxes, transfer taxes and insurance premiums usually are expressed as rates. A rate is expressed as cost per unit; for example, in a certain county tax is computed at the *rate of* $5 per $100 of assessed value. The formula *for computing rates* follows:

$$\frac{value}{unit} \times rate\ per\ unit = total$$

*   A house assessed at $50,000 is taxed at an annual rate of $2.50 per $100 assessed valuation. What is the yearly tax?

$$\frac{\$50,000}{100} \times \$2.50 = total\ annual\ tax$$

$$\$50,000 \div \$100 = 500\ (increments\ of\ \$100)$$

$$500 \times \$2.50 = \$1,250,\ total\ annual\ tax$$

AREA AND VOLUME

Area

People in the real estate profession must know how to compute the area of a parcel of land or to figure the amount of living area in a house. *To compute the area of a square or rectangular parcel,* use this formula:

$$area = length \times width\ (A = l \times w)$$

*   What is the area of a rectangular lot 200 feet long by 100 feet wide?

$$200' \times 100' = 20,000\ square\ feet$$

Area is always expressed in square units.

To compute the width of a rectangular parcel, use

$$\text{width} = \frac{\text{area}}{\text{length}}$$

* What is the width of a rectangular lot that measures 40 feet long and has an area of 3,600 square feet?

$$\frac{3{,}600 \text{ sq. ft.}}{40 \text{ ft.}} = 90 \text{ feet}$$

To compute the amount of surface in a triangular-shaped area, use the formula

$$\text{area} = {}^1\!/_2 \text{ (base} \times \text{height)} \ [A = {}^1\!/_2 (b \times h)]$$

The part of an equation enclosed in parentheses is always computed before any other part of the equation. The base of a triangle is the bottom, the side on which the triangle rests. The height is an imaginary line extending from the point (or vertex) of the uppermost angle straight down (perpendicular) to the base (see Figure 8.2).

Figure 8.2

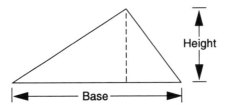

* A triangle has a base of 50 feet and a height of 30 feet. What is the area?

$${}^1\!/_2 (50' \times 30') = \text{area in square feet}$$

$${}^1\!/_2 (1{,}500) = 750 \text{ square feet}$$

To compute the area of an irregular room or parcel of land, divide the shape into regular rectangles, squares or triangles. Next, compute the area of each regular figure and add the areas together to obtain the total area.

* Compute the area in the hallway in Figure 8.3:

Figure 8.3

First, make a rectangle and a triangle by drawing a single line through the figure as shown in Figure 8.4.

Figure 8.4

Compute the area of the rectangle:

$$\text{area} = \text{length} \times \text{width} \qquad 16' \times 6' = 96 \text{ square feet}$$

Compute the area of the triangle:

$$\text{area} = {}^{1}/_{2} (\text{base} \times \text{height}) = {}^{1}/_{2} (4' \times 6') = {}^{1}/_{2} (24) = 12 \text{ square feet}$$

Add the two areas:

$$96 + 12 = 108 \text{ square feet total area}$$

Volume

The cubic capacity of an enclosed space is expressed as volume. Volume is used to describe the amount of space in any three-dimensional area. For example, it would be used in measuring the interior airspace of a room to determine what capacity heating unit is required. *The formula for computing cubic or rectangular volume* is

$$\text{volume} = \text{length} \times \text{width} \times \text{height} \ (V = lwh)$$

* The bedroom of a house is 12 feet long and 8 feet wide and has a ceiling height of 8 feet (Figure 8.5). How many cubic feet does the room contain?

$$8' \times 12' \times 8' = 768 \text{ cubic feet}$$

Figure 8.5

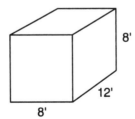

Volume is always expressed in cubic units.

To compute the volume of a triangular space, such as the airspace in a house with a peaked roof, use the following two formulas:

$$V = lwh \text{ and}$$

$$\text{volume} = {}^{1}/_{2} (\text{base} \times \text{height} \times \text{width}) \ [V = {}^{1}/_{2} (bhw)]$$

hat is the volume of airspace in the house shown in Figure 8.6?

First, divide the house into two shapes, rectangular and triangular, as shown in Figure 8.7:

Figure 8.7

Second, find the volume of T.

$$\text{volume} = \frac{1}{2} (\text{base} \times \text{height} \times \text{width})$$

$$\frac{1}{2} (25' \times 10' \times 40') = \frac{1}{2} (10,000) = 5,000 \text{ cubic feet}$$

Third, find the volume of R.

$$25' \times 40' \times 12' = 12,000 \text{ cubic feet}$$

Finally, total volumes *T* and *R*.

$$5,000 + 12,000 = 17,000 \text{ cubic feet of airspace in the house}$$

Cubic measurements of volume are used to compute the construction costs per cubic foot of a building, the amount of airspace being sold in a condominium unit or the heating and cooling requirements for a building.

Be sure that when you compute either area or volume, all dimensions are in the same units of measure. For example, you cannot multiply two feet by six inches; you have to multiply two feet by $\frac{1}{2}$ foot or 24 inches by 6 inches.

PRORATIONS

When closing a real estate transaction, it is generally necessary to divide the financial responsibility between the buyer and seller for items such as taxes, loan interest, fuel bills and rents. Prorations provide for an equitable distribution of income and expenses between the seller and the buyer. Accrued items such as real estate taxes are owed by the seller but will be paid at a later date by the buyer. The seller pays for accrued items by giving the buyer a credit at closing. A prepaid item—such as fuel oil that has not been used—requires a credit to the seller at closing.

Proration may be done through the day prior to closing or through the day of closing. The sales contract (offer to purchase) will generally determine whether the buyer or seller will pay for the actual day of closing. For example, if real estate taxes are prorated through the day of closing, the seller will pay the taxes for the day of closing.

Prorations may be calculated on either a 360-day year (12 months of 30 days each) or a 365-day year. The 365-day year requires determination of the daily charge multiplied by the actual number of days in the proration period. All prorations should be computed by carrying the division to four decimal places. The third and fourth decimal places should not be rounded off to cents until the final proration figure has been determined.

The first step in the proration process is to determine the time period involved in the proration process (the number of days charged to or through the closing date).

The second step is to calculate the dollar amount per day.

The third step is to determine the proration by multiplying the time period by the dollar amount per day.

General Guidelines for Prorations

A.   Because property taxes are paid in arrears, the taxes are prorated through either the day prior to closing or the day of closing. The prorated tax will be credited to the buyer and debited (charged) to the seller.

B.   If a buyer assumes a seller's existing loan, the balance of the loan will be credited to the buyer and debited to the seller. Because interest on the loan is paid in arrears, the amount of interest owed from the day of the last payment through the day of closing will be debited to the seller.

C.   Because a water bill is prepaid, the prepaid time must be computed. The amount of this prepaid item will be debited to the buyer and credited to the seller.

D.   If the buyer assumes the seller's existing fire and hazard insurance policy, the seller is credited for the unused portion of the premium, which is usually paid for in advance.

E.   The broker's commission is debited to the seller.

F.   Items credited to the seller and debited to the buyer generally include

  1. The sales price
  2. Any tax and insurance reserve in the case of a buyer assuming the seller's loan
  3. Prepaid real estate taxes
  4. Any fuel oil remaining in the storage tank on the day of closing

G.   Items credited to the buyer and debited to the seller include

  1. Unpaid utility bills
  2. The buyer's earnest money

3. Tenants' security deposits
4. The unearned portion of rent collected in advance

EXAMPLE:

Using a 365-day year, prorate the taxes for a December 14 closing if the annual tax bill is $1,224 and is prorated through the day of closing.

SOLUTION:

First, determine the time period during which taxes have accrued.

Jan	— 31 days	July	— 31 days		
Feb	— 28 days	Aug	— 31 days		
Mar	— 31 days	Sept	— 30 days		
Apr	— 30 days	Oct	— 31 days		
May	— 31 days	Nov	— 30 days		
June	— 30 days	Dec	— 14 days	Total = 348 days	

Second, divide the annual tax by the days in the year to determine the amount per day.

$$\$1,224 \div 365 \text{ days} = \$3.3534 \text{ per day}$$

Finally, multiply the time period by the amount per day.

$$\$3.3534 \times 348 = \$1,166.99 \text{ debit to the seller and credit to the buyer (rounded)}$$

AMORTIZATION

The majority of mortgage and deed of trust loans are amortized loans. Regular payments are made for up to 30 years with each payment being applied first to interest owed and the balance deducted from the principal. The amount of interest due on a specific payment date is determined by calculating the total yearly interest based on the unpaid loan balance and dividing that figure by the number of payments each year. For example, if the current outstanding loan balance is $100,000 with interest at the rate of 8 percent per year and constant payments of $769, the interest and principal due on the next payment would be calculated as shown below.

$$\$100,000 \times .08 = \$8,000$$

$$\$8,000 \div 12 = \$666.666 \text{ (round to \$666.67)}$$

$769.00	monthly payment
666.67	month's interest
$102.33	month's principal

All interest due and the full amount of principal due will be paid at the end of the term.

Lenders generally use the fully amortized loan plan in which the borrower pays a constant amount that usually is monthly. Each payment is credited first to the interest due with the balance of the payment being applied to the principal amount of the loan. A prepared

ortgage factor chart is used to determine the amount of the
e factor chart indicates the amount of monthly payment per
term and interest rate.

umber of thousands (and fractions thereof) of the amount
iyment chart is shown below.

Monthly Payment Factors

(Per $1,000)

	15 Years	30 Years
7.00	$8.99	$6.65
7.25	9.13	6.82
7.50	9.27	6.70
7.75	9.41	7.16
8.00	9.56	7.34
8.25	9.70	7.51
8.50	9.85	7.69
8.75	10.00	7.87
9.00	10.15	8.05
9.25	10.30	8.23
9.50	10.45	8.41
9.75	10.60	9.60
10.00	10.75	8.78
10.25	10.90	8.97
10.50	11.06	9.15
10.75	11.21	9.34
11.00	11.37	9.53
11.25	11.53	9.72
11.50	11.69	9.91
11.75	11.85	10.10
12.00	12.01	10.29
12.25	12.17	10.48
12.50	12.33	10.68
12.75	12.49	10.87
13.00	12.66	11.07

EXAMPLE:

What is the monthly payment on a $60,000 loan at 9 percent for 30 years?

SOLUTION:

Refer to the mortgage factor chart above. Move down the "Rate" column to 9%. Then move
to the right to the column headed "30 Years" to find the payment on a $1,000 loan ($8.05).
To find the monthly payment on the $60,000 loan:

$$\text{Monthly Payment} = \frac{\text{Amount of Mortgage}}{\$1,000} \times \begin{array}{c}\text{Payment for } \$1,000 \text{ Loan} \\ \text{(from monthly payment factors chart)}\end{array}$$

$$\frac{\$60,000}{\$1,000} \times \$8.05 = 60 \times \$8.05 = \$483.00$$

The $483 monthly payment is for the principal and interest only. The lender might add an amount for insurance and for real estate taxes.

If it is known how much a borrower has available to spend on a monthly loan payment, one may use the mortgage factor chart to determine the amount of the loan that the borrower can afford.

Assume that a prospective buyer can afford $800 per month for principal and interest and the lender will make a loan for 30 years at 8 percent. To find the amount of the loan move down column 1, "Rate," to find the interest rate; then move to the right to find where the rate and the 30-year column meet; you will find $7.34. Every $7.34 of monthly payment will support a loan of $1,000.

$$\begin{array}{c}\text{Amount borrower has available to spend each month for}\\ \text{Amount of Loan} = \text{principal and interest} = \$800 \div 7.34 \text{ Monthly payment per } \$1,000\\ 108.991 \text{ thousands or } \$108,991\end{array}$$

The mortgage factor chart also can be used to determine how much interest will be paid over the life of the loan.

Using the $800 monthly payment figure, what is the total interest paid over the life of this loan?

$$\$800 \text{ (monthly payment)} \times 360 \text{ months} = \$288,000$$

$$\begin{array}{ll}\$288,000 & \text{(Total principal and interest)}\\ \underline{-108,991} & \text{(Amount of principal)}\\ \$179,009 & \text{(Total interest paid over life of loan)}\end{array}$$

MATHEMATICS REVIEW TEST

1. A broker sold a home for $62,000. The broker charged the seller a 7 percent commission and will pay 25 percent of that amount to the listing salesperson and 30 percent to the selling person. What amount of commission will the listing salesperson receive from the sale of the home?

1.	$1,085	3.	$4,340
2.	$1,302	4.	None of the above

2. A man signed an agreement to purchase a home. The contract stipulated that the seller replace the damaged bedroom carpet. The carpet the buyer has chosen costs $14.95 per square yard plus $3.50 per square yard for installation. If the bedroom dimensions are as illustrated in Figure 8.8, how much will the seller have to pay for the job?

1.	$164.45	3.	$222.50
2.	$173.62	4.	$256.27

Figure 8.8

3. Three investors decided to pool their savings and purchase some commercial real estate for $150,000. If one invested $40,000 and the second contributed $20,000, what percentage of ownership was left for the third investor?

1.	60 percent	3.	26 percent
2.	40 percent	4.	13 percent

4. A father is curious to know how much money his son and daughter-in-law still owe on their mortgage loan. The father knows that the interest portion of their last monthly payment was $582.84. If they are paying interest at the rate of 12 percent, what was the approximate outstanding balance of their loan before the last payment was made?

1.	$48,520	3.	$63,583
2.	$58,284	4.	$69,941

5. You bought a house one year ago for $102,900. Property in your neighborhood is said to be increasing in value at a rate of 4 percent annually. If this is true, what is the current market value of your real estate?

1.	$171,600	3.	$107,188
2.	$170,160	4.	$107,016

6. You own a home valued at $75,000. Property in your area is assessed at 80 percent of its value and the local tax rate is $3.25 per $100. What is the amount of your monthly taxes?

    1. $1950.00
    2. $243.75

    3. $195.00
    4. $162.50

7. You are planning to construct a patio in your backyard. An illustration of the surface area to be paved appears in Figure 8.9. If the cement is to be poured as a six-inch slab, how many cubic feet of cement will be poured in your patio?

    1. 64 cubic feet
    2. 244 cubic feet

    3. 384 cubic feet
    4. None of the above

Figure 8.9

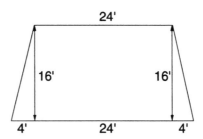

8. You receive a monthly salary of $500 plus 3 percent commission on all of your listings that sell and 2.5 percent on all of your sales. None of the listings you took sold last month, but you received $7,350 in salary and commission. What was the value of the property you sold?

    1. $245,000
    2. $247,000

    3. $274,000
    4. $294,000

9. A residence has proved difficult to sell. The salesperson suggests that it might sell faster if the owners enclosed a portion of the backyard with a privacy fence. If the area to be enclosed is as illustrated in Figure 8.10, how much would the fence cost at $7.25 per linear foot?

    1. $1,051.25
    2. $1,232.50

    3. $1,486.25
    4. $1,667.50

Figure 8.10

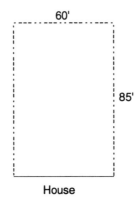

House

10. An owner leases the 24 apartments in his building for a total monthly rental of $6,000. If this figure represents a 9 percent annual return on the owner's investment, what was the original cost of the property?

    1. $800,000
    2. $720,000
    3. $666,667
    4. None of the above

For the following questions regarding closing statement prorations, base your calculations on a 30-day month. Carry all computations to three decimal places and round off after all computations have been made.

11. A sale is to be closed on April 15. Real estate taxes for the current year are $1,860 and have not been paid. What amount of the real estate tax proration will be credited to the buyer?

    1. $434
    2. $542.51
    3. $1,317.49
    4. $1,860

12. You sell your house to a married couple. The buyers are assuming your outstanding mortgage, which had an unpaid balance of $65,400 after the last payment on September 1 and an annual interest rate of 11 percent. Interest is paid in advance each month. The sale is to be closed on September 14. What is the amount of mortgage interest proration to be credited to you at the closing?

    1. $185.44
    2. $279.77
    3. $319.73
    4. $501.98

13. Your brother sells a home on October 10. At the closing, the buyer assumes the seller's three-year fire and hazard insurance policy, which is due to expire at the end of May of next year. The original cost of the premium was $740. What is the amount of insurance proration that will be charged to the buyer at the closing?

    1. $144.76
    2. $158.28
    3. $255.49
    4. None of the above

14. In a sale of residential property, real estate taxes for the current year amounted to $1,630 and already have been paid by the seller. The sale is to be closed on November 4. What is the settlement sheet entry for the tax proration?

    1. $237.19 debit to seller; $237.19 credit to buyer
    2. $253.56 credit to seller; $253.56 debit to buyer
    3. $1,476.05 debit to seller; $153.95 credit to buyer
    4. $253.56 credit to seller, only

15. You are buying a house and assuming the seller's mortgage. The unpaid balance after the most recent payment (August 1, the first of the month) was $64,750. Interest is paid in arrears each month at an annual rate of 12 percent. The sale is to be closed on August 18. What is the amount of the mortgage interest proration to be credited to you at the closing?

    1. $140.72
    2. $388.49
    3. $539.19
    4. None of the above

16. A 200-acre farm is divided into house lots. The streets require one-eighth of the whole farm, and there are 220 lots. How many square feet are there in each lot?

   1. 34,650 square feet   3. 43,916 square feet
   2. 39,784 square feet   4. None of the above

17. The taxes of $2,140 have been paid for the entire calendar year. The seller sells on November 1. What is the amount of the remaining prepaid proration?

   1. $1,961.67   3. $356.67
   2. $1,783.30   4. $178.33

18. A broker received a $28,000 commission check for the sale of a house. The broker's commission was 6 percent of the total sale price. What was the total sale price of the house?

   1. $560,000   3. $297,872
   2. $466,667   4. $168,000

19. A seller wants to sell his house and realize $80,000 from the sale. If his only cost of selling would be a 7 percent commission, what is the minimum amount he could sell his house for and realize his desired net?

   1. $85,600   3. $87,400
   2. $86,022   4. None of the above

20. You have been making constant payments of $623 per month on your mortgage. The balance after your last payment was $59,200. The interest rate on your mortgage is 7 percent. What will be the balance of your mortgage after your next payment?

   1. $55,056   3. $58,922.33
   2. $58,577   4. None of the above

21. Using the mortgage factor chart on page 87, what is the monthly payment for a $150,000 loan at 11.5 percent for 30 years?

   1. $1,429.50   3. $1,525.50
   2. $1,486.50   4. $1,543.50

22. Using the numbers in question 21, what is the total interest paid over the life of the loan?

   1. $150,000   3. $533,653
   2. $385,140   4. None of the above

23. A young couple want to purchase a home and feel that they can afford to pay $990 per month on a loan. They have saved enough to make a $14,000 down payment and pay closing costs. If lenders are offering 30-year loans at 8.25 percent interest, what is the maximum amount this couple can pay for a home? (Refer to the mortgage factor chart on page 87.)

   1. $131,800   3. $145,800
   2. $141,300   4. $155,400

ANSWER KEY WITH EXPLANATIONS

1. $62,000 sales price × 7% commission = $62,000 × 0.07 = $4,340, broker's commission

   $4,340 × 25% = $4,340 × 0.25 = $1,085

   Correct answer: **1**

2. See Figure 8.11.

Figure 8.11

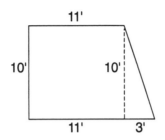

11' × 10′ = 110 square feet, area of rectangle

¹/₂ (3′ × 10′) = ¹/₂ (30′) = 15 square feet, area of triangle

110 + 15 = 125 square feet, total area

Divide by 9 to convert square feet to square yards.

125 ÷ 9 = 13.89 square yards

$14.95 + $3.50 installation = $18.45, cost per square yard

$18.45 × 13.89 square yards = $256.27

Correct answer: **4**

3. $40,000 first investor + $20,000 second investor = $60,000

   $150,000 – $60,000 = $90,000 third investor's contribution

   $$\frac{\text{part}}{\text{total}} = \text{percent}$$

   $90,000 ÷ $150,000 = 0.60, or 60%

   Correct answer: **1**

4. $582.84 × 12 = $6,994.08 annual interest

   $$\frac{\text{part}}{\text{percent}} = \text{total}$$

   $6,994.08 ÷ 12% = $6,994.08 ÷ 0.12 = $58,284

   Correct answer: **2**

5. $102,900 × 4% = $102,900 × 0.04 = $4,116, annual increase in value.

$102,900 + $4,116 = $107,016, current market value

Correct answer: **4**

Read your calculator carefully. Answer choices with the same number combinations can be misleading.

6. $75,000 × 80% = $75,000 × 0.80 = $60,000, assessed value

Divide by 100 because tax rate is stated per $100.

$60,000 ÷ 100 = $600

$600 × $3.25 = $1,950, annual taxes

Divide by 12 to get monthly taxes.

$1,950 ÷ 12 = $162.50

Correct answer: 4

7. See Figure 8.12.

Figure 8.12

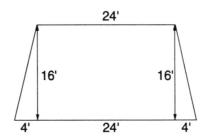

24′ × 16′ = 384 square feet, area of rectangle

^{1}/$_2$ (4′ × 16′) = ^{1}/$_2$ (64′) = 32 square feet, area of each triangle

32 × 2 = 64 square feet, area of two triangles

384 + 64 = 448 square feet, surface area to be paved

6″ deep = ^{1}/$_2$′

448 × ^{1}/$_2$ = 224 cubic feet of cement needed for patio

Correct answer: **4**

8. $7,350 – $500 salary = $6,850 commission on sales

$6,850 ÷ 2.5% = $6,850 ÷ 0.025 = $274,000 value of property sold

Correct answer: **3**

9.   See Figure 8.13.

Figure 8.13

House

Two sides of 85′ plus one side of 60′

85′ × 2 = 170 feet

170 + 60 = 230 linear feet

230 × $7.25 = $1,667.50

Correct answer: **4**

10. $6,000 × 12 = $72,000 annual return

$72,000 ÷ 9% = $72,000 ÷ 0.09 = $800,000, original cost of property

Correct answer: **1**

11. $1,860 ÷ 12 months = $155 per month

$155 ÷ 30 days = $5.167 per day

$155 × 3 months = $465

$5.167 × 15 days = $77.505

$465 + $77.505 = $542.505, rounds to $542.51

Correct answer: **2**

12. $65,400 × 11% = $65,400 × 0.11 = $7,194

$7,194 ÷ 12 months = $599.50 per month

$599.50 ÷ 30 days = $19.983 per day

30-day month − 14 days = 16 days

$19.983 × 16 days = $319.728, rounds to $319.73

Correct answer: **3**

13. $740 ÷ 3 years = $246.667 per year

$246.667 ÷ 12 = $20.556 per month

$20.556 ÷ 30 days = $.685 per day

$20.556 × 7 months = $143.892

$.685 × 20 days = $13.70

$143.892 + $13.70 = $157.592, rounds to $157.95

Correct answer: **4**

14. $1,630 ÷ 12 months = $135.833 per month

$135.833 ÷ 30 days = $4.528 per day

$4.528 × 26 days = $117.728

$135.833 + $117.728 = $253.561, rounds to $253.56

Correct answer: **2**

The taxes have been paid. The seller is entitled to a refund for 1 month and 26 days. He therefore will receive a credit and the buyer will be charged (debited) for the same amount.

15. $64,750 × 12% = $64,750 × 0.12 = $7,770

$7,770 ÷ 12 months = $647.50

$647.50 ÷ 30 days = $21.583 per day

$21.583 × 18 days = $388.494, rounds to $388.49

Correct answer: **2**

16. 43,560 square feet/acre × 200 acres = 8,712,000, total square feet

8,712,000 square feet × $^{1}/_{8}$ = 8,712,000 × 0.125 = 1,089,000 square feet for streets

8,712,000 − 1,089,000 = 7,623,000 square feet for lots

7,623,000 square feet ÷ 220 lots = 34,650 square feet per lot

Correct answer: **1**

17. Time period : 2 months (November/December)

$2,140 per year ÷ 12 = $178.33 per month

$178.33 × 2 = $356.67

Correct answer: **3**

18. Part = $28,000, Percent = 6%

    Part ÷ Percent = Total

    $28,000 ÷ .06 = $466,667

    Correct answer: **2**

19. Part ÷ Percent = Total

    $80,000 ÷ .93 = $86,021.5, rounds to $86,022

    Correct answer: **2**

20. $59,200 × .07 = $4,144.00 annual interest

    $4,144 ÷ 12 = $345.33 interest for one month

    $623.00 P&I − 345.33 = $277.67 principal payoff

    $59,200 − $277.67 = $58,922.33 balance after next payment

    Correct answer: **3**

21. $1,486.50 (150,000 × 9.91)

    Correct answer: **2**

22. $1.486.50 × 360 months = $535,140 total P&I

                  − 150,000 P = $385,140

    Correct answer: **2**

23. The payment chart indicates 8.25 percent loans are 7.51 per $1,000.

    $990 affordable monthly payment / 7.51 = 131.82423

    $131.82423 × 1,000 = $131,824.33 maximum loan amount

    $131,824.33 plus down payment = $145,824.33 maximum selling price of house.

    Correct answer: **3**

PART 9 / VALUATION AND REAL ESTATE ECONOMICS

OUTLINE OF CONCEPTS TO UNDERSTAND

I. Financial Institutions Reform, Recovery, and Enforcement Act (FIRREA) and the appraisal industry

    A. The collapse of many savings and loan associations as a result of the surge into unsound investments was at least partly the consequence of questionable property appraisals.

    B. Congress introduced appraisal regulation by passing FIRREA in 1989.

    C. Appraisals performed as part of a federally related transaction must comply with state standards and must be performed by a state-certified or state-licensed appraiser.

    D. State appraiser licensing requirements and appraisal standards must meet minimum levels set by the Appraisal Standards Board and Appraisal Qualifications Board of the Appraisal Foundation, a national group of representatives of major appraisal and related organizations.

II. Appraisal and value

    A. Appraisal—an estimate or opinion of value; a detailed estimate of a property's value by a professional appraiser

    B. Competitive market analysis (CMA)—used by the broker or the salesperson to help the seller determine a listing price for the property; basically, a comparison of prices of recently sold and currently for sale properties that are similar in location, style and amenities to the property of the listing seller. CMA will generally estimate market value as likely to fall within a range of figures

    C. Value

        1. Definition—the present worth of future benefits arising from the ownership of real property

        2. Characteristics a property must have to have value in the real estate market include

            a. Utility—capacity to satisfy human wants and needs

            b. Scarcity—finite supply

        c.   Effective demand—need supported by purchasing power

        d.   Transferability—transfer of ownership rights with relative ease

D.   Market value

   1.   Most probable price a property will bring in a competitive market, allowing for reasonable time to find a knowledgeable purchaser

       a.   The buyer and seller are not under pressure to act.

       b.   Payment is made in cash or equivalent.

   2.   Typical goal of an appraiser, although a property may have different values at the same time

   3.   Estimated price (compare to *market price,* which is the actual selling price)

III.   Principles of valuation

   A.   Highest and best use—most profitable use to which a property may be adapted, given legal constraints

   B.   Substitution—the value of a property tends to be set by the cost of purchasing an equally desirable substitute.

   C.   Supply and demand—the price of a property will increase if the supply decreases and will decrease if the supply increases.

   D.   Conformity—maximum value is realized if the land use conforms to existing neighborhood standards.

   E.   Increasing and decreasing return—improvements to land and structures produce a proportionate increase in value until some point beyond which the impact of improvements begins to decrease, until improvements cause virtually no change in the property value.

   F.   Competition—high levels of profits attract competitors into an industry; increase in competition results in decreased profits throughout the industry.

   G.   Change—no economic or physical condition remains constant.

   H.   Contribution—the value of any component of property consists of what its addition contributes to the value of the whole property.

   I.   Anticipation—value can increase or decrease in anticipation of some future benefit or detriment that will affect the property.

   J.   Assemblage plottage—the act of combining two or more adjacent parcels of land, with a resulting increase in value

   K.   Balance is achieved when adding improvements to land and structures will increase the property value.

   L.   Regression—the principle between dissimilar properties: the worth of the better property is affected adversely by the presence of the lesser-quality property

   M.   Progression—the worth of a lesser property tends to increase if it is located among better properties.

IV.   Approaches to value

   A.   Cost approach

1. Based on the principle of substitution
2. Steps of cost approach
   a. Estimate the land value.
   b. Estimate the replacement cost of the improvements.
   c. Estimate the depreciation.
   d. Deduct the depreciation from the replacement cost.
   e. Add the land value to the depreciated cost of improvements—do not depreciate land.
3. Depreciation—generally applies to a wasting asset, such as a building.
   a. Physical deterioration (wear, tear, poor maintenance)—may be curable or incurable
   b. Functional obsolescence—may be curable or incurable (outdated items, poor design)
   c. External (economic, environmental or locational) obsolescence—loss of value due to factors outside the property: is incurable only
   d. Most reliable approach for special-purpose buildings such as churches, schools, etc.

B. Market/data approach (sales comparison or direct sales)

1. A value estimate is obtained by comparing the subject property with recent sales of comparable properties through adjustment of sales prices of comparables.
2. Four areas of adjustment
   a. Date of sale
   b. Location
   c. Physical characteristics
   d. Terms of the sale
3. Considered the most reliable of the three approaches in appraising residential property

C. Income capitalization approach

1. Based on the present value of the rights to future income
2. Steps in the income approach
   a. Estimate the annual potential gross income.
   b. Deduct the vacancy and rent loss to arrive at the effective gross income.
   c. Deduct the annual operating expenses to arrive at the annual net operating income.
   d. Estimate the capitalization rate.
   e. Apply the capitalization rate to the annual net income.
3. Formula for capitalization rate: net income ÷ capitalization rate = value
4. As risk increases, the value decreases, and vice versa
5. Gross rent multiplier (GRM)
   a. Used as a substitute for the income approach in appraising a single-family home
   b. Formula for GRM: sales price ÷ monthly rental income = GRM
   c. Monthly rental income × GRM = estimated market value
6. Gross income multiplier (GIM)
   a. Used as a quick way to appraise commercial and industrial properties
   b. Formula for GIM: sales price ÷ annual rental income = GIM

7. Most reliable approach for income-producing property

V. Steps in the appraisal process

A. State the problem.

B. List the types of data needed and the sources.

C. Gather, record and verify the *general* data.

D. Gather, record and verify the *specific* data.

E. Gather, record and verify the data for the valuation approach needed.

F. Analyze and interpret the data.

G. Reconcile the data for the final value estimate.

H. Prepare the appraisal report.

VI. Neighborhood analysis

A. Neighborhood—homogeneous grouping of individuals or businesses within, or as part of, a larger community

B. Residential neighborhoods generally pass through three stages: growth, stability, decline

C. Factors to consider in analysis

1. Physical—street pattern, relation to the rest of the community
2. Economic—rent levels, new construction
3. Social—population density, frequency of crime
4. Governmental—zoning, special assessments

VII. Ethics of appraising

A. The appraiser should have no present or planned interest in the property being appraised.

B. The appraiser should have no personal interest in the property being appraised or the parties involved.

C. The appraiser should not improperly disclose the confidential parts of an appraisal report.

VIII. Real estate economics and urban development

A. Urban development patterns

1. Concentric theory: land uses tend to develop in a definite pattern of concentric circles outward from a central point called the *business district.*
2. Axial theory: land uses tend to develop along major transportation lines outward from the central business district.
3. Sector theory: an established or more efficient artery tends to attract development more than would a newer or less-efficient corridor.
4. Multiple nuclei theory: there is more than one central business district, and land-use patterns will develop outward from these various centers of activity.

B. Economic-base analysis—method of analyzing the economic activity of a community that attracts income from outside its boundaries; used to predict the impact on real estate of population and other variables, based on the analysis of basic and service employment

1. Basic employment—attracts income from outside the borders of the community, for example, employment in a steel plant
2. Service employment—exists because of the population attracted to the community by basic employment, for example, real estate offices, hair salons

IX. Industrial park—an area zoned to provide facilities for an industrial and industry-oriented community with special emphasis given to community compatibility and aesthetics

A. Benefits to industry

1. The readiness of the site reduces the time lag between the decision to locate and the beginning of production.
2. It gives large-scale-operation advantages, such as a railway spur to smaller industries.
3. "Package plan" availability generally relieves the industry of the need to develop the site, handle the legal negotiations, etc.
4. Protection of the investment through covenants designed to guard against the deterioration of the properties in the industrial park

B. Benefits to the community

1. Economy stimulated through new construction activity, increased payroll, and the like
2. Diversification of the economic base usually creates more stability in the labor market.
3. Allows for more efficient extension of municipal services
4. Provides compatibility and soundness in land-use relationships

C. Limitations of the industrial park

1. Lack of suitability to all types of industry; a chemical processor, for example, would have substantial land and utility requirements
2. Unanticipated restrictions on production as a result of conflict between development restrictions and change in production processes
3. Expansion problems if required land not available

X. Other important terms

A. Amenities—intangible benefits of ownership in addition to the property's legal description

B. Capitalization—a mathematical process for estimating a property's value using a proper rate of return on investment and anticipated annual net income

C. Capitalization rate—the rate of return a property will produce on the owner's investment

D. Comparables—properties listed in the appraisal report generally equivalent to the subject property

E. Reconciliation—final step in the appraisal process, in which the appraiser reconciles the estimates of value received from the market data, cost and income approaches to arrive at a final estimate of the market value for the property being appraised

F. Replacement cost—construction cost at current prices of property not necessarily an exact duplicate of the subject property but serving the same purpose or function as the original

G. Reproduction cost—construction cost at current prices of exact duplicate of the subject property

H. Subject property—property being appraised

I. URAR—Uniform Residential Appraisal Report

REVIEW LIST

The student should have an understanding of the following areas of valuation and economics.

1. Concept and purpose of appraisal

2. Difference between comparative market analysis and appraisal

3. The appraisal process

4. Depreciation

5. Neighborhood analysis

6. Ethics of appraising

7. Economic and urban development

DIAGNOSTIC TEST

1. The characteristics required for a property to have value include all of the following **EXCEPT**

    1. effective demand.   3. depreciation.
    2. scarcity.   4. transferability.

2. Which of the following laws require that appraisals performed as part of a federally related transaction must comply with federal standards and be performed by a state-certified or state-licensed appraiser?

    1. Financial Institutions Reform, Recovery, and Enforcement Act (FIRREA)
    2. Regulation Z
    3. RESPA
    4. Statute of Frauds

3. You own land worth $40,000 and your building has a replacement cost of $160,000. What would be the value if the appraiser used a depreciation rate of 30 percent?

    1. $148,000   3. $188,000
    2. $152,000   4. None of the above

4. All of the following apply to the definition of market value **EXCEPT**

    1. both buyer and seller must be well informed.
    2. market value is the average price that a property will bring.
    3. both buyer and seller must act without undue pressure.
    4. payment must be made in cash or its equivalent.

5. The annual net income for an office building is $20,000. If the owner realizes a 9 percent return on his investment, the value of the building is

    1. $1,800.   3. $222,222.
    2. $22,222.   4. $285,714

6. You look at four similar houses for sale in the same area and choose the house with the lowest asking price. You probably are basing your decision on the principle of

   1. highest and best use.
   2. substitution.
   3. contribution.
   4. conformity.

7. A builder developed a subdivision in which the demand for homes was great. He sold the last lot in his subdivision for a much higher price than that for which he had sold the first lot in the area. This example illustrates the principle of

   1. highest and best use.
   2. substitution.
   3. conformity.
   4. supply and demand.

8. In appraising a special-purpose building such as a post office, the most reliable approach to an indication of its value would generally be the

   1. cost approach.
   2. market/data approach.
   3. income approach.
   4. sales comparison.

9. Which of the following is an example of locational obsolescence?

   1. Termite damage
   2. Negligent care of property
   3. A zoning ordinance allowing a decrease in the minimum lot size
   4. Poor architectural design

10. Economic obsolescence does not result from

    1. adverse zoning changes.
    2. a city's leading industries moving out.
    3. an inharmonious land use in a neighborhood.
    4. outdated kitchens.

11. Depreciation generally applies to

    1. the building only.
    2. the land only.
    3. both the land and the building.
    4. the net income of the building.

12. A principal factor for which adjustments must be made in using the market/data approach is

    1. depreciation.
    2. the date of sale.
    3. the amount of real estate taxes.
    4. the cost of replacement.

13. An appraiser is estimating the value of a building that has a net income of $5,000 per quarter and a capitalization rate of 8 percent. What is the value of this property?

    1. $25,000
    2. $62,500
    3. $250,000
    4. $312,500

14. An appraiser is using the gross-rent-multiplier (GRM) method to estimate the market value of a single-family home. The home has an annual gross income of $7,200, with quarterly expenses of $900. The recognized GRM for the neighborhood is 110. The appraiser's estimate of value is likely to be

    1. $22,000.
    2. $33,000.
    3. $66,000.
    4. none of the above.

15. The GRM is used in the

    1. market/data approach.
    2. income approach for office buildings.
    3. cost approach.
    4. income approach for single-family homes.

16. An office building recently sold for $600,000, with a monthly rental income of $5,000. The GIM for the property was

    1. 120.   3. 10.
    2. 100.   4. none of the above.

17. In determining the value of a 20-unit apartment building, the appraiser has established the gross income from rents. After deducting the loss for vacancies and collection losses from this gross income, the appraiser would have established the

    1. net income.   3. gross income.
    2. spendable income.   4. effective gross income.

18. What is the first step an appraiser would take to arrive at an estimated value using the income approach?

    1. Determine gross income.   3. Determine effective gross income.
    2. Determine operating expenses.   4. Determine the vacancy rate.

19. An airport routing was changed, with the result that airplanes flew over a residential area. The subsequent loss in value caused by the airplane noise would be best described as

    1. physical depreciation.   3. economic obsolescence.
    2. functional obsolescence.   4. eminent domain.

20. Which of the following factors would be considered in the market/data approach to value?

    1. Conditions under which property was sold
    2. Annual gross income
    3. Replacement cost
    4. Original cost

21. Outmoded plumbing fixtures are an example of

    1. curable physical deterioration.   3. incurable physical deterioration.
    2. curable functional obsolescence.   4. incurable functional obsolescence.

22. In the income approach to appraisal, if the net income was $42,000 and the capitalization rate was 12 percent, to find the value of the property the appraiser would

    1. multiply the income by the capitalization rate.
    2. multiply the capitalization rate by the net income.
    3. divide the net income by the capitalization rate.
    4. divide the capitalization rate by the net income.

23. The theory of urban development that states that land uses tend to develop outward from the central business district along major transportation lines is known as the

    1. sector theory.
    2. concentric theory.
    3. axial theory.
    4. multiple nuclei theory.

24. Employment that attracts income from outside the boundaries of a community is known as

    1. datum.
    2. basic employment.
    3. secondary employment.
    4. service employment.

25. A man built his dream house for $300,000 in a neighborhood of $100,000 homes and suffered a substantial loss when he had to sell four years later. This is an example of the principle of

    1. anticipation.
    2. competition.
    3. progression.
    4. regression.

ANSWER KEY

Question	Answer	Outline Reference	Question,	Answer	Outline Reference
1.	3	II	14.	3	IV
2.	1	I	15.	4	IV
3.	2	IV	16.	3	IV
4.	2	II	17.	4	IV
5.	3	IV	18.	1	IV
6.	2	III	19.	3	IV
7.	4	III	20.	1	IV
8.	1	IV	21.	2	IV
9.	3	IV	22.	3	IV
10.	4	IV	23.	3	VIII
11.	1	IV	24.	2	VIII
12.	2	IV	25.	4	III
13.	3	IV			

VALUATION AND REAL ESTATE ECONOMICS

Rating	Test Score Range	Your Score	
GOOD = 80% to 100%	20–25	Total number	25
FAIR = 60% to 80%	15–19	Total wrong	–__
NEEDS IMPROVEMENT = Below 60%	14 or less	Total right	__

Passing requirement— 20 or better

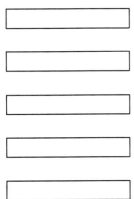

PART 10 / FINANCE

OUTLINE OF CONCEPTS TO UNDERSTAND

I. Theories of mortgage law

    A. Lien theory—the mortgage is viewed as a lien on real property in many states.

    B. Title theory—the lender is viewed as the owner of mortgaged land in some states.

    C. Intermediate theory—a number of states allow the lender to take possession of the mortgaged real estate on default.

II. Mortgage loan

    A. Mortgage—the mortgagor (borrower) gives a lien on the property to the mortgagee (lender) as security for debt.

    B. Note—promise to repay debt in definite installments with interest; a negotiable instrument

III. Trust deed—three-party instrument used in place of a mortgage in some areas of the country

    A. Conveys real estate as security for loan to a third party, the trustee

    B. Trustee holds the title on behalf of the lender, known as the *beneficiary*; the trustee is the legal owner, and the beneficiary is the holder of the note; the borrower retains the equitable title to the property, and the deed of the trust becomes the lien against it

    C. The trustee may take foreclosure action if the borrower (trustor) defaults.

IV. Payment plans

    A. Constant amount—payment credited first to interest due, then applied to the loan balance (amortized loan payment plan)

    B. Differing installments—each payment consists of the fixed amount credited toward the principal, as well as the additional amount for the interest due on the loan balance.

C. Flexible payment—allows for smaller payments in early years, larger payments in later years (graduated payment mortgage)

D. Straight term payment—allows for periodic payments of interest only with lump-sum payment at the maturity of all principal

E. Balloon payment—payments of principal and interest are paid to the lender over a relatively short period; the outstanding balance is due in a lump sum at a predetermined future date (partially amortized loan payment plan).

F. Amortization—loan payment process

1. Mortgage loans are repaid in equal monthly payments.
2. The monthly payment is a fixed amount that both reduces the principal and pays interest on the unpaid balance.

V. Mortgage provisions

A. Acceleration clause—if the borrower defaults, the lender has the right to declare the entire debt due and payable.

B. Assignment—the mortgagee becomes the assignor and executes assignment to the assignee, who becomes the new owner of the mortgage and debt.

C. Defeasance clause—the mortgagee is required to execute the release or satisfaction of the mortgage when the note is fully paid.

D. Alienation (due-on-sale) clause—if the borrower sells the property on any terms, the lender has the choice of either declaring the entire debt due and payable or allowing the buyer to assume the loan.

E. Buying "subject to" versus assuming—if the property is sold "subject to" the mortgage, the buyer is not personally liable to pay the entire debt (the seller remains liable); if the buyer assumes the mortgage, he or she becomes personally liable for payment of the entire debt. The seller is secondarily liable.

VI. Mortgage foreclosure and redemption

A. Judicial foreclosure

1. Lender sues the borrower in court; obtains judgment and court order to sell
2. Property sold at public sale to the highest bidder

B. Nonjudicial foreclosure

1. The mortgage generally must include a power-of-sale clause.
2. A notice of default must be recorded and a public sale advertised in the newspaper.
3. Property sold at a public sale to highest bidder

C. Strict foreclosure—the court may award title to the lender.

D. Redemption—process by which the borrower regains interest in the property

1. Equitable redemption
   a. Occurs prior to public sale
   b. If the borrower pays the amount due plus the costs prior to the public sale, the mortgage is reinstated.

    c. If not redeemed, the property is sold at a public sale to the highest bidder.

   2. Statutory redemption

    a. Occurs after public sales in some states and continues for a period of time specified by law

    b. The borrower may pay the sale price in full plus costs.

  E. Deficiency judgment—if the property is sold and the proceeds are insufficient to pay the mortgage and foreclosure costs, the difference is a deficiency; the lender usually can sue the original borrower for the difference (process of deficiency judgment).

VII. Types of mortgages

  A. Conventional

   1. Payment of the debt based solely on the borrower's ability to pay, with security provided by the mortgage; neither insured nor guaranteed by government agency

   2. Lender sets the terms subject to the law and policy

   3. Ratio of the loan to value lower than with insured and guaranteed loans

   4. If the loan-to-value ratio exceeds a given level, the lender may require private mortgage insurance (PMI).

  B. Federal Housing Administration (FHA) insured

   1. FHA insures lenders against loss on loans made on real property.

   2. Interest rates are set by the lender.

   3. The borrower pays the FHA insurance premium (up to 2.25 percent of the mortgage amount) either at the time of closing or financed into the loan amount; the borrower also pays the monthly insurance premium of up to $1/2$ of 1 percent of the mortgage amount over the first few years of the loan, depending on the amount of the down payment and length of loan.

   4. Mortgaged property must be appraised by an FHA-approved appraiser.

   5. Generally, the loan-to-value ratio cannot exceed 97 percent on the first $25,000 of the appraised value and 95 percent on the next $100,000 and 90 percent on amounts more than $125,000, up to the allowable maximum in the area; the only exception is loans on a property with an appraisal value of $50,000 or less where the loan value cannot exceed 98.75 percent. There is a limitation that the loan amount for any loan more than $50,000 cannot exceed 97.75 percent of the purchase price or appraised value, whichever is less.

   6. FHA does not allow a prepayment penalty.

   7. FHA mortgages are assumable with qualification.

   8. Discount points generally used to reduce the interest rate (1 point = 1 percent of the loan balance); generally negotiated between the seller and the buyer.

  C. DVA guaranteed (DVA loans)

   1. DVA does not allow a prepayment penalty.

   2. A DVA loan may be assumed by a nonveteran.

   3. DVA guarantees home loans for eligible veterans or eligible dependents with little or no down payment.

   4. The interest rate is set by the lender.

5. DVA does not charge the borrower for the guarantee; however, the borrower must pay up to 3 percent in funding fees on the loan amount to the DVA, in addition to any other fees.
6. Mortgaged property must be appraised by a DVA-approved appraiser.
7. DVA sets a limitation on the loan amount of up to four times the amount of the veteran's entitlement.
8. DVA guarantees the lender up to $50,750 of the loan balance.
    a. 50 percent of the loan balance, up to $50,000
    b. 40 percent of the loan balance, up to $144,000
    c. 25 percent of the loan balance, up to $203,000
9. Discount points generally are negotiated between the seller and the buyer.
10. In some cases, the DVA will make direct loans to eligible veterans or their dependents.
11. DVA requires appraisers to complete a Certificate of Reasonable Value (CRV); the DVA guarantee is based on either the amount of the CRV or the selling price, whichever is less.
12. National Guard members and reservists with at least six years of service now are eligible for DVA-guaranteed loans.

D. Rural Development and Farm Agency (formerly Farmers Home Administration)

1. Rural Development makes and guarantees housing loans to low-income people in rural areas in communities of 10,000 population or less.
2. Farm Service Agency makes and guarantees loans to farmers and ranchers.

E. Rural Economic and Community Development services makes and guarantees loans to homeowners in rural areas.

F. Privately insured

1. The buyer may obtain a conventional mortgage for up to 95 percent of the appraised value with PMI insurance.
2. The buyer is charged the market rate of interest plus reasonable insurance premium costs.
3. The borrower's insurance protects the lender against loss on the upper 20 to 25 percent portion of the loan.
4. PMI premiums vary among the insurers. The general rule is
    a. The first-year premium is approximately 1 percent of the loan amount.
    b. Subsequent years are $\frac{1}{4}$ of 1 percent (.0025) of the loan amount.
    c. Many insurers now charge monthly premiums with no premium deposits up front.
5. As property values rise and the loan-to-value ratio is 80 percent or less, the PMI insurance may be dropped.
    a. Requires lender approval and new appraisal
    b. Insurance must be held for two years, and the mortgagor must have a 25 percent equity position to drop the insurance.

G. Purchase-money mortgage—given by the buyer to the seller as part of the purchase price (owner financing); legal title passes to the buyer

H. Blanket mortgage—covers more than one property or lot; generally includes a partial release clause

I. Package mortgage—includes real estate and (expressly) all fixtures and appliances located on the property

J. Open-end mortgage

1. Secures the note executed by the borrower to the lender and any future advances of funds by the lender to the borrower
2. Terms usually restrict an increase in debt to a limit of either the original debt or a specified amount in the mortgage.
3. Additional loan amounts are figured at prevailing interest rates.

K. Construction loans

1. Generally short-term or interim loan to finance construction of an improvement
2. Periodic payments or draws made by the lender to the owner for work completed since the previous payment

L. Wraparound mortgage (all-inclusive deed of trust)

1. Allows the borrower who is paying an existing mortgage to obtain additional financing from a second lender
2. New lender assumes payment of the existing loan; gives the borrower a new, increased loan at a higher interest rate
3. The new lender makes payments on the original loan; the borrower makes payments to the new lender on the larger loan on the increased amount.

M. Graduated payment mortgage

1. Initial payments are low, but increase over the life of the loan.
2. Allows the buyer to purchase a home with monthly payments lower than those on a level payment
3. Aimed at helping first-time buyers who have increasing income potential

N. Adjustable-rate mortgage

1. Contains interest-rate provision related to the selected index
2. The interest rate may be adjusted periodically (either up or down). A margin is added to the index to determine the interest rate.

O. Reverse annuity mortgage

1. Allows the borrower to receive periodic payments from the lender on the equity in the home
2. The note becomes due on a specific date, the sale of the property or the death of the borrower.

P. Participation mortgage—lender receives interest and an equity position in project known as equity kicker or a percentage of the income of the property.

VIII. The money market

A. General characteristics

1. Money may be viewed as a means of payment, storehouse of purchasing power, standard value

        2. Money market is regulated by the federal government through the Federal Reserve System and the U.S. Treasury.

  B. Federal Reserve System (FED)

        1. Regulates the flow of money through member banks by controlling their reserve requirements and discount rates
        2. Tempers the economy through open-market operations

  C. U.S. Treasury

        1. In effect, our nation's banker and fiscal manager
        2. Responsible for supervising the daily fiscal operations of the federal government

IX. Sources of real estate financing

  A. Savings and loan associations

        1. Principal function: to promote thrift and home ownership
        2. Regulated on the national level by the Office of Thrift Supervision
        3. Deposits are insured by the Savings Association Insurance Fund (SAIF) for up to $100,000 per account; SAIF is part of the FDIC.
        4. Local in nature

  B. Commercial banks

        1. Prefer short-term loans but have been significant participants in residential mortgage lending
        2. Deposits are insured by the Bank Insurance Fund (BIF) for up to $100,000 per account; BIF is part of the FDIC.

  C. Mutual savings banks

        1. Primarily savings institutions in the northeastern United States
        2. Active in mortgage market
        3. Prefer FHA and DVA loans

  D. Life insurance companies

        1. Prefer long-term commercial, industrial loans
        2. Seek equity position in projects financed
        3. Regulated by state law

  E. Mortgage banking companies

        1. Originate loans with their own money and money belonging to other institutions and from other sources (pension funds, private individuals)
        2. Service loans they originate

  F. Mortgage brokers—originate loans for other lenders but do not service loans

  G. Sale of state mortgage bonds

        1. Authorized by federal government
        2. Lower interest rates are usually charged to low-income and moderate-income buyers.
        3. Usually for first-time buyers only

H. Owner assisted

    1. Contract for deed, land contract
    2. Take back second mortgage

X. Secondary mortgage market

A. Market in which loans are bought and sold after they have been originated and funded

B. Warehousing agencies play a major role in the secondary market by purchasing a number of mortgage loans and assembling them into packages for resale to investors.

C. Major warehousing agencies

    1. Federal National Mortgage Association (FNMA)—Fannie Mae.
        a. Privately owned corporation authorized to purchase conventional as well as FHA and DVA loans
        b. Raises funds to purchase loans by selling government-guaranteed FNMA bonds at market interest rates
    2. Government National Mortgage Association (GNMA)— Ginnie Mae
        a. Federal agency designed to administer a special assistance program and to work with the FNMA in secondary market activities
        b. Can join forces with the FNMA in times of tight money and high interest rates; through a tandem plan, the FNMA can purchase high-risk, low-yield loans at full market rates, while the GNMA guarantees payment and absorbs the difference between low-yield and current market prices
    3. Federal Home Loan Mortgage Corporation (FHLMC)—Freddie Mac.
        a. Government chartered corporation created to provide secondary mortgage market for conventional loans
        b. Has the authority to purchase conventional, FHA and DVA mortgages; pool them; and sell bonds in the open market with mortgages as security

XI. Closing statements (settlement statement or adjustment sheet)

A. Related to the completion of the real estate transaction, when the seller delivers title to the buyer in exchange for payment of the purchase price by the buyer

B. Detailed accounting of real estate transaction; shows all cash received, all charges and credits made, all cash paid out

C. Prepared by the broker, escrow office, attorney or any other person designated to process the details of the sale

D. Indicates how all closing costs plus prepaid and unpaid expenses are allocated between the buyer and the seller

E. Closing statement procedures generally reflect local custom as well as state and federal laws (for example, RESPA).

XII.   Other important terms

    A.   Amortized mortgage (direct-reduction loans)—regular monthly payments, applied first to the interest with the balance to the principal, over the term of the loan

    B.   Balloon payment—final payment of the loan, larger than previous payments and repays the debt in full

    C.   Equity—value of the owner's interest in the property; the difference between the value of the property and all the liens on the property

    D.   Subordination agreement—changes the order of priority of the liens between two creditors

    E.   Usury—rate of interest in excess of the maximum rate allowed by state law

    F.   Seller financing—the seller of the real estate provides financing for the sale by taking back a secured note in the form of a purchase-money mortgage, land contract or deed of trust.

    G.   Disintermediation— process by which investors place funds directly rather than in financial institutions for investment; reduces the availability of mortgage money

    H.   Arbitrage—difference between interest rates in financing arrangements such as wraparound mortgages.

    I.   Hypothecation—pledging property as security for the loan without losing possession of it, such as in lien theory states

    J.   Impound account—trust account created to set aside funds for the future needs of a property; for example, to provide funds for the payment of real estate taxes and renewal premiums for insurance

REVIEW LIST

The student should have an understanding of the following areas of finance:

1. Policies and procedures used by mortgage lending agencies

2. Government mortgage institutions

3. Mathematics of financial practice

4. Truth-in-lending laws

DIAGNOSTIC TEST

1. All of the following statements concerning real estate financing are correct **EXCEPT**

    1. the mortgage generally is considered a lien.
    2. the mortgagee is the lender.
    3. an owner of property by whom the mortgage is executed is called a mortgagor.
    4. a promissory note is security for a mortgage.

2. A promissory note is not

    1. a negotiable instrument.
    2. evidence of debt.
    3. a document in which the debtor agrees to repay the stated loan.
    4. evidence of title.

3. Which of the following payment plans allows for periodic payments of interest *only*, with the principal due as a lump sum payment at maturity?

    1. Amortized
    2. Flexible
    3. Straight
    4. Balloon

4. All of the following are participants in the secondary mortgage market **EXCEPT**

    1. FHLMC.
    2. FNMA.
    3. FDIC.
    4. GNMA.

5. All of the following are characteristics of a conventional loan **EXCEPT**

    1. it is neither insured nor guaranteed by public agency. (govt)
    2. security rests on the borrower's ability to pay and the collateral pledged.
    3. it is never insured by a private agency. it is insured
    4. the ratio of the loan to the value of the property usually does not exceed 80 percent without private mortgage insurance.

6. Department of Veterans Affairs (DVA) guarantees a lender from 25 to 50 percent of the loan balance on a Veterans Administration (VA) loan, up to

    1. $25,000.
    2. $36,000.
    3. $46,000.
    4. $50,750.

7. All of the following are characteristics of a Federal Housing Administration (FHA) loan **EXCEPT**

    1. a mortgage insurance premium is charged.
    2. lender is insured against loss.
    3. maximum mortgage debt is determined by a formula.
    4. FHA provides the money for the loan.

8. The following are characteristics of a DVA loan **EXCEPT**

    1. the loan is guaranteed.
    2. only an eligible veteran or eligible dependents of veterans, as well as reservists and National Guardsmen who have served for six years, may qualify for the loan.
    3. the loan is insured.
    4. little or no down payment is required.

9. A mortgage that covers more than one piece of real property is

    1. a junior mortgage.   3. a package mortgage.
    2. a blanket mortgage.   4. an open-end mortgage.

10. Granting a conventional loan requires that the borrower provide the lender with which of the following?

    1. Sales contract and hypothecation instrument
    2. Mortgage and promissory note
    3. Deed of trust and sales contract
    4. Mortgage and letter of intent

11. A graduated-payment mortgage

    1. contains an interest-rate provision related to a selected index.
    2. is granted for a term of three to five years and is secured by a long-term mortgage of up to 30 years.
    3. allows a buyer to purchase a home with initial monthly payments lower than the level payment, amortized mortgage.
    4. allows the mortgagor to borrow additional money during the term of the loan, up to the original amount of the mortgage.

12. Under judicial foreclosure, the

    1. mortgage generally must include a power-of-sale clause.
    2. court may award title to the lender.
    3. lender sues the borrower in court and obtains a judgment and court order to sell.
    4. lender may sell the property without obtaining a judgment.

13. The process by which a mortgagor regains his or her interest in a property is called

    1. foreclosure.   3. a deficiency judgment.
    2. redemption.   4. laches.

14. You financed the purchase of a home by means of a trust deed. Until you pay off the trust deed, title will be held by the

    1. trustee.
    2. trustor.
    3. seller.
    4. beneficiary.

15. The tandem plan involves

    1. VA and FHA.
    2. Fannie Mae and Freddie Mac.
    3. Fannie Mae and Ginnie Mae.
    4. Ginnie Mae and Freddie Mac.

16. All of the following statements about FHA mortgages are true **EXCEPT**

    1. FHA mortgages require a larger down payment than VA mortgages do.
    2. there is no prepayment penalty.
    3. FHA mortgages are assumable with qualification.
    4. FHA mortgages are not assumable.

17. The difference between interest rates in financing arrangements such as a wraparound mortgage is called

    1. equity.
    2. usury.
    3. disintermediation.
    4. arbitrage.

18. On an FHA loan, the buyer would NOT be required to

    1. provide mortgage insurance to protect the lender.
    2. meet FHA credit standards.
    3. find an approved lender willing to make the loan.
    4. make a 20 percent down payment on the loan.

19. A mortgage on four lots with a partial release clause would be

    1. a wraparound mortgage.
    2. a blanket mortgage.
    3. a package mortgage.
    4. an open-end mortgage.

20. Funds for DVA loans usually are provided by

    1. HUD.
    2. the secondary mortgage market.
    3. Freddie Mac.
    4. approved lenders.

21. Charging a rate of interest in excess of the maximum rate allowed by law is

    1. laches.
    2. hypothecation.
    3. subordination.
    4. usury.

22. Pledging property as security for a loan without losing possession of it is

    1. a subordination agreement.
    2. hypothecation.
    3. an impound account.
    4. seller financing.

23. A veteran buys a home with a DVA-guaranteed loan. Two years later, the veteran sells his home to a buyer who, with the lender's approval, assumes the veteran's loan. In this situation, the veteran is

    1. responsible for paying an insurance fee charged by the DVA.
    2. responsible for paying the loan origination fee.
    3. no longer financially responsible if the buyer defaults six months later.
    4. financially responsible if the buyer defaults six months later.

24. If a lender charges a borrower two points on a $60,000 loan, what will be the service charge for points?

    1. $120   3. $2,400
    2. $1,200   4. None of the above

25. Reserve requirements for banks are controlled by which of the following federal agencies?

    1. FNMA
    2. HUD
    3. Federal Deposit Insurance Corporation (FDIC)
    4. The "Fed"

ANSWER KEY

Question	Answer	Outline Reference		Question	Answer	Outline Reference
1.	4	II		14.	1	III
2.	4	II		15.	3	X
3.	3	IV		16.	4	V
4.	3	X		17.	4	XII
5.	3	VII		18.	4	VII
6.	4	VII		19.	2	VII
7.	4	VII		20.	4	VI
8.	3	VII		21.	4	XII
9.	2	VII		22.	2	VI
10.	2	II		23.	3	V
11.	3	VII		24.	2	VII
12.	3	VI		25.	4	VIII
13.	2	VI				

FINANCE

Test Score

Rating	Range	Your Score	
GOOD = 80% to 100%	20–25	Total number	25
FAIR = 70% to 79%	17–19	Total wrong	–__
NEEDS IMPROVEMENT = Below 70%	16 or less	Total right	__

Passing requirement—
17 or better

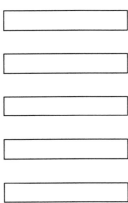

PART 11 / LAND-USE CONTROLS AND REGULATIONS

OUTLINE OF CONCEPTS TO UNDERSTAND

I. Local, state and federal government land rights

    A. Police power—power of the state to set laws aimed at promoting the general welfare and protecting public health and safety; examples of the use of police power include zoning, building codes, environmental protection

    B. Taxation—power to tax real estate to meet the public needs of the government

    C. Eminent domain—power of the government to acquire private property for public use while providing just compensation for the property owner

    D. Escheat—state laws that provide for ownership of real estate to revert to the state when the owner dies intestate and leaves no heirs or when the property is abandoned

    E. Water rights—ownership of water and land adjacent to it as determined by state law, which is based on either the doctrines of riparian and littoral rights or on the doctrine of prior appropriation; owners generally have the right to use water so long as they do not pollute or interrupt the flow

        1. Riparian rights—granted to owners along a river or stream
        2. Littoral rights—granted to owners along an ocean or large lake
        3. Prior appropriation—the right to use water is controlled by the state rather than by the adjacent landowner. A person must show a beneficial use for the water, such as crop irrigation, in order to secure water rights.

II. Control of land use

    A. Public land-use controls—under police power, each state has the authority to adjust regulations required for protecting public health, safety and the general welfare.

        1. Zoning—local laws that regulate and control the use of land within specified areas, for example, residential or commercial areas; generally pertain to the height, bulk and use of the buildings. Powers to zone are conferred on municipal governments by state enabling acts.

         a.   Nonconforming use—use in existence prior to the passage of a zoning ordinance and allowed to continue even though it does not conform
              1)   If property that exists as nonconforming is destroyed, it cannot be rebuilt without the approval of the zoning authority.
         b.   Variance—allows an individual to deviate from the zoning requirement
         c.   Conditional use permit—allows for a use that does not conform with existing zoning but is necessary for the common good, such as locating a medical clinic in a primarily residential neighborhood
         d.   Downzoning—land zoned for residential or commercial use is rezoned for conservation only; it also applies to changes from dense to less-dense usage. The state generally is not responsible for compensating property owners for any loss of value unless the court finds that a "taking" of value has occurred such as land being rezoned from residential to conservancy.
         e.   Buffer zone—a land area that separates one land use from another; a part that separates a residential neighborhood from a shopping center
         f.   Spot zoning—reclassification of a small area of land for use that does not conform to the zoning of the rest of the area
         g.   Planned unit development (PUD)—planned mix of diverse land uses such as housing and recreation in one comprehensive plan
  2. Building codes—ordinances that specify standards for both construction, maintenance and demolition
  3. City plan specifications—a master plan to guide physical development of a community
  4. Subdivision regulations—apply to the location of streets, minimum lot size, etc.
  5. Environmental protection laws
         a.   Federal—examples include National Environmental Policy Act, Clean Air Act
         b.   State—many states, counties and cities have passed their own environmental legislation.

B.   Private land-use controls—restrictions specified by the owner in the deed when conveying the property

C.   If conflict exists between a zoning ordinance and a deed restriction, the more restrictive of the two takes precedence.

D.   Taxation on real estate
  1. Real estate taxes generally take priority over other liens; may be enforced by the court sale of real estate that is free of other liens
  2. Ad valorem tax (Latin for "according to the value")—includes taxes levied on real estate by various governmental units and municipalities
  3. Assessment—appraisal of value for tax purposes by an assessor representing the municipality in which the property is located
  4. Equalization factor—used in some states to correct general inequalities in statewide tax assessment
  5. Computation of tax rate
         a.   The taxing district adopts a budget that identifies the amount of income to be raised from real estate taxes.

b. To arrive at the tax rate, divide the amount of money required for the budget by the total assessed value. For example, if the taxing district must raise $600,000 from real estate taxes and the total assessed value is $10,000,000, the tax rate would be $600,000 ÷ $10,000,000 = 0.06, or 6 percent.

c. The tax rate may be expressed in mills (a mill is 1/1,000 of a dollar, or $0.001); the tax rate in (b) would be 60 mills ($6) per $100 of the assessed value or $60 per $1,000 of the assessed value.

d. The tax bill for a property is calculated by applying the tax rate to the assessed valuation of the property; for example, a home assessed for tax purposes at $60,000 at a rate of 6 percent, or 60 mills, would have a tax bill of $3,600.

6. Special assessments—special taxes levied on real estate; require property owners to pay for improvements that specifically benefit their real estate (installation of a curb and gutter, streets, water system, sewers, etc.)

III. Floodplain, wetlands and shoreline regulations

A. Floodplain—portions of land located near running bodies of water, such as rivers or lakes, that are subject to flooding; government controls generally restrict building in a floodplain

B. Wetlands—areas of land where groundwater is close to or at the surface of the ground for a period of time each year that may produce swamps, floodplains or marshes; because these areas of land are prone to flooding, they are covered by various federal, state and local controls, such as zoning for conservation

C. Shoreline regulation—zoning laws that reflect environmental as well as health and safety concerns; usually require zoning of all lands within a given distance of all navigable waters in each state; generally include tree-cutting rules, setback requirements for structures, filling and grading controls, dredging regulations, minimum standards for water supply and waste disposal, minimum lot sizes and widths, and subdivision regulations

IV. Health and safety codes

A. Building codes

1. Specify construction standards that must be met when erecting, maintaining or demolishing buildings.

2. Generally identify requirements for electrical wiring, sanitary equipment and fire-prevention standards

3. Enforced by issuing building permits that verify compliance with building codes and zoning ordinances

4. The building inspector issues a certificate of occupancy when the completed structure has been inspected and found satisfactory.

5. Issuing a building permit does not take precedence over the violation of a deed restriction.

V. Environmental concerns

A. Pollution and environmental risks in real estate transactions

1. Increasing public awareness of and concern about pollution problems and their health and economic effects have had significant consequences on real estate sales and values.

2. The actual dollar value of real property can be affected significantly by both real and perceived pollution.

3. The cost of cleaning up and removing pollution may be much greater than the dollar value of the property before pollution occurred.

4. In some areas of the United States, mortgage and title insurance approval may depend on the inspection of the property for hazardous substances and proof of their absence.

B. Role of real estate licensees regarding environmental risks in real estate transactions

1. Be alert to the possibility of pollution and hazardous substances on the property being sold.

2. Ask clients about the possibility of hazardous substances associated with the property.

3. Expect increasing numbers of questions from customers concerned about pollution.

4. Consider the consequences of the potential liability in real estate transactions where hazardous substances may be involved.

5. Contact government agencies and private consulting firms for information, guidance and detailed study; real estate licensees often, however, do not have the technical expertise required to determine if hazardous material is present on or near the property.

6. Be scrupulous in considering environmental issues and exercise a high degree of care in all real estate transactions.

C. Hazardous substances of concern to real estate professionals

1. Radon gas—an odorless radioactive gas produced by the decay of other radioactive materials in rocks under the earth's surface
    a. Radon is released from the rocks and finds its way to the surface; usually it is released into the atmosphere. Radon comes into a house through the foundation or basement or crawl space.
    b. Long-term exposure is said to cause lung cancer.
    c. The U.S. Environmental Protection Agency (E.P.A.) has established radon levels that are felt to be unsafe.
    d. Testing techniques have been developed that allow homeowners to determine the exact quantity of radon in their homes.
    e. If a home is determined to have radon gas, the seller is obligated to find a way to eliminate the hazard, whether the danger is actual or only perceived.
    f. Most homes with elevated levels of radon can be fixed for between $500 and $2,500, with an average cost of about $1,200.

2. Asbestos—material used for many years as insulation on plumbing pipes and heat ducts and as general insulation because it is a poor heat conductor; also was used in floor tile and roofing material
    a. Relatively harmless if not disturbed; can become life-threatening during its removal because of accompanying dust
    b. Exposure to asbestos dust can come if
        1) The asbestos gets old and starts to disintegrate
        2) Remodeling projects include the removal of asbestos shingles, roof tile or insulation that can cause the dust to form in the air and expose people in the area to the health hazard

3. Urea-formaldehyde foam insulation (UFFI)—a synthetic material generally used to insulate buildings
   a. Typically pumped between walls as a foam that later hardens and acts as an insulating material
   b. Becomes dangerous because of gases released from the material after it hardens
4. Lead poisoning—lead is a mineral that has been used extensively because of its pliability and its ability to impede water flow.
   a. Becomes a health hazard when ingested.
   b. Sources of lead poisoning
      1) Peeling or flaking paint
      2) Plumbing systems
   c. Federal regulations on lead-based paint disclosure
      1) Owners of residential properties built before 1978, when the use of lead-based paint was common, will have to disclose to buyers or renters the presence of known lead-based paint hazards.
      2) A lead-based paint disclosure statement must be attached as a separate item to all real estate sales and lease contracts on pre-1978 residential properties.
      3) Real estate practitioners must distribute to buyers and renters a federal lead hazard pamphlet but won't be responsible for ensuring that people read and understand the brochure.
      4) Buyers will have up to 10 days to have a lead-risk assessment performed on the property if they want one.
      5) Exemptions from the regulations are provided for housing for the elderly and disabled, provided children are not regularly present; for vacation homes and short-term rentals; for foreclosure sales; and for single-room rentals within dwellings.
5. PCBs (Polychlorinated biphenyls)—used in the manufacture of electrical products such as voltage regulators as well as in paints and caulking materials
   a. PCBs haven't been used since 1977; however, they are still dangerous because many of the products are still being used.
   b. An environmental consultant can assess the property and recommend procedures for cleanup.
6. Waste-disposal sites—landfill operations
   a. Landfill—a specific site that has been excavated and lined with either a clay or a synthetic liner to prevent leakage of waste material into the local water system
   b. Construction and maintenance of a landfill operation heavily regulated by state and federal authorities
   c. Landfills at improper locations and improperly managed sites have been sources of major problems; for example, landfills constructed on the wrong type of soil will leak waste into nearby wells, causing major damage.
   d. Real estate licensees must be aware of such facilities within their areas and take appropriate action when dealing with potential clients.
7. Underground storage tanks—used in residential and commercial settings for many years

        a.   An estimated 3 million to 5 million underground storage tanks exist in the United States that hold hazardous substances such as gasoline.

        b.   Risk occurs when containers become old, rust and start to leak.

        c.   Toxic material may enter the groundwater, contaminate the wells and pollute the soil.

        d.   Sources of pollution

              1)   Older gas stations with steel tanks that develop leaks through oxidation (rusting)

              2)   Underground containers used to hold fuel oil for older homes

        e.   Recent federal legislation calls for removal of such tanks and all the polluted soil around them.

    8. Groundwater contamination

        a.   Groundwater includes runoff at ground level as well as underground water systems that are sources of wells for both private and public facilities.

        b.   Sources of contamination

               1)   Waste-disposal sites

              2)   Underground storage tanks

              3)   Pesticides and herbicides typically used in farming communities

        c.   The only protection for the general public against water contamination is heavy government regulation.

        d.   Once contamination is identified, its source can be eliminated; the process often is time-consuming and very expensive.

D.   Agencies administering federal environmental laws

    1. Environmental Protection Agency

        a.   Toxic Substance Control Act

        b.   Resources Conservation and Recovery Act

        c.   Federal Clean Water Act

    2. U.S. Department of Transportation—administers the Hazardous Materials Transportation Act

    3. The Occupational Safety and Health Administration (OSHA) and the U.S. Department of Labor—administer standards for all employees working in the manufacturing sector

    4. Federal government encourages state and local governments to prepare legislation in their areas.

E.   Statutory law

    1. Resource Conservation and Recovery Act (RCRA) of 1976—created to regulate the generation, transportation, storage, use, treatment, disposal and cleanup of hazardous waste

    2. The Comprehensive Environmental Response Compensation and Liability Act (CERCLA) was created in 1980.

        a.   Established fund of $9 billion called Superfund to clean up uncontrolled hazardous waste dumps and respond to spills

        b.   Created a process for identifying liable parties and ordering them to take responsibility for the cleanup

        c.   Liability under Superfund considered to be strict, joint and several, and retroactive

               1)   Strict liability—owner is responsible to the injured party without excuse

          2) Joint and several liability—each individual owner is personally responsible for the damages in whole; if only one owner is financially able to handle the total damage, then that owner will have to pay all and attempt to collect the proportionate share of the rest of the owners from them.

          3) Retroactive liability—liability not limited to the person who currently owns the property; also extends to people who have owned the site in the past

   3. Leaking Underground Storage Tanks (LUST) regulations—established in 1984

      a. Governs the installation, maintenance, monitoring and failure of underground storage tanks

      b. Aimed at protecting groundwater in the United States through release prevention, detection and correction

   4. Superfund Amendments and Reauthorization Act (SARA)—created in 1986

      a. Established stronger cleanup standards for contaminated sites

      b. Substantially increased the funding of the Superfund

      c. Attempted to clarify the obligation of the lenders

      d. Created the concept called *innocent landowner immunity*

F. Common law

   1. Provides the backdrop for existing legislation to catch situations that do not specifically fall within the law

   2. California case of *Easton v. Strassburger* (1986) led to state laws requiring that all real estate agents conduct a "reasonably diligent and competent inspection" of the property for sale, examining for potential problems dealing with pollution, and mandating the use of disclosure forms that must be presented to the prospective purchaser.

VI. Deed restrictions

A. Private restrictions written into deeds or leases that limit the use of property, for example, restrictions on the type or the size of the building

B. May be terminated by a quitclaim deed executed by the necessary parties

C. Generally enforced by means of a court injunction

D. Adjoining lot owners in a subdivision can lose the right to the court's injunction by inaction, under the doctrine of laches (the loss of a right through undue delay or failure to assert the right).

REVIEW LIST

The student should have an understanding of the following areas of land-use controls and regulation:

1.   Planning and zoning

2.   Property taxation

3.   Floodplain, wetlands and shoreline regulations

4.   Health and safety codes

5.   Environmental concerns

6.   Deed restrictions

DIAGNOSTIC TEST

1.   When the county board acquires land for a freeway, it is exercising the power of

   1.   zoning.
   2.   environmental protection laws.
   3.   escheat.
   4.   eminent domain.

2.   One example of the use of police power by a city is

   1.   taxation.
   2.   eminent domain.
   3.   laches.
   4.   environmental protection laws.

3.   An insurance agency existed before the land was zoned residential by a new zoning ordinance. The insurance agency is an example of

   1.   a variance.
   2.   a nonconforming use.
   3.   spot zoning.
   4.   a planned unit development.

4.   An investor purchased a large parcel of land zoned for commercial development, but the land was rezoned by the city to recreational right after the purchase was made. This was an example of

   1.   eminent domain.
   2.   downzoning.
   3.   nonconforming use.
   4.   a planned unit development.

5.   Zoning laws that include tree-cutting rules, dredging regulations and waste disposal exemplify

   1.   subdivision regulations.
   2.   city plan specifications.
   3.   shoreline regulations.
   4.   deed restrictions.

6.   Radon enters a house through the

   1.   roof.
   2.   foundation.
   3.   chimney.
   4.   windows.

7. A mineral used for many years as insulation on heat ducts is

   1. asbestos.
   2. lead.
   3. urea-formaldehyde foam.
   4. radon.

8. Which of the following is typically pumped between the walls of a house to act as an insulating material?

   1. Asbestos
   2. Radon
   3. Urea-formaldehyde foam
   4. Lead

9. A material that has been used extensively because of its ability to impede water flow is

   1. lead.
   2. asbestos.
   3. urea-formaldehyde foam.
   4. radon.

10. Which of the following statements most correctly describes a waste-disposal site?

    1. Construction is relatively unregulated by state authorities.
    2. Landfills at appropriate locations have been sources of major problems.
    3. Real estate licensees need not be concerned about such facilities within their areas.
    4. Landfills constructed on the wrong type of soil may leak water into nearby wells, causing major damage.

11. All of the following may be sources of groundwater contamination **EXCEPT**

    1. underground storage tanks.
    2. waste-disposal sites.
    3. use of pesticides on farms.
    4. cement.

12. All of the following requirements generally are covered by building codes **EXCEPT**

    1. fire-prevention standards.
    2. electrical wiring.
    3. sanitary equipment.
    4. minimum number of square feet of land area per apartment unit.

13. Strict liability means that

    1. an owner is responsible to an injured party without excuse.
    2. each owner is personally responsible for damages as a whole.
    3. liability extends to people who have owned the site in the past.
    4. an owner is not responsible to an injured party.

14. State laws that require real estate agents to conduct a reasonably diligent and competent inspection of the property for sale, examining for potential problems dealing with pollution, are a result of

    1. *Jones v. Mayer.*
    2. *Easton v. Strassburger.*
    3. the Superfund Amendments and Reauthorization Act.
    4. the Resource Conservation and Recovery Act.

15. All of the following statements concerning deed restrictions are true **EXCEPT**

    1. violation of a restrictive condition may result in the forfeiture of title to real property.
    2. encumbrances in the form of restrictive conditions generally run with restricted land into the indefinite future.
    3. the penalty for violation or breach of a restrictive covenant is more severe than that for breach of a restrictive condition.
    4. The goal of deed restrictions generally is to protect the value of all properties in a development.

16. Which of the following best describes a buffer zone?

    1. An industrial park located between a shopping center and a residential neighborhood
    2. A high-rise apartment complex located between a commercial development and a town-house subdivision
    3. A recreational area located between a residential area and an office park
    4. A sound barrier located alongside a major highway

17. Police-power controls include all of the following **EXCEPT**

    1. city plan specifications.
    2. building codes.
    3. zoning.
    4. deed restrictions.

18. A tire company has a manufacturing plant located in an area that recently has been zoned residential. The company is allowed to operate under the new zoning ordinance. If the plant is destroyed by fire, the company may

    1. appeal for an exculpatory provision.
    2. not construct another tire plant in the neighborhood without being granted a zoning variance.
    3. not construct another tire plant in the neighborhood under any conditions.
    4. reconstruct the tire company in the same neighborhood.

19. Which of the following provides for monetary compensation to an owner in the event of a loss of property value?

    1. Taxation
    2. Eminent domain
    3. Escheat
    4. Police power

20. A recorded restriction is best described as

    1. a limitation on use.
    2. a condition.
    3. a lien.
    4. a lien and an encumbrance.

ANSWER KEY

Question	Answer	Outline Reference	Question	Answer	Outline Reference
1.	4	I	11.	4	V
2.	4	I	12.	4	IV
3.	2	II	13.	1	V
4.	2	II	14.	2	V
5.	3	III	15.	3	VI
6.	2	V	16.	3	II
7.	1	V	17.	4	I
8.	3	V	18.	2	I
9.	1	V	19.	2	II
10.	4	V	20.	1	IV

LAND-USE CONTROLS AND REGULATIONS

Rating	Test Score Range	Your Score	
GOOD = 80% to 100%	16–20	Total number	20
FAIR = 70% to 79%	14–15	Total wrong	–__
NEEDS IMPROVEMENT = Below 70%	13 or less	Total right	__

**Passing requirement—
17 or better**

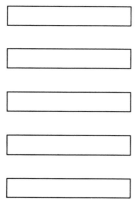

PART 12 / BROKERAGE MANAGEMENT

OUTLINE OF CONCEPTS TO UNDERSTAND

I.   Types of ownership

    A.   Sole proprietorship

        1. Provides broker with flexibility and control, while trading off protection against personal liability

        2. Appropriate for the broker who desires a small operation and sales staff

    B.   Joint or multiple ownership—appropriate for the broker interested in growth and expansion as well as joint ownership; five primary forms of multiple ownership

        1. Corporation

            a. Advantages

                1) Limited liability—any liability incurred by a corporation through judgments, bankruptcies, etc., limited to the investment of a shareholder in a corporation; does not affect a shareholder's personal assets

                2) Centralized management—shareholders elect a board of directors, who elect officers to manage the company; a licensed broker-director is responsible for the real estate brokerage phase of the business.

                3) Continuity of life—a corporation is a legal entity that never dies; its officers may be continually replaced if necessary.

                4) No income limitations—no upper limit on the amount of income a corporation may earn or the number of shareholders it may have

                5) Transferability—corporate stock may be freely transferred from one shareholder to another.

            b. Disadvantages

                1) Double taxation—profits taxed at both the corporate and individual levels

                2) Treatment of losses—corporation losses may not be passed on to shareholders; they may be applied to future earnings of the corporation.

                3) Capital gains—passed on to shareholders as ordinary income

2. S corporation
   a. Advantages
      1) No double taxation—income, losses and capital gains passed directly to the shareholders
      2) Centralized management and continuity of life—similar to the typical corporation
      3) Limited liability with shareholders' interests freely transferable
   b. Disadvantages
      1) Ownership limited to 35 shareholders
      2) Not more than 20 percent of income may be from passive investments, that is, investments that are income-related, such as stock dividends or interest from deposits.
3. General partnership
   a. Advantages
      1) No double taxation—income directly taxable to each partner
      2) Capital gains or losses pass directly to the partners.
   b. Disadvantages
      1) Problems arising from the death, bankruptcy, etc., of the partner(s)
      2) Ownership not freely transferable
4. Limited partnership
   a. Rarely used in an active brokerage firm
   b. Used primarily to acquire investments such as syndicates, joint ventures
   c. One or more general partners have unlimited liability; are responsible for the operation of the business
   d. Limited partners generally have no say in the business operation.
   e. Limited partners' liability is limited to the amount of the investment.
5. Limited liability companies
   a. Offer advantages of the single-level taxation of a partnership and the limited liability of a corporation
   b. Avoid some of the restrictions that are imposed on an S corporation
   c. Must generally have at least one member; members may be corporations, individuals, limited or general partnerships, a trust or foreign persons
   d. May be directly managed by members, or responsibility may be delegated to a property manager

C. Franchises and alternatives—the broker may choose among various types of operations.

   1. Remain independent—provides pride of ownership
   2. Become a member of a referral system
   3. Franchise membership—for example, Century 21 and Electronic Realty Associates (ERA)
      a. Advantages
         1) Approaches to management and marketing—members pay an initial fee and a percentage of the profits in return for franchise "expertise."
         2) Client referral system
         3) Economics of volume purchasing of equipment, signs, etc.
         4) National advertising and promotion

         b.   Disadvantages
           1)   Loss of individual identity
           2)   High initial fees and franchise fees
           3)   Possibly limited geographic area

4. Quasi-franchise membership—for example: Better Homes and Gardens and Gallery of Homes
   a. The broker may retain the name as part of the firm identification.
   b. Offer varied services that are less extensive than those of a franchise operation—for example: Help-U-Sell
   c. The owner is guided by a broker on how to sell property.
   d. The seller takes on part of the broker's responsibility such as showing the property.
5. The seller generally pays a commission less than that charged by a traditional broker.
6. Advantages
   a. The broker's monetary investment and time are less.
   b. Greater exposure to FSBOs (For Sale by Owner)
7. Disadvantages
   a. Lower fees require increased business activity.
   b. Increased pressure to earn a profit
   c. May retain offices while pooling advertising outlays and sharing in the profits of the cooperative
8. Membership in broker association—single office composed of a group of individual brokers who share office space and expenses
9. 100-percent commission office
   a. Landlord-broker owns the office and facilities; rents the office to other brokers or associates on a per-desk basis
   b. Each broker or associate pays a monthly fee to cover the landlord's office expenses and a small percentage of the commission for the benefit of all the brokers and associates; the 100-percent concept often is used in combination with other forms of operation.

D. Internal structure of organization

1. One-person organization
2. One-to-ten-agent organization
   a. A small, centralized operation in which the capacity for doing business grows as the size of the organization grows
   b. Management responsibility, as well as the need for office space and equipment, will increase the cost of doing business.
3. Monolithic organization
   a. Functions as single unit, though it normally consists of a number of work groups
   b. There is a single source of authority at the top of the organization.
4. Decentralized organization—fewer levels of management, thus the managers have the authority to operate essentially as individual business units

II. Sales associate relationship

A. Independent contractor

1. Salesperson under limited supervision

2. The salesperson contracts with the broker to produce specific outcomes, for example, leasing commissions and real estate sales.
3. The process by which a salesperson produces a commission cannot be controlled by the broker except within the guidelines of the contract.
4. The broker may not unduly restrict the methods that the associate may use.
5. The broker may not withhold federal and state income taxes, Social Security taxes or state unemployment insurance from commissions.
6. The broker may not provide health insurance or pension plans.
7. The salesperson must pay his or her own license fees and board dues.
8. The salesperson is responsible for car and transportation expenses.
9. The salesperson may not be required to attend sales meetings.
10. The salesperson may not be required to follow a set work schedule.

B. Employee

1. The broker can employ, guide the activities of, maintain the standards of conduct of or terminate an employee at will.
2. The broker is required to withhold federal and state income taxes, pay an employee's share of Social Security taxes and withhold state unemployment insurance from commissions.
3. The broker may choose to provide fringe benefits such as health insurance.
4. The broker may require attendance at sales meetings.

C. Federal income tax requirements to be classified as an independent contractor—see "VI. IRS regulations," in "Outline of Concepts to Understand" for Part 7.

III. Developing plans

A. Purpose—to commit broker's financial and human resources to those activities that will produce highest return on investment

1. Plans tell what broker's company wants to accomplish and provide general framework for how organization will follow through
2. The broker must have specific goals for the company to accomplish.

B. Business plan—generally a three-year to five-year blueprint for the organization.

C. Short-range plan—tells company what it should be doing in the coming year.

D. Mission statement—states what a company's purpose is for doing business, specifically, what the business does and where the company intends to be in the future

IV. Risk management

A. Management styles

1. Dictatorial style—the manager has total control over the organization.
2. Autocratic style—managers are authoritarian but more benevolent than dictatorial managers.
3. Participative style—more democratic than above styles; utilizes talents of people to a greater extent than is common in other styles of management

4. Laissez-faire—manager doesn't exercise any authority; style characterized by nonintervention and indifference.

B. Benefits of training program

1. Reputation—reputation for good program attracts new salespeople
2. Supervision—need for close supervision reduced
3. Selection—helps the broker select the most promising salespeople
4. Motivation—motivates salespeople to try out what they have learned
5. Morale—aids the retention of salespeople by helping them to be productive as quickly as possible
6. Less turnover—provides the knowledge that is necessary for salespeople to succeed, thus reducing the need to terminate the unproductive

C. Objectives of a training program

1. Good habits—primary objective to develop good working habits in trainees
2. Increased profits—provides well-chosen salespeople with greater profits
3. Better production—providing salespeople with training as well as attention increases their productivity.
4. Better time management—lessens the need for salespeople to depend on brokers, thus allowing greater sales production
5. Learning from mistakes—makes salespeople aware of the need to learn from mistakes

D. Personal assistants

1. Personal assistants may handle the non-sales-related aspects of real estate transactions.
2. Personal assistants have enhanced the productivity of salespeople as well as the profitability of brokerage firms.
3. State licensing laws may address the numerous issues posed by the use of personal assistants.
4. Personal assistants are generally hired and supervised by a salesperson.
5. The broker's policies and procedures should define how salespersons' assistants are handled in an organization.

E. Record keeping

1. Method of keeping financial records
   a. Cash method—records income as received and expenses when actually paid
   b. Accrual method—records income when earned and expenses when incurred (Most firms begin operating under the cash method because the accrual method is more complicated.)
2. Financial analysis guidelines
   a. Provides standardized method of classifying income and expenses; accounting functions are becoming computerized.
   b. Once expense categories are established and income categories assigned, the coding of deposit slips and checks written can provide the basis for the development of financial statements, balance sheets and profit-and-loss statements.
3. Typical bookkeeping system
   a. Records of income—can be entered on a ledger page as in a checkbook register or on a computer.

      b. Record of payments—carbon copy of entries, duplicate of check or computer record is sufficient.

      c. Accounts payable—list all the bills received and the date of payment in the file or book.

      d. Payroll card—shows the gross and net salaries plus the federal and state tax deductions for all employees.

      e. Commission records—indicate the amounts of all commissions paid to each salesperson, with each transaction identified.

      f. Advertising—newspaper, Internet, cable TV, etc., ads are checked for accuracy and charted to keep track of calls received.

      g. Telephone—outgoing personal calls should be discouraged as much as possible by logging incoming and outgoing calls or by computer printouts.

      h. Supplies—a sign-in/sign-out sheet should be used to keep track of such items as lawn signs and lock boxes.

  4. Miscellaneous

      a. Licensing requirements—brokers should make sure that salespeople are properly licensed.

      b. Contracts—each person in the office should sign the contract; this is essential for the independent contractor.

      c. Policy manual—the office policy and procedure manual should be ready when a brokerage office is opened.

      d. Legal advice—brokers should retain good attorneys for sound legal advice.

V.   Trust accounts

  A. Commingling business monies with escrow monies is illegal.

  B. Trust account records must be kept of the names of parties for whose benefit the trust account is created; most brokers maintain trust account records on computer.

  C. Notation of the date of receipt of any sum and the record of the date and manner of disbursement of funds held in trust should be maintained.

  D. All disbursement notations should include the check number and the name of the payee.

  E. Trust funds should be deposited in a checking account maintained especially for this purpose.

VI.   Basic financial concepts

  A. Cash flow—net spendable income from the investment calculated by deducting all the operating and fixed expenses from the gross income

  B. Company dollar—amount of income that remains after subtracting all the commissions from the gross income

  C. Gross income—revenue earned from all sources, including sales, appraisals, management fees, etc.

  D. Budget—a quantified business plan

E. Budgeting process—mechanism through which a broker can design a firm's activities and assign dollar costs and anticipated revenues to their implementation

F. Zero-base budgeting—requires that all budgeted costs for the planning period be justified each time a new budget is developed

G. Desk cost—the cost of providing the opportunity for salespeople to conduct business is calculated by dividing the total operating expenses of the firm (including salaries, rent, insurance, etc.) by the number of salespeople. (The number of desks is not considered in the calculation. For example, if the broker's annual overhead is $60,000 and there are two desks, each accommodating two salespeople, the desk cost for the firm is $15,000. On a 50/50 split, each salesperson does not begin to earn a profit for the broker until each has brought in a total of $30,000 in gross commissions for the year.)

REVIEW LIST

The student should have an understanding of the following areas of brokerage management:

1. Types of ownership

2. Sales associate relationships

   a. Independent contractor
   b. Employee

3. Risk management

   a. Agent supervision
   b. Record keeping

4. Trust accounts

5. Basic financial concepts

DIAGNOSTIC TEST

1. Ownership in an S Corporation is limited to

   1. 20 stockholders.
   2. 25 stockholders.
   3. 35 stockholders.
   4. 100 stockholders.

2. All of the following are advantages of the corporation form of ownership **EXCEPT**

   1. limited liability.
   2. centralized management.
   3. no income limitations.
   4. double taxation.

3. All of the following statements correctly describe a limited partnership **EXCEPT**

   1. a limited partnership is a popular form of ownership for active brokerage firms.
   2. limited partners generally have no say in business operations.
   3. the general partner has unlimited liability.
   4. limited partnerships primarily are used to acquire investments such as syndicates.

4. Which of the following is a quasi-franchise?

   1. Electronic Realty Associates (ERA)
   2. Better Homes and Gardens
   3. Century 21
   4. Re/Max

5. A landlord-broker generally would be found in a

   1. sole proprietorship.
   2. limited partnership.
   3. general partnership.
   4. 100-percent commission office.

6. All of the following statements correctly describe the independent contractor relationship **EXCEPT**

   1. the salesperson is under limited supervision.
   2. the salesperson is responsible for car and transportation expenses.
   3. the broker must provide health insurance.
   4. the broker may not withhold federal income taxes from commissions.

7. A broker has an annual overhead of $300,000, and there are ten desks, each accommodating two salespeople. The broker's desk cost is

   1. $15,000
   2. $20,000

   3. $25,000
   4. $30,000

8. The person who manages your brokerage firm exercises total control over the organization. This type of management style would be called

   1. autocratic.
   2. dictatorial.

   3. participative.
   4. laissez-faire.

9. All of the following statements correctly describe the methods of keeping financial records **EXCEPT**

   1. the cash method records income as it is received.
   2. the accrual method records income when it is earned.
   3. most firms begin operating under the accrual method.
   4. the accrual method records expenses when they are incurred.

10. All of the following are objectives of a training program **EXCEPT**

    1. increased profits.
    2. better time management.
    3. good habits.
    4. preparation for passing the license exam.

11. Benefits of a training program include all of the following **EXCEPT**

    1. supervision.
    2. motivation.

    3. morale.
    4. handling of personal problems.

12. A typical bookkeeping system includes all of the following **EXCEPT**

    1. records of income.
    2. accounts payable.

    3. payroll cards.
    4. a policy manual.

13. Trust account notations include all of the following **EXCEPT**

    1. the receipt of any monies belonging to others.
    2. a record of the date of the disbursement of the funds.
    3. the manner in which the funds are disbursed.
    4. a record of appointments to show homes.

14. All of the following statements correctly describe trust accounts **EXCEPT**

    1. commingling of business funds with escrow funds is illegal.
    2. trust funds should be deposited in a business account.
    3. trust account records must be kept of the names of the parties for whose benefit the trust account is created.
    4. all disbursement notations should include the check number and the name of payee.

15. Miscellaneous record keeping for a broker includes all of the following **EXCEPT**

1. providing a policy manual.
2. making sure that salespeople are properly licensed.
3. retaining an attorney to provide sound legal advise.
4. making sure that salespeople are staying up-to-date in their field.

ANSWER KEY

Question	Answer	Outline Reference	Question,	Answer	Outline Reference
1.	3	I	9.	3	IV
2.	4	I	10.	4	IV
3.	1	I	11.	4	IV
4.	2	I	12.	4	IV
5.	4	I	13.	4	V
6.	3	II	14.	2	V
7.	1	V	15.	4	IV
8.	2	II			

BROKERAGE MANAGEMENT

Rating	Test Score Range	Your Score	
GOOD = 80% to 100%	12–15	Total number	15
FAIR = 70% to 79%	10–11	Total wrong	–__
NEEDS IMPROVEMENT = Below 70%	9 or less	Total right	__

Passing requirement—
10 or better

PART 13 / SALESPERSON EXAMINATIONS

The sample examinations that follow evaluate your general real estate knowledge and test-taking ability. Simulate as closely as possible the actual test conditions (see Part 1, "Use of the Manual"); avoid distractions; and use only those tools permitted by your state. These exams contain 100 questions. Circle your answer for each question. Remember that the PSI exam includes an additional 40- to 50-question portion that tests your knowledge of your state's real estate laws and specific real estate practices.

After completing and grading this sample exam, carefully analyze your results. Did you complete all the questions in the allotted time? Did you answer a minimum of 81 questions correctly? It will be useful to mark in the answer key all the questions you missed. The answers and explanations are keyed to topics in the concepts-to-understand outlines for each part. The pattern of your errors should immediately suggest which areas require additional study. For example, if you missed more than three of the first 12 questions (more than 20 percent), you should review Part 4.

As a final check, you may wish to review all the exam questions in the *Guide* that relate to a specific topic. Feel free to test and retest yourself. The greater your familiarity with the scope and style of the PSI exam, the better you are likely to perform.

SALESPERSON EXAMINATION I

1. A man gave his best friend the right to go hunting on his farm. This would be an example of an

   1. easement by prescription.
   2. easement of gross.
   3. easement of necessity.
   4. easement of appurtenant.

2. A state wants to build a publicly owned convention center to attract private development in its largest city. Can the state use eminent domain to acquire the land?

   1. No, because private investments would not be allowed.
   2. Yes, if just compensation is paid to the owners of the land.
   3. No, because eminent domain can only be used for highway expansion.
   4. Yes, if the owners hold fee simple interest in the land.

3. A broker sold a home for $146,000. The broker charged the owner a 6 percent commission and will pay 25 percent of that amount to the listing salesperson and 30 percent to the selling salesperson. What amount of commission will the listing salesperson receive from the sale?

   1. $2,058
   2. $2,190
   3. $2,628
   4. None of the above

4. Salesperson *A* for broker *B* has listed a home. Salesperson *C* for broker *D* is trying to sell the home to his own buyer. Salesperson *C* is primarily responsible to

   1. his own buyer.
   2. salesperson *A*.
   3. broker *B*.
   4. broker *D*.

5. The listing broker owes a fiduciary duty to

   1. the customer.
   2. the listing salesperson.
   3. the client.
   4. the buyer.

6. You are a broker holding an open house for your seller when an old friend stops by and asks you to show her the property. Your friend likes the property and asks you to write up an offer to purchase. Which of the following statements would describe your relationship with your friend?

   1. Your friend is your principal.
   2. Your friend is a customer.
   3. You have a fiduciary relationship with your friend.
   4. Your friend is your client.

7. You are working as a buyer's broker for a client. Which of the following would NOT describe your role as a buyer's broker?

   1. You should show the buyer properties in which your commission is protected, such as MLS-listed properties.
   2. You should counsel the buyer about developing accurate objectives.
   3. You should search for the best properties for your buyer to inspect, widening the marketplace to include homes for sale by owners (FSBOs).
   4. You should help the buyer prepare the strongest offer.

8. A claim based on adverse possession of property must NOT be

   1. notorious.
   2. open.
   3. hostile.
   4. secretive.

9. All of the following statements concerning encumbrances are true **EXCEPT**

   1. all encumbrances are liens.
   2. all liens are encumbrances.
   3. restrictions beneficial to the grantee are encumbrances.
   4. an easement is a physical encumbrance.

10. You and your husband own your house in a form of ownership in which neither of you can sell the house individually. Your form of ownership is most likely

    1. tenancy by the entirety.
    2. in severalty.
    3. joint tenancy.
    4. tenancy in common.

11. A man has his property listed with a broker. On June 23, a fire causes considerable damage to the property. On June 25, the owner revokes the listing. On June 29, the broker is deemed incompetent. Two days later, on July 1, the listing expires. On what date was the listing terminated?

1. June 23
2. June 25
3. June 29
4. On the expiration date included in the listing agreement

12. You bought a home one year ago for $83,500. Property in your neighborhood is said to be increasing in value at a rate of 6 percent annually. If this is true, what is the current value of your real estate?

1. $86,840   3. $88,510
2. $87,675   4. None of the above

13. You are appraising a property in which seller motivation is a significant factor. The motivation would be most important in utilizing which of the following?

1. Cost approach   3. Income approach
2. Gross-rent-multiplier method   4. Sales-comparison approach

14. Which of the following is a similarity between an exclusive-right-to-sell listing and an exclusive-agency listing?

1. Under both, the seller avoids paying the broker a commission if the seller sells the property without the help of the broker.
2. Both give the responsibility of representing the seller to just one broker.
3. Both are net listings.
4. Under both, the seller authorizes one specific salesperson to show the property.

15. A home is valued at $92,000. Property in this city is assessed at 70 percent of its value and the local tax rate is $3.40 per $100. What is the amount of the owner's monthly taxes?

1. $182.47   3. $2,189.60
2. $260.67   4. None of the above

16. Using the mortgage factor chart on page 87, what is the monthly payment for a $150,000 loan at 11.5 percent for 30 years?

1. $1,429.50   3. $1,525.50
2. $1,486.50   4. $1,581.00

17. Using the information in question 16, what is the total interest paid over the life of the loan?

1. $297,300   3. $535,140
2. $371,625   4. None of the above

18. A broker has just listed a property and written an offer on it. Which of the following statements would describe the agency relationship?

    1. The broker is required to charge a commission.
    2. The commission will be set by the local board of realtors.
    3. The commission may not be based on a flat fee.
    4. The buyer and the customer are the same party.

19. How must a licensed broker handle earnest money deposits?

    1. The broker should deposit the money in his or her business account.
    2. When the seller directs, the broker should keep the earnest money attached to the sales contract in her or his safe until the sale is closed.
    3. The broker should not deposit the money in her or his special account until the offer is accepted and all contingencies are removed by the buyer.
    4. The broker should promptly deposit the money in his or her special account following acceptance of the contract.

20. A developer was able to buy two adjoining single-family lots for $20,000 each. He combined the lots into one parcel with a value of $90,000. The developer's action reflects the process of

    1. accession.
    2. attachment.
    3. exchange.
    4. plottage.

21. Lenders are required to prepare a loan closing on HUD Form 1 by

    1. the Civil Rights Act of 1866.
    2. Regulation Z.
    3. RESPA.
    4. federal fair housing laws.

22. The Housing and Community Development Act, passed in 1974, provides that it is unlawful to discriminate on the basis of

    1. sexual orientation.
    2. age.
    3. sex.
    4. marital status.

23. You signed a lease for one year and took possession of an apartment. When the lease expired, you continued to live in the apartment without the owner's consent. Your tenancy would be considered to be a(n)

    1. estate for years.
    2. estate from year to year.
    3. tenancy at will.
    4. tenancy at sufferance.

24. The Civil Rights Act of 1866 prohibits discrimination based on

    1. handicap.
    2. familial status.
    3. race.
    4. sex.

25. All of the following would be a benefit to an industry being located in an industrial park **EXCEPT**

    1. protection of investment through covenants designed to guard against deterioration of industrial park properties.
    2. advantage of large-scale operation.
    3. more efficient extension of municipal services.
    4. "package plan" availability, which generally relieves industry of the need to develop a site.

26. A salesperson is working for a broker. The salesperson is required to attend all sales meetings and take ten hours of floor time each week. The salesperson is most likely

    1. an employee.
    2. a manager.
    3. an independent contractor.
    4. a branch manager.

27. A broker who knowingly violates the provisions of the Truth-in-Lending Law relating to advertising properties and is guilty of a first offense may have to

    1. pay a fine of up to $1,000.
    2. pay a fine of up to $5,000.
    3. serve a jail sentence of up to six months.
    4. pay actual damages.

28. You have entered into a lease that requires you to pay 20 percent of the owner's expenses. Your lease would be an example of a

    1. variable lease.
    2. net lease.
    3. percentage lease.
    4. gross lease. (fixed rent)

29. Tax-deferred exchanges are covered in

    1. IRC Section 7082.
    2. IRC Section 1031. Tax deferred
    3. IRC Section 1445. Foreign
    4. IRC Section 1099.

30. Riparian rights would exist in a

    1. condominium on a bay.
    2. house on a bay.
    3. hotel whose land abuts a large lake.
    4. cooperative on a river.

31. A contract in which both parties have fulfilled their promises is

    1. an executory contract.
    2. a bilateral contract.
    3. an expressed contract.
    4. an executed contract.

32. An option, prior to being exercised, is an example of

    1. an executory contract.
    2. a unilateral contract.
    3. a bilateral contract.
    4. an executed contract.

33. You wrote an offer on a house for $214,000. The seller gave you a counteroffer for $218,000. The seller may withdraw the counteroffer

    1. within 72 hours after acceptance.
    2. prior to your acceptance.
    3. prior to removal of all contingencies in the offer.
    4. prior to closing.

34. You have an exclusive-right-to-sell listing on a house when you are informed by your aunt that one of her coworkers would be interested in buying the house. Your aunt wants $1,000 for providing the name of the coworker to you. Which of the following statements correctly describes the situation?

    1. You may pay the finder's fee.
    2. You may not pay the finder's fee. In most states, however, you could buy her a television set.
    3. You may not pay the finder's fee to your aunt, but you could pay it to the coworker, should the coworker buy the house.
    4. You may not legally pay a finder's fee to your aunt.

35. A meat-packing plant has just been built one block from where your house is located. The strong odors are lowering property values in your neighborhood. The loss in value would be classified as

    1. functional obsolescence.
    2. physical deterioration.
    3. the principal of change.
    4. external obsolescence.

36. What is the actual value of your property if the annual taxes are $2,880 and real estate is assessed at 30 percent of actual value? (Figure a levy of 48 mills per $1 of assessed value.)

    1. $86,400
    2. $120,000
    3. $200,000
    4. None of the above

37. You have a mortgage in which you make the same payment each month for principal and interest, with the principal payment increasing and the interest payment decreasing from month-to-month. This is called a(n)

    1. amortized mortgage.
    2. term mortgage.
    3. reverse annuity mortgage.
    4. partially amortized mortgage.

38. Which of the following grants zoning authority to municipal governments?

    1. Eminent domain
    2. State enabling acts
    3. Laches
    4. Escheat

39. A buyer has entered into an agreement with more than one buyer's agent at the same time but owes compensation only if she uses the services of a buyer's broker. This arrangement is known as a(n)

    1. multiple-listing agreement.
    2. exclusive right agreement.
    3. exclusive agency agreement.
    4. open agreement.

40. You have just made the final payment on your mortgage loan to the bank. Regardless of this, the bank still will hold a lien on your mortgaged property until which of the following is recorded?

   1. Satisfaction of the mortgage instrument
   2. Reconveyance of the mortgage instrument
   3. Alienation of the mortgage instrument
   4. Reversion of the mortgage instrument

41. All of the following agencies are included in the secondary mortgage market **EXCEPT**

   1. FHA.   3. GNMA.
   2. FNMA.   4. FHLMC.

42. A husband and wife own an apartment building. The husband owns an undivided three-fourths interest and the wife owns a one-fourth interest. This type of tenancy is a

   1. leasehold estate.   3. tenancy in common.
   2. joint tenancy.   4. tenancy by the entirety.

43. A broker was employed by an owner to sell her home. All of the following statements correctly describe the broker's relationship to the owner **EXCEPT**

   1. the broker has become the seller's agent.
   2. the broker owes fiduciary duty to the seller.
   3. the broker is a special agent.
   4. the broker is a general agent.

44. According to the law of agency, a real estate broker does NOT owe the principal the duty of

   1. exercising reasonable care.
   2. acting in good faith.
   3. conforming with the principal's legal instructions.
   4. offering legal advice.

45. All of the following describe violations of antitrust laws **EXCEPT**

   1. two brokers agree that they both will pay 2.5 percent of the sales price to cooperating brokers on all listings published in an MLS after the date of the specified agreement.
   2. two brokers agree to pay just $40 to Reliance Title Company for closings.
   3. two brokers agree not to cooperate with a flat-fee broker.
   4. a broker refuses to cooperate with a flat-fee broker.

46. The IRS has how many requirements for establishing an independent-contractor status?

   1. One   3. Three
   2. Two   4. Four

47. You listed a home that was subsequently shown by six cooperating brokers and two buyer's brokers. How many agents were involved in this transaction?

   1. One   3. Seven
   2. Three   4. Nine

48. Three investors decided to pool their savings and buy some commercial real estate for $180,000. If one invested $60,000 and the second invested $40,000, what percentage of ownership was left for the third investor?

    1. 22.2 percent
    2. 33 percent
    3. 44.4 percent
    4. None of the above

49. A mother wants to know how much money her son owes on his mortgage loan. The mother knows that the interest part of the last monthly payment was $473.26. If her son is paying interest at the rate of 9 percent, what was the approximate outstanding balance of the loan before that last payment was made?

    1. $52,584.44
    2. $55,921.03
    3. $63,101.33
    4. None of the above

50. A salesperson listed a home for sale and transferred to another brokerage firm two weeks later. Which of the following statements describes the status of the listing?

    1. The listing is terminated.
    2. The listing is transferred to the new broker.
    3. The two brokers will negotiate to determine who will hold the listing.
    4. The listing will stay with the former broker of the salesperson.

51. If the Federal Reserve Board raises its discount rate, which of the following is likely to occur?

    1. Mortgage money will become more available.
    2. Interest rates will stay the same.
    3. Mortgage money will become less available.
    4. Interest rates will decline.

52. A person who receives property by will is called a

    1. testator.
    2. devise.
    3. hypothecate.
    4. devisee.

53. A broker has listed a home for sale. The broker will earn a commission

    1. when an offer to purchase has been presented to the client.
    2. when title has been transferred to the buyer.
    3. when the seller accepts and signs an offer to purchase.
    4. when a "ready, willing and able buyer" signs an offer to purchase that meets the terms of the listing contract.

54. The highest form of ownership interest a person may hold in real estate is a

    1. life estate.
    2. fee simple.
    3. legal life estate.
    4. base fee.

55. Which of the following parties would probably be treated as an independent contractor?

    1. Listing broker
    2. Closing officer
    3. Cooperating broker
    4. Salesperson

56. Two unrelated people own a three-unit apartment building as tenants in common. One wants to sell but the other does not. Which of the following statements describes the legal rights of the party who wants to sell?

   1. The party may partition the building.
   2. The party may require the co-owner to sell.
   3. The party may record a lis pendens on the property.
   4. The party may refinance the mortgage in her or his own name, thus eliminating the co-owner's interest in the property.

57. You have entered into a land contract for the sale of your home. Which of the following is NOT correct?

   1. The buyer is the vendee.
   2. The buyer will take possession when the contract is signed by both parties.
   3. The buyer will hold legal title during the term of the contract.
   4. The buyer will hold equitable title during the term of the contract.

58. A farmer was unable to secure credit from other sources, so he probably got a mortgage loan from which of the following?

   1. FHA
   2. Savings and loan
   3. Farm Service Agency
   4. Commercial bank

59. A McDonald's restaurant opened in a neighborhood and was enjoying substantial profits. Within a year a Burger King was built across the street from McDonald's and resulted in McDonald's losing 30 percent of its profits in the next year. This is an example of the principle of

   1. competition.
   2. conformity.
   3. highest and best use.
   4. progression.

60. You sign an agreement to purchase a home. The contract requires that the seller replace the damaged living room carpet. The carpet you have chosen costs $16.95 per square yard plus $4.50 per square yard for installation. If the living room dimensions are as illustrated in Figure 13.1, how much will the seller have to pay for the job?

   1. $357.50
   2. $314.60
   3. $353.93
   4. None of the above

Figure 13.1

61. A broker acting as the agent of a principal

   1. can agree to a change in price without the principal's approval.
   2. may share her commission with the salesperson of another broker.
   3. must report all offers to the principal unless instructed otherwise.
   4. can make a profit in addition to her commission.

62. A broker listed an owner's home for $85,900. One week later the broker presented the owner with an offer to purchase for $85,900, which met all the terms of the listing contract that the owner had signed. The owner thanked the broker but said that because of family problems, she no longer wished to sell her home. The owner told the broker that she would pay him $500 for his time and trouble. All of the following statements correctly describe the rights of the broker **EXCEPT**

1. because he did not sell the property, the broker is entitled to nothing.
2. the owner does not have to accept the offer to purchase, but she does have to pay the broker the commission agreed to in the listing.
3. if the owner fails to pay a commission, the broker may sue her for his commission.
4. the broker earned his commission when he presented the owner with an offer to purchase from a "ready, willing and able" buyer.

63. Personal property is generally conveyed by a

1. bill of sale.
2. certificate of title.
3. quitclaim deed.
4. trust deed.

64. All of the following statements correctly describe a legal life estate **EXCEPT**

1. the life tenant is generally answerable to the holder of the future interest.
2. the life tenant may not commit any acts that would permanently injure the property.
3. there may be a reversionary interest.
4. there may be a remainder interest.

65. Which of the following is NOT a leasehold estate?

1. An estate for years
2. Periodic estate
3. Time-share estate
4. Estate from year to year

66. In the appraisal of a public building, an appraiser would use the

1. cost approach.
2. income capitalization approach.
3. sale comparison approach.
4. gross rent multiplier.

67. All of the following are specific liens **EXCEPT**

1. mortgage liens.
2. state inheritance taxes.
3. real estate taxes.
4. mechanics' liens.

68. The servient estate in an easement appurtenant is the property

1. owned by the landlord.
2. on which the easement is placed.
3. owned by the tenant.
4. that benefits from the easement.

69. Broker *X* is showing buyer *Y,* an Asian, homes only in Asian neighborhoods. The broker may be guilty of

1. arbitrage.
2. blockbusting.
3. redlining.
4. steering.

70. Brokers who violate the Sherman Antitrust Act may be punished by a maximum fine of

1. $10,000.
2. $25,000.
3. $50,000.
4. $100,000.

71. A sale is to close on June 23. Real estate taxes of $2,640 for the current year have NOT been paid. What is the amount of the real estate tax proration to be credited to the buyer? (Use a 30-day month for calculation.)

    1. $168.67
    2. $868.67
    3. $1,268.66
    4. None of the above

72. A four-bedroom house with one bathroom would be an example of

    1. physical deterioration.
    2. functional obsolescence.
    3. economic obsolescence.
    4. environmental obsolescence.

73. Which of the following situations would NOT be covered by RESPA?

    1. The borrower must be provided with a good-faith estimate of closing costs by the lender.
    2. The loan closing must be prepared on a Uniform Settlement Statement.
    3. The broker lowers her commission so that the seller is willing to accept an offer to purchase.
    4. A broker is unable to receive a referral fee because he did not render any services.

74. A broker listed a property under a valid written listing agreement. After the sale was completed, the owner refused to pay the broker's fee. Which of the following can the broker do?

    1. She probably can take the seller to court and sue for the commission.
    2. She is entitled to a lien on the seller's property for the amount of the commission.
    3. She can go to court and stop the transaction until she is paid.
    4. She can collect the commission from the buyer.

75. Which of the following is NOT a stage in the appraisal process?

    1. State the problem.
    2. Analyze the tax consequences of the property owner.
    3. Reconcile the data for the final value estimate.
    4. Analyze and interpret the data.

76. You are selling your house to two brothers. The buyers will assume your outstanding mortgage, which had an unpaid balance of $58,700 after the last payment on August 1 and an annual interest rate of 9 percent. Interest is paid in advance each month. The sale is to be closed on August 18. What is the amount of mortgage interest to be credited to you at the closing?

    1. $161.43
    2. $176.10
    3. $190.78
    4. None of the above

77. An appraiser uses the cost approach in appraising a home. The appraiser should NOT use which of the following types of information?

    1. Physical deterioration
    2. Cost of replacement of house
    3. Depreciation on land
    4. Economic obsolescence

78. Which of the following would NOT be considered real property?

    1. Mineral rights
    2. A leasehold estate
    3. Fixtures
    4. Air

79. Which of the following agencies would be involved in administering special assistance programs for housing?

    1. Fannie Mae
    2. Ginnie Mae
    3. Freddie Mac
    4. The "Fed"

80. A broker listed a property for 90 days. Soon after the listing expired, the owner sold the property to someone who had been shown the property by the broker during the listing period. The owner was obligated to pay the broker a commission on this. This obligation is covered in which clause of the listing agreement?

    1. Alienation
    2. Acceleration
    3. Protection
    4. Defeasance

81. The city in which you live has a zoning ordinance. The basis for the city to have such an ordinance is

    1. eminent domain.
    2. escheat.
    3. police power.
    4. riparian rights.

82. A bill of sale would be used to convey ownership for a

    1. chattel.
    2. easement in gross.
    3. fixture.
    4. house.

83. You receive a monthly salary of $600 plus 3.5 percent commission on all of your listings that sell and 2.5 percent on all of your sales. None of the listings that you took sold last month, but you received $8,460 in salary and commission. What was the value of the property you sold?

    1. $131,000
    2. $224,571
    3. $314,400
    4. None of the above

84. A house has been difficult to sell. The salesperson suggests it might sell faster if the owners enclosed a portion of the backyard with a privacy fence. If the area to be enclosed is as illustrated in Figure 13.2, how much would the fence cost at $8.40 per linear foot?

    1. $546
    2. $1,512
    3. $2,058
    4. None of the above

Figure 13.2

65'

90'

House

85. Strict liability under Superfund means that

    1. each of the individual owners is personally responsible for the damages in whole.
    2. the owner is responsible to the injured party without excuse.
    3. the liability is not limited to the person who currently owns the property but also includes people who have owned the site in the past.
    4. the owner is not responsible to the injured party unless it can be proved that the owner was aware of the problem.

86. Your aunt died intestate and you inherited her house. The way in which you acquired the title to her house is by

    1. curtesy.   3. escheat.
    2. descent.   4. laches.

87. You and two friends have entered into a partnership to buy a motel. You will be a general partner in charge of running the business. Which of the following describes your partnership?

    1. A corporation   3. A limited partnership
    2. A general partnership   4. A tenancy in common

88. Which of the following terms are NOT related?

    1. Freehold estate—fee simple
    2. Grantor—person conveying title
    3. Leasehold estate—personal property
    4. Police power—deed restriction

89. Your neighbor has given you permission to go hunting on his farm. He has also stated that he reserves the right to cancel the agreement. You have a(n)

    1. leasehold estate.   3. license.
    2. easement appurtenant.   4. defeasible fee estate.

90. All of the following correctly describe how real estate licensees should handle the possibility of hazardous substances on a property being sold **EXCEPT**

    1. clients should be asked about the possibility of hazardous substances being on the property.
    2. licensees should consider the consequences of potential liability.
    3. licensees should be scrupulous in considering environmental issues.
    4. licensees should not disclose the problem because it might harm the seller.

91. Sources of groundwater contamination do not include

    1. waste disposal sites.
    2. underground storage tanks.
    3. use of pesticides in farming communities.
    4. radon.

92. You are purchasing a home and the seller asks you which type of deed you prefer. You tell the seller that you prefer the most protective type of deed, which is the

    1. bargain and sale deed.   3. quitclaim deed.
    2. general warranty deed.   4. special warranty deed.

93. You are preparing a competitive market analysis on a house that you hope to list for sale. Which of the following approaches to value will be used in the development of the estimated value?

    1. Cost approach
    2. Gross income multiplier
    3. Income approach
    4. Sales comparison approach

94. You have just purchased a home and recorded your deed. Recording the deed provides what is called

    1. validation of the agreement between the parties.
    2. a writ of attachment.
    3. certificate of title.
    4. constructive notice.

95. According to the 1988 amendment to the Fair Housing Act of 1968, a person found guilty of violating the law can receive a civil penalty not exceeding

    1. $5,000 for the first offense.
    2. $10,000 for the first offense.
    3. $25,000 for the first offense.
    4. $50,000 for the first offense.

96. A salesperson received an earnest money payment for $2,000. The salesperson should

    1. hold the payment until the buyer has received a financing commitment.
    2. give the earnest money to his broker.
    3. open up a trust account and deposit the payment in it.
    4. deposit the payment in the seller's checking account.

97. A lease that allows rent to be increased or decreased periodically based on changes in government statistics is a(n)

    1. graduated lease.
    2. gross lease.
    3. percentage lease.
    4. index lease.

98. You are considering taking legal action on a business transaction that took place three years ago, but you would like to know the period of time during which you may commence legal action. The law that will identify the time limit is the statute of

    1. descent and distribution.
    2. frauds.
    3. laches.
    4. limitations.

99. Bank A holds a lien on a home on which Bank B already had a lien. The lenders subsequently entered into an agreement in which Bank A moved into a first lien position. This is an example of a

    1. hypothecation agreement.
    2. disintermediation agreement.
    3. reverse annuity mortgage.
    4. subordination agreement.

100. Your house is the least expensive home in your neighborhood, but over the years it has grown substantially in value because of the more expensive homes in the area. This growth in value is an example of

    1. the principle of anticipation.
    2. the principle of competition.
    3. the principle of progression.
    4. the principle of highest and best use.

SALESPERSON EXAMINATION I ANSWER KEY WITH EXPLANATIONS

NOTE: The information in parentheses at the end of each explanation refers to the part number and outline reference where this material is discussed. For example: (4–VI) = Part 4, outline reference VI.

1. **2.** An easement in gross is the personal interest to use the land of another. An easement appurtenant requires two tracts of land with one of the tracts benefiting from the easement. An easement by necessity is used where the owner is landlocked, and an easement by prescription involves hostile use of another's land. (4–V)

2. **2.** The government has the right to acquire private property for public use while paying just compensation to the owner. The convention center would attract private development of hotels and retail establishments. The type of estate held by owners would not prevent the state from acquiring the land. (4–V)

3. **2.** $146,000 sales price × 6% commission
$146,000 × 0.06 = $8,760 × 0.25 = $2,190 (8)

4. **4.** Salesperson *C* is an agent of his broker *D* and a subagent of the listing broker *B*. (5–II)

5. **3.** The fiduciary relationship of trust and confidence exists between the agent and the principal (client). The listing salesperson is a subagent of the client. The listing broker does not have a fiduciary responsibility to the buyer or customer. (5–I)

6. **2.** The seller is your client. The customer is a third party for whom a service is provided. (5–I)

7. **1.** The buyer's broker has a fiduciary relationship with the buyer. (6–VII)

8. **4.** A claim based on adverse possession must be notorious, open and hostile. (4–VI)

9. **1.** Encumbrances may be either liens, which affect the title, or physical encumbrances, which affect the condition of the land. (4–III)

10. **1.** Severalty refers to one owner, while joint tenants and tenants in common may convey individual interests. (4–V)

11. **1.** Destruction of the property on June 23 is an example of an operation of law that will act to terminate the agency. Revocation of the listing by the seller could result in damage to the broker if done arbitrarily; thus, the broker might be able to recover damages through litigation. Incompetency of the broker would be grounds for termination. Expiration of the contract on July 1 would, of course, have terminated the listing. (6–VIII)

12. **3.** $83,500 × 6% (0.06) = $5,010, annual increase in value
$83,500 + $5,010 = $88,510, current market value (8)

13. **4.** The sales comparison approach relies on comparable sales, sales that involve willing buyers and sellers with neither being under abnormal pressure. (9–IV)

14. **2.** The exclusive-agency listing allows the seller to sell his own house without paying the broker a commission. The broker under an exclusive-right-to-sell listing receives a commission regardless of who sells the property. Either type is given to only one broker. (6–VII)

15. **1.** $92,000 × 70% (0.70) = $64,400, assessed value

    Divide by 100 because the tax rate is stated per $100

    $64,400 ÷ 100 = $644

    $644 × $3.40 = $2,189.60, annual taxes

    Divide by 12 to get the monthly taxes.

    $2,189.60 ÷ 12 = $182.47 (8)

16. **2.** $150,000 ÷ 1,000 = 150 × 9.91 = $1,486.50 (8)

17. **4.** $1486.50 × 360 months =

    $ 535,140   Total principal and interest

    – 150,000   Amount of loan

    $ 385,140   Total interest paid over the life of the loan (8)

18. **4.** The broker is not required to charge a commission; the commission is negotiable. (5–I)

19. **4.** The license laws generally require the broker to deposit funds that are not to be immediately released to escrow into a trust fund account with a bank within one business day after receipt. (5–I)

20. **4.** Accession refers to acquiring title to real property through the annexation of a fixture. Attachment is the act of taking a person's property into legal custody by a court. An exchange is a transaction in which part or all of the consideration is the transfer of like-kind property. (9–III)

21. **3.** RESPA provides for use of a HUD form. The Civil Rights Act of 1866 and federal fair housing laws are aimed at preventing discrimination in housing. Regulation Z is aimed at providing borrowers and customers with full disclosure of the cost of credit. (7–III)

22. **3.** The fair housing laws do not include age, marital status or sexual orientation in their protected categories. (7–I)

23. **4.** A tenant at sufferance continues to hold possession without consent of the landlord. (4–V)

24. **3.** Sex became a protected class in 1974, while familial status and handicap became protected classes in 1989. (7–I)

25. **3.** More efficient extension of municipal service is a benefit to the community. (9–IX)

26. **1.** An employee can be told what to do and when as compared to an independent contractor, who cannot. (7–V)

27. **2.** *Willful* violation is a misdemeanor punishable by a fine of up to $5,000 or one year of imprisonment, or both. (7–II)

28. **2.** A tenant in a net lease pays rent plus all or part of the property charges. A tenant in a gross lease pays a fixed rent, while the landlord pays all of her own expenses. (4–V)

29. **2.** IRC Section 1031 is covered in 7–V.

30. **4.** Riparian rights are water rights granted to owners along a river or stream. (11–I)

31. **4.** A contract in which both parties have fulfilled their promises is an executed contract. Something remains to be done in an executory contract. A bilateral contract is one in which promises are exchanged. An expressed contract is one in which the parties show their intentions by words. (6–III)

32. **2.** An option is an example of a unilateral contract. An option is an agreement to keep open for a specified period an offer to sell or purchase property. When an option is exercised by the optionee, it becomes a bilateral contract. The other choices are explained in the preceding solution. (6–X)

33. **2.** Any offer or counteroffer may be withdrawn at any time prior to acceptance by the offeree. (6–II)

34. **4.** The payment of a finder's fee generally is prohibited by state license law, regardless of whether the compensation is monetary or nonmonetary. (5–I)

35. **4.** Functional obsolescence and physical deterioration refer to a loss of value within the property, while external obsolescence refers to a loss of value outside the property. (9–IV)

36. **3.** $2,880 ÷ 0.048 = $60,000, assessed value (8)

    $60,000 ÷ 30% = $60,000 ÷ 0.30 = $200,000, market value (8)

37. **1.** A term mortgage allows for payment of interest only with a lump-sum payment at maturity. A partially amortized loan also involves a lump-sum, or balloon, payment at maturity. (10–IV)

38. **2.** Eminent domain, laches and escheat were defined earlier. (11–I)

39. **4.** The buyer agency open agreement is similar to an open listing seller agency agreement. (6–VII)

40. **1.** An alienation clause states that if the borrower sells the property, the lender has the choice of either declaring the entire debt due and payable or allowing the buyer to assume the loan. A reconveyance clause is used in a trust deed. A reversion clause could be used in a deed and stipulates that if not complied with, the property reverts

to the grantor. A satisfaction of mortgage is a certificate issued by the mortgagee when a mortgage is paid in full. The satisfaction states that the mortgage has been paid and that the mortgagee consents that it be discharged of record. (10–V)

41. **1.** The FHA insures mortgages made in the primary mortgage market. FNMA, GNMA and FHLMC are major warehousing agencies in the secondary mortgage market. (10–VII)

42. **3.** A leasehold estate is a personal property interest. Joint tenancy and tenancy by the entirety require equal interests. (4–V)

43. **4.** A real estate broker is a special agent authorized to represent the principal in one specific transaction. (5–I)

44. **4.** The broker may not offer legal advice; only a licensed attorney may do so. (5–I)

45. **4.** The first three choices are examples of price fixing or boycotts. (7–VI)

46. **3.** The requirements are covered in 7–V.

47. **2.** The six cooperating brokers were subagents of the seller. (5–I)

48. **3.** $60,000 first investor + $40,000 second investor = $100,000

   $180,000 – $100,000 = $80,000, third investor's contribution

   $$\frac{part}{total} = percent$$

   $80,000 ÷ $180,000 = 44.4% (8)

49. **3.** $473.26 × 12 = $5,679.12, annual interest

   $$\frac{part}{percent} = total$$

   $5,679.12 ÷ 9% (0.09) = $63,101.33 (8)

50. **4.** The salesperson's listing of the home created an agency relationship between the seller and the salesperson's broker. The listing belongs to the broker. (5–II)

51. **3.** Raising the discount rate would increase interest rates and make mortgage money less available. (10–VIII)

52. **4.** A testator is a person who makes a will. Devise refers to a transfer of real property under a will. Hypothecate refers to the pledging of property as security for a debt without giving up possession. (4–V)

53. **4.** The broker earns a commission when he produces a "ready, willing and able" buyer. (5–I)

54. **2.** A fee simple is the highest form of interest. A base fee is subject to certain limitations imposed by the owner. A life estate is limited to the life of an owner or some other person. Legal life estates are created by state law. (4–IV)

55. **4.** A salesperson can work under a broker as either an employee or an independent contractor. A closing officer would be an employee of the broker. (4–II)

56. **1.** Tenants in common may partition the property. (4–V)

57. **3.** The buyer (vendee) will not receive the deed to the property until the entire purchase price has been paid. (6–XII)

58. **3.** Farm Service Agency makes and guarantees loans to farmers unable to secure credit from other sources. (10–VII)

59. **1.** The principle of competition states that excess profits create ruinous competition. (9–III)

60. **4.** See Figure 13.3.

Figure 13.3

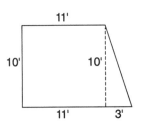

11′ × 10′ = 110 square feet, area of rectangle

½ (3′ × 10′) = ½ (30′) = 15 square feet, area of triangle

110 + 15 = 125 square feet

To convert square feet to square yards, divide by 9

125 ÷ 9 = 13.888 square yards

$16.95 + 4.50 installation = $21.45, cost per square yard

$21.45 × 13.888 square yards = $297.92 (8)

61. **3.** Unless instructed otherwise, the broker is responsible for submitting all offers to his or her principal. (5–I)

62. **1.** When the broker provided a ''ready, willing and able'' buyer, he earned and must be paid a commission. (5–I)

63. **1.** Real property is conveyed by deed. (4–I)

64. **1.** The life tenant is generally not answerable to the holder of the future interest. (4–IV)

65. **3.** A time-share estate includes a fee simple interest in condominium ownership. (4–V)

66. **1.** The cost approach is considered most reliable in the appraisal of special-purpose buildings such as churches and schools. (9–IV)

67. **2.** State inheritance taxes are a general lien and affect all the debtor's property. (4–III)

68. **2.** A servient estate also is referred to as a servient tenement. The property that benefits from the easement is known as the dominant tenement. (4–III)

69. **4.** Blockbusting and redlining are violations of the Federal Fair Housing Act of 1968, which was discussed above. Arbitrage refers to the difference between interest rates in financing arrangements. (7–I)

70. **4.** The Sherman Antitrust Act is described in 7–VI.

71. **3.** $2,640 ÷ 12 months = $220 per month

    $220 ÷ 30 days = $7.333 per day

    $220 × 5 months = $1,100

    $7.333 × 23 = $168.66

    $1,100 + $168.66 = $1,268.66 (8)

72. **2.** Functional obsolescence is a loss in the value of a property resulting from a deficiency in the floor plan of a house, etc. One bathroom would be inadequate for a four-bedroom house. (9–IV)

73. **3.** The commission agreement between the broker and client is negotiable and not subject to RESPA. (7–IV)

74. **1.** The broker has no lien on a property for a commission due on negotiating the sale of that property. Accordingly, the broker may not go to court to stop the transaction. The broker cannot collect the commission from the buyer because the buyer is not in the agency relationship between the seller and the broker. (5–I)

75. **2.** The appraisal process is discussed in 9–V.

76. **2.** $58,700 × 9% (0.09) = $5,283

    $5,283 ÷ 12 months = $440.25 per month

    $440.25 ÷ 30 days = $14.675 per day

    30-day month − 18 days = 12 days

    $14.675 × 12 days = $176.10 (8)

77. **3.** Depreciation generally is applied to a wasting asset such as a building. Land is not considered a wasting asset. (9–IV)

78. **2.** A leasehold estate is a nonfreehold estate involving the tenant's right to occupy the real estate during the term of the lease. (4–V)

79. **2.** Ginnie Mae administers special assistance programs and works with Fannie Mae in secondary market actitivies. (10–X)

80. **3.** Standard listings contain a clause that stipulates that if the property is sold to someone who was introduced to the property by the broker, even after the listing has expired, the broker is entitled to a commission. Usually, there is a time period written into the

clause. This is called the protection clause. The other answers are clauses found in mortgages. (5–I)

81. **3.** Police power is the power of the state to establish legislation to protect public health and safety and promote general welfare. (4–IV)

82. **1.** A chattel is personal property. (4–I)

83. **3.** $8,460 – $600 = $7,860, commission on sales

$7,860 ÷ 2.5% (0.025) = $314,400, value of property sold (8)

84. **3.** See Figure 13.4.

Figure 13.4

House

2 sides of 90′ + one side of 65′

180′ + 65′ = 245 linear feet

245 × $8.40 = $2,058 (8)

85. **2.** The different types of liability are described in 11–V.

86. **2.** When a person dies intestate, the decedent's real estate and personal property pass to his or her heirs according to the statutes. (4–V)

87. **3.** A limited partnership includes a general as well as a limited, or silent, partner. (4–V)

88. **4.** Police power is a public-land-use control, and a deed restriction is a private-land-use control. (4–IV)

89. **3.** License is permission to enter the land of another for a specific purpose. (4–III)

90. **4.** The first three answers describe how licensees should handle this type of transaction. (11–V)

91. **4.** Sources of groundwater contamination are described in 11–V.

92. **2.** The quitclaim deed is the least protective. (4–VI)

93. **4.** The competitive market analysis is described in 9–II.

94. **4.** Deeds are recorded to establish priority and provide protection against third parties. (4–VIII)

95. **2.** The remedies under the amendments are listed in 7–I.

96. **2.** Earnest money must be placed in the broker's trust account. (4–VIII)

97. **4.** An index lease is adjusted periodically based on changes in a government cost-of-living index. (4–V)

98. **4.** The various terms are covered in 4–VIII.

99. **4.** The subordination agreement is discussed in 10–XII.

100. **3.** The principles of valuation are discussed in 9–III.

SALESPERSON EXAMINATION II

1. A grantor wishes to convey title to a grantee in a deed that creates the least protection for the grantee. The grantor should give the grantee a

   1. bargain and sale deed.
   2. quitclaim deed.
   3. general warranty deed.
   4. special warranty deed.

2. Of the following liens, which generally would be given the highest priority?

   1. A judgment issued last year
   2. A mortgage recorded four years ago
   3. A special assessment
   4. A mechanic's lien for work begun two months ago

3. You are showing a house which you have listed to a customer. During the showing you tell her that the house is located in the nicest neighborhood in the city. The customer subsequently buys the house and learns that two other neighborhoods are considered to be nicer. Which of the following statements describes your situation?

   1. You are guilty of misrepresentation.
   2. You are not guilty because you were only puffing.
   3. You are guilty of unintentional misrepresentation.
   4. You would generally be in violation of most state license laws covering real estate agents.

4. An appraiser is developing an operating statement to determine effective gross income. The appraiser should

   1. deduct vacancy and rent loss from annual potential gross income.
   2. deduct annual operating expenses from the annual potential gross income.
   3. divide the annual potential gross income by the capitalization rate.
   4. divide the annual net operating income by the capitalization rate.

5. You are chairperson of the Democratic party in your state and you also own an eight-unit apartment building that you currently rent out. You are taking a rental application from a prospective tenant when she informs you that she works for the Republican party of your state. You inform her that all the apartments have been rented even though you know that they have not been rented. Which of the following statements correctly describes your situation?

   1. You have violated Regulation Z.
   2. You have violated the federal fair housing law.
   3. You have exercised your rights as an owner of private property.
   4. You have violated RESPA.

6. The broker protection clause in the listing contract
   1. protects the broker against any lawsuits filed by the client.
   2. allows the broker to buy the listed property if the broker is unable to sell it.
   3. automatically extends the listing for six months if the broker is unable to see the property.
   4. states that the owner will pay a commission to the listing broker if the property is sold to a buyer with whom the broker negotiated during the listing term within a specified time after the listing expires.

7. The rights of a surviving wife in real estate owned by her deceased husband during their marriage are classified as a
   1. defeasible fee.   3. homestead.
   2. curtesy.   4. dower.

8. Which of the following would not be considered to be real property?
   1. Trees.   3. Trade fixtures.
   2. Buildings.   4. Water rights.

9. A sale is to be closed on June 23. Real estate taxes of $3,760 for the current year have NOT been paid. What is the amount of the real estate tax proration to be credited to the buyer? (Use a 30-day month for calculation.)
   1. $1,566.65   3. $1,879.98
   2. $1,806.86   4. None of the above

10. The giver of an option is called the
    1. vendor.   3. vendee.
    2. optionor.   4. optionee.

11. The SE¼ of the NW¼ of the NE¼ of Section 9 contains how many acres?
    1. 5   3. 20
    2. 10   4. 40

12. Which of the following would be a lien on personal property?
    1. Mortgage   3. Trust Deed
    2. Encroachment   4. Chattel Mortgage

13. Which of the following types of depreciation is generally incurable?
    1. Physical deterioration   3. Functional obsolescence
    2. Economic obsolescence   4. Physical depreciation

14. Three investors decided to pool their savings and buy a motel for $330,000. If one invested $90,000 and the second contributed $50,000, what percentage of ownership was left for the third investor?
    1. 14.1   3. 57.6
    2. 27.3   4. None of the above

15. The provision that gives the lender the right to declare the entire debt due and payable if the mortgaged property is sold is called the

1. acceleration clause.
2. equitable redemption.
3. defeasance clause.
4. alienation clause. ✓

16. In a community property state

1. a husband may have sale ownership of property acquired during marriage.
2. husband and wife are equal partners in property acquired prior to marriage.
3. the survivor, upon the death of one spouse, automatically owns all of the community property.
4. the property that a person acquired prior to marriage is called separate property. ✓

17. A woman owns a tract of land with a servient tenement. This easement is a(an)

1. lien.
2. encumbrance. ✓
3. license.
4. encroachment.

18. In the traditional exclusive right-to-sell listing agreement, how many *agents* are involved?

1. Two
2. One ✓
3. As many as the owner/lister chooses
4. As many salespeople as the broker has in his or her office

19. The broker has listed an owner's home. This agreement will be terminated by all of the following **EXCEPT**

1. death of the listing salesperson. ✓
2. death of the owner.
3. death of the broker.
4. bankruptcy of the broker.

20. A drunken man signed an offer to purchase. The contract that he signed is

1. valid.
2. void.
3. voidable. ✓
4. unenforceable.

21. You sign an agreement to purchase a home. The contract requires that the seller replace the damaged living room carpet. The carpet you have chosen costs $18.95 per square yard plus $5.50 per square yard for installation. If the living room dimensions are as illustrated in Figure 13.5, how much will the seller have to pay for the job?

1. $315.82
2. $407.34 ✓
3. $490.81
4. None of the above

Figure 13.5

22. You have just participated as the cooperating broker in a real estate transaction. Which of the following would not describe your role in the transaction?

    1. Buyer's broker
    2. Subagent
    3. Selling broker
    4. Listing broker

23. An appraiser is trying to determine the value of an income property by capitalizing the income stream. Which of the following factors will the appraiser use?

    1. Mortgage interest
    2. Net income
    3. Replacement cost
    4. Income taxes

24. Theories of urban development do not include

    1. sector theory.
    2. axial theory.
    3. multiple nuclei theory.
    4. competition.

25. A partial release clause is generally found in a

    1. construction mortgage.
    2. package mortgage.
    3. blanket mortgage.
    4. wraparound mortgage.

26. Which of the following scenarios would not be considered discriminatory under the federal fair housing law?

    1. A man owns and lives in his four-unit apartment building, and he refuses to rent to families with children.
    2. A landlord charges higher security deposits to tenants with children.
    3. A landlord places all families in selected buildings in his apartment complex.
    4. A landlord refuses to rent to a pregnant woman.

27. Which of the following is a requirement for a valid deed?

    1. The grantee must sign deed.
    2. The consideration must be in dollars.
    3. It must contain a subordination clause. *priority of lien clause*
    4. It must contain a granting clause.

28. A salesperson would like to be classified as an independent contractor by her broker. To be eligible for independent contractor status, what percentage of her income has to be based on sales production?

    1. 70
    2. 80
    3. 90
    4. 100

29. You bought a home one year ago for $115,900. Property in your neighborhood is said to be increasing in value at a rate of 8 percent annually. If this is true, what is the current value of your real estate?

    1. $125,172
    2. $134,444
    3. $144,063
    4. None of the above

30. An enforceable contract may contain any of the following as consideration EXCEPT

    1. money.
    2. love.
    3. affection.
    4. duress.

31. Which of the following is an economic characteristic of land?

    1. Immobility
    2. Situs
    3. Non-homogeneity
    4. Indestructibility

32. IRS Form 8288-A must be used in which of the following types of transactions?

    1. Foreign Investment and Real Property Act transactions
    2. Independent contractor agreements
    3. Assignment of imputed interest on installment contracts
    4. Tax-deferred exchanges

33. When she died, a broker had exclusive-right-to-sell listings on 20 residential properties. Her daughter took over the business as the new broker. With respect to these 20 listings, the new broker now must

    1. file a court action to transfer the listings to herself.
    2. advise the owners that the original broker's death will have no effect on the listings as far as the owners are concerned.
    3. negotiate new listing agreements with each property owner.
    4. notify each property owner that because she has inherited the business, all commissions due the original broker now are due her.

34. You have just given an option to buy your restaurant to your friend. Which of the following statements is not correct?

    1. Your friend is the optionee.
    2. You are the optionor.
    3. Your friend is obligated to buy your house.
    4. Your friend will have to pay a fee for the option right.

35. A broker listed a home under the condition that the owner receive $210,000 from the sale, with the broker being able to sell the property for as much as possible and to keep the difference as the commission. This agreement is an example of

    1. an exclusive-agency listing.
    2. an exclusive-right-to-sell listing.
    3. a net listing.
    4. an option listing.

36. A broker was offered a listing by homeowners who stated that they would not sell to a minority. The broker should

    1. accept the listing and allow the owners the right to choose the buyer.
    2. file a complaint with the local board of realtors.
    3. accept the listing and make sure that no minorities are shown the property.
    4. refuse to accept the listing based on this condition.

37. All of the following would be public land use controls **EXCEPT**

    1. zoning.
    2. environmental protection laws.
    3. subdivision regulations.
    4. deed restrictions.

38. A home is valued at $103,000. Property in this city is assessed at 80 percent of its value and the local tax rate is $3.60 per $100. What is the amount of the owner's monthly taxes?

    1. $247.20
    2. $824
    3. $2,966.40
    4. None of the above

39. Which of the following persons would NOT be protected under the familial status definition according to the federal fair housing law?

    1. A 19-year-old girl living with her mother
    2. A 17-year-old boy living with his father
    3. A 14-year-old girl living with a person who is seeking legal custody of her
    4. A 21 year old woman who is pregnant

40. You are working as a salesperson for a broker and you have just sold a home. You will receive your share of the commission on the sale from:

    1. cooperating broker.   3. your broker.
    2. the seller.   4. the buyer.

41. You have been given oral permission to park in a friend's driveway while attending a football game. This right is a(an)

    1. easement appurtenant.   3. license.
    2. encroachment.   4. littoral right.

42. Charging a rate of interest in excess of the maximum rate allowed by law is

    1. novation.   3. laches.
    2. subordination.   4. usury.

43. An amendment to the federal fair housing law which became effective in 1989 prohibits discrimination on the basis of

    1. familial status.   3. sex.
    2. race.   4. sexual orientation.

44. Using the mortgage factor chart on page 87, what is the monthly payment for a $170,000 loan at 8.5 percent for 30 years?

    1. $1,247.80   3. $1,307.30
    2. $1,276.70   4. $1,337.90

45. Using the information in question 44 above, what is the total interest paid over the life of the loan?

    1. $279,208   3. $311,644
    2. $300,628   4. None of the above

46. A real estate development corporation purchased land for a condominium project. The corporation most likely took title to the land

    1. as a syndication.   3. as joint tenants.
    2. as a general partnership.   4. in severalty.

47. A broker listed a home for sale under an exclusive-right-to-sell listing. A second broker cooperated with the listing broker and sold the home. The house was sold and the commission split between the listing broker and the selling broker. Which of the following is FALSE?

1. The selling broker is an agent of the listing broker.
2. The listing broker is an agent of the seller.
3. The selling broker is a subagent of the seller.
4. A broker who is not the seller's agent cannot receive any part of the commission.

48. The requirement that a lender prepare a loan closing on a Uniform Settlement Statement is based on

1. IRS regulations.
2. RESPA.
3. Regulation Z.
4. Federal Housing Administration (FHA) regulations.

49. All of the following would be considered a lien except a(an)

1. encroachment.
2. judgment.
3. mechanic's lien.
4. mortgage.

50. The borrower under a note secured by a mortgage is the

1. mortgagor.
2. trustee.
3. mortgagee.
4. vendee.

51. A general agent would be a

1. broker.
2. property manager.
3. cooperative broker.
4. listing salesperson.

52. The relationship of trust and confidence that a broker has with a principal is called a(an)

1. fiduciary relationship.
2. hypothecation.
3. escrow.
4. trustor relationship.

53. An estate in land refers to all of the following measures of interests in land **EXCEPT**

1. extent.
2. degree.
3. nature.
4. physical quantity.

54. A 500-acre farm is divided into house lots. The streets require one-eighth of the whole farm and there are 300 lots. How many square feet are in each lot?

1. 48,636
2. 55,584
3. 63,525
4. 72,600

55. You received a mortgage loan from a savings and loan association in which the lender was privately insured against loss in the event of default and foreclosure. The loan would have been which of the following?

1. Conventional loan
2. FHA loan
3. VA loan
4. Rural Development

56. You received a mortgage loan from a bank that was guaranteed by the government against loss. The loan was

    1. an FHA loan.
    2. a conventional loan.
    3. a DVA loan.
    4. a privately insured loan.

57. The maximum interest rate on a mortgage loan is set by HUD on which of the following?

    1. Conventional loan
    2. FHA loan
    3. DVA loan
    4. None of the above

58. You receive a monthly salary of $1,200 plus a 3 percent commission on all of your listings that sell and 2.5 percent on all of your sales. None of the listings that you took sold last month, but you receive $6,300 in salary and commission. What is the value of the property that sold?

    1. $170,000
    2. $204,000
    3. $252,000
    4. None of the above

59. The nation's banker and fiscal manager is

    1. SAIF.
    2. the U.S. Treasury.
    3. the Federal Reserve System.
    4. FNMA.

60. A mortgage in which the lender receives an equity position as well as interest on the mortgage is a(an)

    1. adjustable-rate mortgage.
    2. participation mortgage.
    3. reverse annuity mortgage.
    4. wraparound mortgage.

61. A sale closed on July 21. Real estate taxes of $3,420 for the current year have not been paid. What is the settlement sheet entry for the proration of the real estate taxes?

    1. Credit seller $1,985.50; debit buyer $1,988.50.
    2. Debit seller $1,995; credit buyer $1,995.
    3. Debit seller $1,909.50; credit buyer $1,909.50.
    4. Debit buyer $00.00; credit seller $1,710.

62. *A,* who works for broker *C* on a 50-50 basis, sold a house listed by broker *E* for $193,950. The seller agreed to pay a 6 percent commission but stipulated in the listing that 60 percent was to go to the selling broker. How much commission (to nearest dollar) will *A* make on this sale?

    1. $2,327.40
    2. $2,909.25
    3. $3,491.10
    4. $4,189.32

63. You tore out an old furnace and installed a new furnace with central air-conditioning in your home. This newly installed personal property becomes a

    1. trade fixture.
    2. chattel fixture.
    3. fixture.
    4. physical trade fixture.

64. An easement would generally be utilized in which of the following?

    1. Accession
    2. Novation
    3. Partition
    4. Right of way

65. A broker has been found guilty of discrimination under the federal fair housing laws. This is the first time the broker has been found guilty of such a violation. The broker will be subject to a civil penalty not exceeding

    1. $5,000.
    2. $10,000.
    3. $25,000.
    4. $50,000.

66. All of the following are life estates **EXCEPT**

    1. an estate for years.
    2. dower.
    3. homestead.
    4. curtesy.

67. Dower is an example of a

    1. defeasible fee estate.
    2. fee simple state.
    3. life estate.
    4. legal life estate.

68. You have sold your home and taken back a mortgage from the seller for part of the balance due. They type of mortgage you hold is a

    1. blanket mortgage.
    2. purchase money mortgage.
    3. participation mortgage.
    4. wraparound mortgage.

69. The Foreign Investment and Real Property Tax Act is found in

    1. IRC Section 1445.
    2. IRC Section 1031.
    3. IRC Section 1099.
    4. IRC Section 7088.

70. You had an exclusive right-to-sell listing with a seller who openly negotiated with a buyer during the listing term to buy the property after the listing had expired. You have witnesses to document that the seller blatantly conspired with the buyer to avoid paying you a commission. Given the circumstances, you may

    1. collect a commission from the buyer.
    2. sue the seller for commission.
    3. file a complaint against the seller with the state licensing board.
    4. sue the buyer for commission.

71. Which of the following would not be an example of economic obsolescence?

    1. Changing land uses in a neighborhood
    2. The major employer in the city going out of business
    3. A poor floor plan
    4. A nearby landfill contaminating the ground waste

72. An insurance company that refuses to provide homeowners insurance to people living in a minority neighborhood would be

    1. engaged in an acceptable business practice.
    2. blockbusting.
    3. redlining.
    4. steering.

73. A house located next to an airport would be an example of

    1. functional obsolescence.
    2. economic obsolescence.
    3. physical deterioration.
    4. physical depreciation.

74. An odorless radioactive gas produced by the decay of other radioactive materials in rocks under the earth's surface is which of the following?

   1. Asbestos   3. Lead
   2. UFFI   4. Radon

75. Within the field of real estate finance, what does *secondary mortgage market* refer to?

   1. Placing of junior liens
   2. Transferability of mortgages among mortgagees
   3. Transferability of mortgages among mortgagors
   4. None of the above

76. Which of the following types of depreciation contains elements that are incurable only?

   1. Physical deterioration   3. Functional obsolescence
   2. Economic obsolescence   4. Physical depreciation

77. A woman wants to know how much money she owes on her mortgage loan. She know that the interest part of the last monthly payment was $647.91. If she was paying interest at the rate of 9 percent, what was the outstanding balance of her loan before that last payment was made?

   1. $64,791.10   3. $86,388
   2. $77,749.20   4. $97,186.50

78. Brokers who violate the Sherman Antitrust Act may be punished by being sentenced to

   1. three years in prison.   3. six years in prison.
   2. five years in prison.   4. ten years in prison.

79. You list your property for sale with a broker. The listing contract stipulates that the seller will receive $110,000 "net," with all proceeds over $110,000 being the broker's commission. This type of listing is

   1. an open listing.   3. an exclusive-right-to-sell listing.
   2. an exclusive-agency listing.   4. a net listing.

80. Which of the following factors would not be considered by an appraiser in conducting a neighborhood analysis?

   1. Relation to the rest of the community
   2. Rent levels
   3. Racial characteristics of the residents
   4. Zoning

81. An arrangement in which brokers pool their listings, and their commissions are divided between the listing broker and the selling broker is

   1. an open listing.   3. an exclusive-agency listing.
   2. a multiple listing system.   4. an exclusive-right-to-sell listing.

82. A contract in which the intentions of the parties are shown by their conduct is

   1. an expressed contract.   3. a bilateral contract.
   2. an implied contract.   4. an executory contract.

83. All of the following are considered agents **EXCEPT**

   1. a broker who has listed an owner's home for sale.
   2. a property manager.
   3. a salesperson employed by a broker.
   4. a personal assistant.

84. Which of the following would be a violation of antitrust law?

   1. A broker chooses to discontinue her membership in the multiple listing service.
   2. One broker refuses to cooperate with another broker who is charging all of her sellers the same commission.
   3. Two brokerage firms agree to not advertise in the local newspaper for one year.
   4. A broker decides to offer a lower commission split to one of the other brokers in the multiple listing service.

85. A house with outdated architecture is an example of

   1. physical deterioration.   3. economic obsolescence.
   2. functional obsolescence.   4. external obsolescence.

86. Deed restrictions may NOT

   1. restrict the size of a building.
   2. be terminated by a quitclaim deed executed by the necessary parties.
   3. be enforced by means of a court injunction.
   4. restrict occupancy on the basis of race.

87. You are NOT entitled to be paid a commission by the owner for selling the owner's home, if you

   1. acted in good faith.   3. are employed by the owner.
   2. are a licensed broker.   4. are a licensed salesperson.

88. A salesperson

   1. may receive a commission directly from a seller.
   2. can carry out activities in his or her own name.
   3. is responsible only to the broker under whom he or she is licensed.
   4. may place a blind ad.

89. A seller employed broker *A* to sell her house under an open listing for six months. The next day she employed broker *B* to sell the same property under an exclusive-right-to-sell listing contract. Ten days later broker *A* brought an offer for the house to the seller that she accepted. The seller must pay

   1. a full commission only to broker *A*, because *A* sold the house.
   2. a full commission to broker *B* only, because *B* has a valid exclusive-right-to-sell agreement.
   3. one-half of the commission to each broker.
   4. a full commission to each broker.

90. IRS rules require closing agents to report details of closings for sales or exchanges of residents with

   1. two or fewer units.
   2. four or fewer units.
   3. eight or fewer units.
   4. sixteen or fewer units.

91. Which of the following statements does not correctly describe a tax-deferred exchange?

   1. It is covered under Section 1031 of the IRC.
   2. Like-kind property includes dealer property.
   3. Tax on an exchange is deferred.
   4. Like-kind refers to any real property held for income purposes.

92. What is the biggest problem that faces a broker who is helping a relative purchase a home?

   1. The relative will expect part of the commission.
   2. It will create trouble within the family.
   3. It will create an undisclosed dual agency.
   4. Dealing with relatives takes more time than dealing with others.

93. A river has overflowed and flooded your farm, washing away the topsoil. This loss of land is called

   1. accretion.
   2. avulsion.
   3. erosion.
   4. partition.

94. You have purchased three lots zoned for single-family use and combined them into one large parcel to build an apartment building. This is an example of

   1. the principle of progression.
   2. assemblage.
   3. the principle of substitution.
   4. plottage.

95. A summary of all the recorded instruments affecting the title to a property is called a(n)

   1. abstract of title.
   2. certificate of title.
   3. escrow.
   4. title insurance policy.

96. A contract in which one party promises to do something if the other party performs a specific act is a(n)

   1. unenforceable contract.
   2. unilateral contract.
   3. void contract.
   4. bilateral contract.

97. The real estate market in your town is characterized by an excess of demand over supply resulting in the prices of properties increasing. This market is an example of a

   1. marginal market.
   2. seller's market.
   3. classical market.
   4. buyer's market.

98. Discrimination on the basis of sex became a protected class under the federal fair housing law in

   1. 1866.
   2. 1968.
   3. 1974.
   4. 1989.

99. The form of listing that provides the most protection to the broker is the

   1. exclusive agency.   3. net listing.
   2. exclusive right-to-sell.   4. open listing.

100. Which of the following statements does NOT correctly describe PCBs?

   1. PCBs were used in the manufacture of paints and caulking materials.
   2. PBCs can cause cancer.
   3. PBCs haven't been used since 1967.
   4. An environmental consultant can assess the property and recommend procedures for cleanup.

SALESPERSON EXAMINATION II
ANSWER KEY WITH EXPLANATIONS

NOTE: The information in parentheses at the end of each explanation refers to the part number and outline reference where this material is discussed. For example: (4–VI) = Part 4, outline reference VI.

1. **2.** The general warranty and special warranty deeds contain an expressed warranty. A bargain and sale deed has an implied warranty. A quitclaim deed contains no form of warranty. (4–V)

2. **3.** Special assessments and real estate taxes take priority over all other liens, regardless of the date of recording. (4–III)

3. **2.** You have given an opinion which would be an example of puffing. (5–III)

4. **1.** The operating statement is described in 9–IV.

5. **3.** Political belief is not a protected class under the federal fair-housing laws. (7–I)

6. **4.** The broker protection clause refers to the broker's commission. (5–I)

7. **4.** Curtesy refers to the husband's rights in the real estate owned by his wife. A defeasible fee estate is an estate that continues for an indefinite period while a homestead is the tract of land owned and occupied as the family home. (4–IV)

8. **3.** Trade fixtures are items installed by a tenant for conducting a business. (4–I)

9. **2.** $3760 ÷ 12 months = $313.33 per month

    $313.33 ÷ days = $10.444 per day

    $313.33 × 5 months = $1,566.65

    $10.444 × 23 = $240.21

    $1,566.65 + $240.21 = $1,806.86 (8)

10. **2.** The giver of an option is the optionor, while the buyer is the optionee. The vendor is a seller of realty; the vendee is the purchaser of realty. (6–XI)

11. **2.** There are 640 acres in a section

    $\frac{1}{4} \times \frac{1}{4} \times \frac{1}{4}$ or $4 \times 4 \times 4 = 64$

    $640 ÷ 64 = 10$ acres (4–II)

12. **4.** Mortgages and trust deeds create liens on real property while an encroachment is an encumbrance. (4–I)

13. **2.** Physical deterioration or depreciation and functional obsolescence *may* be incurable, while economic obsolescence generally is incurable. (9–IV)

14. **3.** $90,000 (first investor) + $50,000 (second investor) = $140,000

$330,000 – $140,000 = $190,000 third investor's contribution

part ÷ total = percent

$190,000 ÷ $330,000 = 0.5757 or 57.6% (8)

15. **4.** An acceleration clause states that if the borrower defaults, the lender has the right to declare the entire debit due and payable. The defeasance clause requires the lender to execute a satisfaction of mortgage when the note is fully paid. Equitable redemption refers to the right of the borrower to redeem his interest in his property prior to a public foreclosure sale. (10–V)

16. **4.** The husband and wife are equal partners in property acquired during the marriage. The surviving spouse owns one half of the community property. (4–V)

17. **2.** The tract of land over which an easement appurtenant runs is the servient tenement; an easement appurtenant is an encumbrance as are the lien, license and encroachment. (4–III)

18. **2.** In an exclusive-right-to-sell listing, there is only one agent. All other brokers and salespeople involved in the transaction are subagents of the seller. (5–II)

19. **1.** The listing salesperson is a subagent whose death will not affect the listing contract. (5–I)

20. **3.** A voidable contract may be disaffirmed because one of the parties signed when under duress. (6–IV)

21. **2.** See Figure 13.6.

Figure 13.6

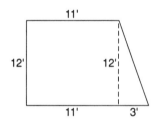

11′ × 12′ = 132 square feet, area of rectangle

½ (3′ × 12′) = ½ (36′) = 18 square feet, area of triangle

132 + 18 = 150 square feet

To convert square feet to square yards divide number of square feet by 9

150 ÷ 9 = 16.666 square yards

$18.95 + $5.50 = $24.45 cost per square yard

$24.45 × 16.66 square yards = $407.34 (8)

22. **4.** The listing broker would be the agent of the seller and thus not be the cooperating broker. (5–I)

23. **2.** Net income in the operating statement does not reflect interest and taxes. (9–IV)

24. **4.** *1, 2* and *3* are three of the recognized theories of how cities grow. (9–VIII)

25. **3.** A blanket mortgage covers more than one property or lot; it is typically used to finance the development of a subdivision. (10–VII)

26. **1.** Rentals of rooms in an owner-occupied one-family to four-family dwelling are exempt from the federal fair housing law. (7–I)

27. **4.** The grantor must sign the deed. Consideration can be monetary or nonmonetary. Subordination clauses are used in mortgages. (4–VIII)

28. **3.** The requirements for an independent contractor are covered in 7–V.

29. **1.** $115,900 × 8% (0.08) = $9,272 annual increase in value

    $115,900 + $9,272 = $125,172, current market value (8)

30. **4.** A valid contract must be based on good or valuable consideration. If duress is involved, however, there would not be a meeting of the minds; thus, the contract would not be valid. (6–II)

31. **2.** Immobility, nonhomogeneity, and indestructibility are physical characteristics of land. (4–II)

32. **1.** The foreign Investment and Real Property Tax Act requires that buyers or other transferees of a U.S. real property interest must file an IRS Form 8288-A to show the amount withheld. (7–V)

33. **3.** A listing agreement may be terminated by death or insanity of either the broker or seller. The broker's death has terminated her listings; therefore, the daughter will have to negotiate new listing agreements. (6–VIII)

34. **3.** The optionee (prospective buyer) pays for the option right but assumes no obligation to make any other payments until she decides whether or not to exercise her option right. (6–XI)

35. **3.** The other listings would include a commission agreed on in advance in terms of a percentage or dollar amount. (5–I)

36. **4.** The federal fair housing law provides that it is unlawful to discriminate on the basis of race, when selling residential property. The broker must refuse to accept the listing based on this condition. (7–I)

37. **4.** Zoning, environmental protection laws and subdivision regulations are public land-use controls. (11–I)

38. **1.** $103,000 × 80% (0.80) = $82,400 assessed value

    Divide by 100 because the tax rate is stated per $100

    $82,400 ÷ 100 = $824.00

    $824.00 × $3.60 = $2,966.40, annual tax

    $2,966.40 ÷ 12 = $247.20 (8)

39. **1.** The familial status category protects individuals who have not reached the age of 18, under certain circumstances. (7–I)

40. **3.** The salesperson can only receive compensation from the broker for whom she works. (5–II)

41. **3.** A license provides permission to enter the land of another for a specific purpose. Littoral rights involve water rights. An encroachment is an illegal extension of the building beyond the land of its owner. An easement appurtenant requires two tracts of land. (4–III)

42. **4.** Charging a rate of interest in excess of the maximum rate allowed by law is known as usury. Novation refers to an agreement in which a new debtor is accepted in place of an old one. Laches is a court doctrine used to bar a legal claim because of undue delay in asserting the claim. Subordination refers to an agreement that changes the order of priority of liens between two creditors. (10–V)

43. **1.** Race became a protected class in 1968 and sex in 1974. Sexual orientation is not a protected class under the federal fair housing law. (7–I)

44. **3.** $170,000 \div 1,000 = 170 \times 7.69 = \$1,307.30$ (8)

45. **2.** $\$1,307.30 \times 360$ months =

$ 470,628	Total principal and interest
– 170,000	Amount of loan
$ 300,628	Total interest paid over the life of the loan (8)

46. **4.** Corporations are considered by law to be a single entity, ownership in severalty involves one owner. The other answers involve coownership. (4–V)

47. **4.** The cobroker is an agent of the listing broker as well as a subagent of the seller. A broker need not be the seller's agent to receive part of the commission. (5–I)

48. **2.** The other choices do not have requirements on what closing form should be used. (7–IV)

49. **1.** An encroachment is an encumbrance. (4–III)

50. **1.** The borrower under a note secured by a mortgage is the mortgagor. The lender is the mortgagee. The trustee holds real estate as a security for the loan under a trust deed. The vendee is the buyer in a real estate contract. (10–III)

51. **2.** The broker is a special agent while the cooperative broker and listing salesperson are subagents. (5–I)

52. **1.** Hypothecation is the pledging of property as security for a loan without losing possession of it. Escrow is a third party agreement while the trustor is the borrower in a trust deed. (5–I)

53. **4.** An estate in land refers to the degree, extent and nature of an interest in land. (4–IV)

for streets

. ft. for lots

. ft. per lot (8)

loans. All non-FHA and non-DVA loans

he lender, as described in answer 55 above.

VA loans no longer is set by HUD. HUD
rates that may be charged by lenders on
(10–VII)

n sales

,000 value of property sold (8)

ervising the daily fiscal operations of the
gs-and-loan association deposits while
secondary mortgage market. The Federal
rough member banks. (10–VIII)

60. **2.** A participation mortgage provides the lender with a percentage of cash flow beyond the interest paid by the borrower. (10–VII)

61. **3.** $3,420 ÷ 12 months = $285 per month

$285 ÷ 30 days = $9.50 per day

$285 × 6 months = $1,710

$9.50 × 21 days = $199.50

$1,710 + $199.50 = $1,909.50

The taxes for the year have not been paid. When they are paid, the buyer will be in possession and have to pay the bill. The seller, therefore, must pay (be debited) for the portion of the year that she occupied the property. The buyer receives a credit for the same amount. (8)

62. **3.** $193,950 sales price × 6% commission =

$193,950 × 0.06 = $11,637 broker commission

$11,637 × 60% = $6,982.20 × 0.05 = $3,491.10, selling salesperson's commission. (8)

63. **3.** A trade fixture is attached to real property for the purpose of carrying on a business. A chattel fixture is an item of personal property. (4–I)

64. **4.** A commercial easement in gross would be used for right-of-way. (4–III)

65. **2.** Penalties for subsequent violations within a seven year period would be either $25,000 or $50,000 depending on the circumstances. (7–I)

66. **1.** An estate for years is a leasehold estate (less than freehold). (4–V)

67. **4.** Dower is the wife's life estate in all inheritable real estate of the deceased husband. (4–IV)

68. **2.** A purchase money mortgage involves seller financing in which the legal title passes to the buyer. (10–VII)

69. **1.** The act is covered in 7–IV.

70. 2. The seller appears to have committed fraud and would be liable for the commission. (5–I)

71. **3.** Economic obsolescence is a loss in value due to factors outside the property. (9–IV)

72. **3.** Redlining refers to discriminatory denial of loans or insurance to people in selected areas, regardless of their qualifications. (7–1)

73. **2.** Economic or environmental obsolescence is a loss in value resulting from a factor external to the property, such as being located next to an airport. (9–IV)

74. **4.** Radon is discussed in 11–V.

75. **2.** The secondary mortgage market deals only with first mortgages of mortgagors (borrowers) transferred among mortgagees (lenders). (10–X)

76. **2.** Economic obsolescence occurs outside the property. (9–IV)

77. **3.** $647.91 \times 12 = \$7,774.92$

    $\$7,774.92 \div 9\% \ (0.09) = \$86,388 \ (8)$

78. **1.** See 7–VI.

79. **4.** Under a net listing, the broker may retain as compensation all the money received in excess of the "net" set by the seller; the compensation is not definitely specified. This type of listing is either prohibited or discouraged by licensing authorities in many states. (6–VII)

80. **3.** Appraisers are not allowed to discuss racial characteristics in an appraisal report. (7–I)

81. **2.** The exclusive-right-to-sell listing generally serves as the basis for the multiple listing system arrangement. (6–VII)

82. **2.** A contract in which the parties show their intentions by conduct is an implied contract; intention is shown by words in an expressed contract. Promises are exchanged in a bilateral contract. Something remains to be performed in an executory contract. (6–III)

83.   **4.** A personal assistant would be an employee of the broker. (5–I)

84.   **3.** When two or more businesses conspire against other businesses to reduce competition they are guilty of boycotting. (7–VII)

85.   **2.** Functional obsolescence is a loss in value, due to a deficiency in the floor plan or design of a house. (9–IV)

86.   **4.** Deed restrictions are described in 11–VI. In the event of a conflict between a deed restriction and a zoning ordinance, the more restrictive of the two takes precedence.

87.   **4.** The commission must be paid to your broker. (5–I)

88.   **3.** The duties of a salesperson are described in 5–II.

89.   **4.** Both brokers are protected under the language in their listing contracts. (6–VII)

90.   **2.** IRS Form 1099S must be submitted to the IRS. (7–VI)

91.   **2.** Like-kind excludes dealer property and residence. (7–VI)

92.   **3.** The broker owes fiduciary duties to his or her principal (the seller). The broker must be very careful not to show favoritism to relatives, disclose information or act in a manner that would violate the agent's duties. It is very easy to become a dual agent by accident. (5–I)

93.   **2.** Avulsion is the *sudden* tearing away of land by the action of water while erosion is the *gradual* wearing away of land by water or wind. (4–VI)

94.   **2.** Plottage is the value increment resulting from assemblage. (9–III)

95.   **1.** A buyer's attorney examines the abstract for flaws and prepares a written opinion of the condition of ownership. (4–VIII)

96.   **2.** The various classifications of contracts are discussed in 6–III.

97.   **2.** A buyer's market would result in a lowering of prices. (9–III)

98.   **3.** The federal fair housing law is discussed in 7–I.

99.   **2.** Under an exclusive-right-to-sell listing, the broker receives a commission regardless of who sells the property. (6–VII)

100.   **3.** PCBs haven't been used since 1977. (11–V)

PART 14 / BROKER EXAMINATIONS

The PSI broker examination, like the salesperson exam, consists of two parts: a 100-question national exam and a 25- to 50-question state exam. Both tests must be completed within a period of up to five hours. The national exam covers generic real estate brokerage practices on a national scale. The state exam covers the listing contract, sales contract and settlement statement, as well as state real estate practices, license law, and rules and regulations.

The national portion of the broker examination contains 100 questions and closely resembles the national salesperson exam in that with the exception of broker management, both exams cover the same categories. The differences between the two exams involve slight variations in weighting the categories, and brokerage management is covered only on the broker's exam. The subject area and number of questions in each area on the broker examination varies from state to state but in general they are as follows:

Property Ownership	10 questions
Laws of Agency	18 questions
Contracts	14 questions
Federal Laws and Regulations	13 questions
Real Estate Mathematics	9 questions
Valuation and Real Estate Economics	9 questions
Financing	10 questions
Land-Use Controls and Regulations	7 questions
Brokerage Management	10 questions

The two sample broker examinations that follow evaluate your general real estate knowledge and your test taking ability.

BROKER EXAMINATION I

1. Which of the following would be considered to be real property?

   1. A leasehold estate
   2. Fixtures
   3. Chattels
   4. Trade fixtures

2. Your uncle died without a will and you inherited his estate. The way in which you would acquire his estate is by

   1. accession.
   2. devise.
   3. escheat.
   4. novation.

3. Loans to low-income people in rural areas are made and guaranteed by

   1. The Federal Home Loan Mortgage Corporation (FHLMC).
   2. Rural Development.
   3. Farm Service Agency.
   4. The Federal Housing Administration (FHA).

4. A man receives possession of property under a deed that states that he will own the property as long as the present building standing on the property is not torn down. The type of estate the man holds is which of the following?

   1. Life estate
   2. Nondestructible estate
   3. Fee simple estate
   4. Determinable fee estate

5. You would like to hire more than one broker to sell your house and be able to sell the house yourself without paying a commission to a broker. Which of the following listing agreements should you choose?

   1. Exclusive agency
   2. Exclusive-right-to-sell
   3. Multiple
   4. Open

6. If a broker is found guilty of two or more discriminating practices within the past seven years, he may be given a civil penalty not exceeding

   1. $5,000.
   2. $10,000.
   3. $25,000.
   4. $50,000.

7. You have been making constant payments of $653 per month on your mortgage. The balance after your last payment was $80,300. The interest rate on your mortgage is 8 percent. What will the balance of your mortgage be after your next payment?

   1. $79,647.00
   2. $80,067.32
   3. $80,182.33
   4. $80,300.00

8. Using the mortgage factor chart on page 87, what is the monthly payment for $121,000 at 7 percent for 30 years?

   1. $773.19
   2. $804.65
   3. $816.75
   4. $847.00

9. Using the numbers in question 8, what is the total interest paid over the life of the loan?

   1. $166,709.23
   2. $167,514.74
   3. $168,319.46
   4. $168,674.00

10. Which of the following statements correctly describes conventional mortgages?

   1. They are assumable.
   2. There is no down payment.
   3. They are guaranteed by the federal government.
   4. The interest rate is set by the lender.

11. You are concerned that the house you are buying may have an encroachment. The best way to discover the existence of an encroachment is through a(n)

   1. abstract of title.
   2. appraisal.
   3. certificate of title.
   4. survey.

12. A broker has been showing homes to some prospects. The prospects have learned of a home for sale by its owner, which they are interested in visiting. The broker calls the owner to arrange a showing, although the owner will not list with the broker. The broker shows the home and writes the offer to purchase, which is accepted by the owner. Which of the following statements correctly describes this situation?

   1. The owner is legally bound to pay the broker a commission.
   2. The prospects are responsible for paying a commission to the broker.
   3. The owner and the prospects are legally bound to pay a commission to the broker.
   4. Neither the owner nor the prospects are legally bound to pay a commission to the broker.

13. A veteran wishes to receive a loan for $70,000 to buy a home. The home has been appraised by the DVA at $68,000. Which of the following statements most accurately describes the veteran's situation?

   1. The veteran may buy the home with a DVA loan only if he is able to lower the purchase price to $68,000.
   2. The veteran may buy the home with a DVA loan if the seller agrees to hold a second mortgage for $2,000.
   3. The veteran may buy the home with a DVA loan if he makes a down payment of $2,000.
   4. The veteran may not buy the home.

14. You are paying interest only on a $75,000 mortgage for three years after which the entire loan is due. This is called a(an)

   1. amortized mortgage.
   3. graduated payment mortgage.
   2. purchase money mortgage.
   4. term mortgage.

15. A farmer is unable to pay the county taxes on his farm. The delinquent taxes would be considered

   1. a lien.
   2. an attachment.
   3. an easement.
   4. an appurtenance.

16. June, a salesperson, is helping her cousin buy a home. Her broker has entered into a buyer's broker agreement with the cousin. At a regular office sales meeting, another salesperson tells the group about a "sweet" deal that he just listed and that the sellers are anxious to sell at any price. If June tells her cousin about this property and a sale is made, at a very low price, which of the following is correct?

    1. June, under her fiduciary duties, is acting in the best interest of her client, her cousin.
    2. June has violated her agency relationship with the seller.
    3. June's broker is a dual agent.
    4. June cannot show this property to her cousin.

17. Commissions paid to salespeople by brokers must be reported to the IRS on

    1. Form 1099 A.   3. Form 1099 S.
    2. Form 1099 B.   4. Form 1099 MISC.

18. A retired woman owns her home free and clear and is looking for a mortgage that would provide her with monthly payments until she dies. This type of mortgage is called a

    1. guaranteed payment mortgage.   3. participation mortgage.
    2. blanket mortgage.   4. reverse annuity mortgage.

19. A man leased a store with the agreement that he would pay a fixed rent with the landlord paying all operating expenses. This would be an example of a

    1. gross lease.   3. net lease.
    2. graduated lease.   4. percentage lease.

20. You have entered into a land contract for the sale of your home. Which of the following statements is not correct?

    1. The seller is the vendor.
    2. The seller will retain possession until the contract has been executed.
    3. The seller will hold legal title during the term of the contract.
    4. The buyer is the vendee.

21. You have received a mortgage loan from a lender that has an interest rate that exceeds the limit set by law. This is a violation of

    1. the Statute of Frauds.   3. Regulation Z.
    2. RESPA.   4. the usury statutes.

22. Which of the following statements correctly describes the way in which a listing broker should represent her client?

    1. The listing broker can tell a prospective buyer the lowest price her client will accept.
    2. The listing broker may choose which offers to present to her client.
    3. The listing broker with two offers may hold back on presenting the second offer until her client has responded to the first offer.
    4. The listing broker must present all offers to her client promptly when received.

23. Which of the following is true as it relates to an easement appurtenant?

    1. This easement may be acquired only by prescription.
    2. The easement right cannot be terminated.
    3. The dominant tenement owner pays taxes only on the dominant estate.
    4. The easement right reverts to the owner of the servient estate on the death of the owner of the dominant estate.

24. Generally, the transferee of any U.S. real property interest is required to withhold a tax equal to a percentage of the amount realized by a foreign transferor on the disposition of the property. The percentage to be deducted is

    1. 5 percent.   3. 15 percent.
    2. 10 percent.   4. 20 percent.

25. A buyer broker has entered into an agreement with a client in which the buyer must compensate her agent whenever she purchases a property of the type described within the time period described. This arrangement is known as a(n)

    1. exclusive agency agreement.   3. open agreement.
    2. exclusive right agreement.   4. multiple-listing agreement.

26. A mortgage is all of the following **EXCEPT**

    1. an encumbrance.
    2. a lien on real property.
    3. a recordable legal document.
    4. an example of involuntary alienation.

27. Three investors decided to pool their savings and buy an office building for $200,000. If one invested $70,000 and the second contributed $40,000, what percentage of ownership was left for the third investor?

    1. 20 percent   3. 45 percent
    2. 35 percent   4. None of the above

28. A broker is selling a home for $85,900. The owner tells the broker that the roof needs repair, the basement leaks, the house is a nonconforming use and that she will accept an offer well below $85,900. The broker now is negotiating with a prospect for the sale of the home. The broker should NOT tell the prospect that the

    1. roof needs repair.
    2. basement leaks.
    3. house is a nonconforming use.
    4. seller will accept an offer well below $85,900.

29. You listed a home for sale and showed the property to a man who wrote an offer that was rejected by the owner. The owner subsequently sold his house to a woman who then sold one month later to the man for whom the broker had written an offer. Are you entitled to a commission from the original owner?

    1. Yes, because the man was covered by the broker protection clause.
    2. Yes, because the man bought the house.
    3. No, because the listing contract was between you and the original owner.
    4. No, because the listing contract had terminated.

30. An investor finds that the cost of installing an air-conditioning system in an office building is greater than is justified by the rental increase that might result from the improvement to the property. The investor's decision is most reflective of the principle of

    1. supply and demand.
    2. competition.
    3. increasing and decreasing returns.
    4. contribution.

31. *A* loaned money to his sister and in return took a mortgage as security for the debt. He immediately recorded the mortgage. Thereafter, *B* loaned money to the sister, took a mortgage and recorded it. The sister later defaulted, and a court determined that *B*'s interest had priority over *A*'s interest. Under these circumstances, chances are that

    1. *A* knew *B* was going to make a loan before *A* made his own loan.
    2. *B*'s loan was larger than *A*'s loan.
    3. *A* had signed a subordination agreement in favor of *B*.
    4. *B* had signed a satisfaction.

32. A sale closed on July 29. Real estate taxes of $2,380 for the current year have not been paid. What is the settlement sheet entry for the proration of the real estate taxes?

    1. Credit seller $1,381.70; debit buyer $1,381.70
    2. Debit seller $998.30; credit buyer $1,381.70
    3. Debit seller $1,381.70; credit buyer $1,381.70
    4. Debit buyer $00.00; credit seller $2,380.00

33. You receive a monthly salary of $600 plus 3 percent commission on all your listings that sell and 3.5 percent on all of your sales. None of the listings that you took sold last month, but you received $4,100 in salary and commission. What was the value of the property you sold?

    1. $100,000
    2. $116,666
    3. $117,142
    4. None of the above

34. A broker has been asked to serve as an agent of a friend who wishes to sell his home. Prior to listing the friend's home, the broker is asked by another friend to serve as her agent in finding a home. Relatives of the two friends also have asked the broker to serve as their agent in helping them find homes. Which of the following statements is correct?

    1. The broker is not allowed to work with the relatives because he would have a conflict of interest.
    2. The broker may not serve as agent to the various parties unless he gets permission from all of the parties.
    3. The broker may serve only as an agent of the seller.
    4. The broker may serve as agent for any of the buyers and sellers.

35. Which of the following types of depreciation is incurable?

    1. A leaky roof
    2. A worn-out water heater
    3. A zoning variance of the neighbor's property for commercial use
    4. Warped doors

36. A salesperson would like to be classified as an independent contractor by his broker. What percentage of his income must be based on sales production for him to qualify for independent-contractor status?

    1.   60 percent   3.   80 percent
    2.   70 percent   4.   90 percent

37. A couple is interested in buying a property located in a economically distressed section of town. Although the couple has an excellent credit history, the couple has been refused a loan by three different lenders. Such action by the lenders

    1.   is a violation of fair housing laws.
    2.   violates the Equal Credit Opportunity Act.
    3.   violates both Regulation Z and RESPA.
    4.   is most likely an economic-based business decision of the bank and does not violate any laws.

38. You have listed a property. The seller told you that he must net at least $14,000 after all fees and expenses are paid. You estimate the seller's closing cost to be $3,500 and he must pay off an existing loan of $108,750. In addition, you are going to charge 7 percent commission on the sale. What is the least amount that the property can sell for to return the seller's desired net?

    1. $126,250   3. $135,088
    2. $134,310   4.   None of the above

39. Which approach to value is an appraiser most likely to emphasize in the appraisal of a single family home?

    1.   cost approach   3.   income capitalization approach
    2.   gross income multiplier approach   4.   sales comparison approach

40. All of the following installment sales amounts are covered by the imputed interest law **EXCEPT**

    1. $2,000.   3. $9,000.
    2. $4,000.   4. $10,000.

41. The tax on the profit realized from an exchange of property is

    1.   ordinary income in the year of the exchange.
    2.   deferred.
    3.   eliminated.
    4.   None of the above

42. You own an apartment building that provides you with a gross income of $40,000 a year. Your annual expenses are $10,000 a year. The value of your real estate if you need a 12 percent return on your investment is

    1. $83,333.   3. $333,333.
    2. $250,000.   4. $444,444.

43. Which of the following statements do not correctly describe joint tenancy?

    1. It is a form of co-ownership.
    2. Owners have the right of survivorship.
    3. Owners must be husband and wife.
    4. Owners may partition the property.

44. All of the following statements correctly describe radon gas **EXCEPT**

    1. as radon is released from the rocks, it finds its way to the surface and usually is released into the atmosphere.
    2. radon enters a house through the roof vents.
    3. radon can become concentrated in the crawl space.
    4. long-term exposure to radon gas is said to cause lung cancer.

45. Strict liability under Superfund means that

    1. each individual owner is personally responsible for the damages in whole.
    2. the owner is responsible to the injured party without excuse.
    3. the liability is not limited to the person who currently owns the property but also to people who have owned the site in the past.
    4. anyone who has been involved in the transaction will be liable for damages.

46. Deed restrictions may

    1. restrict the height of a building.
    2. not be terminated by a quitclaim deed executed by the necessary parties.
    3. not be enforced by means of a court injunction.
    4. not control the square footage of a building.

47. A form of ownership with centralized management limited to no more than 35 shareholders is a

    1. corporation.   3. general partnership.
    2. S corporation.   4. limited partnership.

48. The rent on a house is $400 a month or $4,800 a year, and the house recently sold for $52,000. The gross rent multiplier on the house was

    1. 10.8.   3. 130.
    2. 108.   4. 130.8.

49. The rate of return an investor will require to invest in real estate is called

    1. a gross rent multiplier.   3. a capitalization rate.
    2. a gross income multiplier.   4. an assemblage.

50. National advertising and economies of volume purchasing are advantages for

    1. franchises.   3. broker cooperatives.
    2. quasi-franchises.   4. broker associations.

51. A broker requires that all budgeted costs for the planning period be justified each time a new budget is developed. This requirement reflects

    1. the cash method of keeping financial records.
    2. the concept of cash flow.
    3. the concept of desk cost.
    4. the concept of zero-base budgeting.

52. All of the following statements correctly describe the independent-contractor relationship **EXCEPT**

    1. salesperson contracts with a broker to produce specific outcomes such as commission.
    2. broker may not tell salespeople how to sell real estate.
    3. broker must provide a pension plan.
    4. salesperson must pay his or her board dues.

53. A salesperson works for a broker. The salesperson may

    1. work for the broker as an independent contractor.
    2. place an ad without identifying the broker.
    3. receive a commission directly from a seller.
    4. receive a commission directly from another broker.

54. A broker has listed a home. The broker generally will earn his commission when

    1. he submits an offer to purchase to the seller.
    2. the seller indicates that she feels an offer to purchase is acceptable.
    3. he finds a ''buyer ready, willing and able'' to buy on the terms of the listing.
    4. the closing takes place.

55. A Hispanic buyer has asked a broker to show her homes in a white neighborhood. The broker's response to the buyer should be

    1. "I think you would be happier in a neighborhood with people of a similar background."
    2. "I don't think you would be comfortable with the people in that neighborhood because they do not welcome outsiders."
    3. "I'll be happy to show you homes in that neighborhood but I think you could do better than that."
    4. "I'll be happy to show you homes in that neighborhood or any other neighborhood."

56. During a listing presentation, the seller tells the broker that she will not sell to Hispanics. Should the broker follow the seller's instructions?

    1. Yes. The owner has the right to choose prospective buyers.
    2. Yes. The broker is the seller's agent and must honor his fiduciary responsibility.
    3. No. The broker might lose any commission by limiting potential buyers.
    4. No. The broker should not accept the listing.

57. You are appraising a two-story, three-bedroom house with one bathroom on the first floor and all of the bedrooms on the second floor. This is an example of

    1. economic obsolescence.
    2. escheat.
    3. functional obsolescence.
    4. physical deterioration.

58. Which of the following is NOT an example of real property?

    1. A neighbor's strawberry bush, which she calls "fructus naturales"
    2. Percolating water
    3. Unexcavated clay
    4. The clay bricks that you will use to build your patio wall

59. Which of the following is a violation of the broker's fiduciary relationship?

    1. The broker charges no commission.
    2. The broker charges a 40 percent commission.
    3. The broker tells a prospective buyer the lowest price the seller will accept.
    4. The broker tells a prospective buyer the highest price the seller will accept.

60. A competitive market analysis

    1. uses all three approaches to value.
    2. generally results in a range of figures.
    3. must be performed by a certified appraiser.
    4. is usually based on the cost approach to value.

61. Which of the following forms of ownership is characterized by double taxation?

    1. Corporation   3. S corporation
    2. Sole proprietorship   4. General proprietorship

62. A man wants to know how much money he owes on his mortgage loan. He knows that the interest part of the last monthly payment was $608.52. If he was paying interest at the rate of 10 percent, what was the outstanding balance of his loan before that last payment was made?

    1. $60,852.20   3. $73,022.40
    2. $66,937.20   4. $77,942.26

63. Your aunt bought her house one year ago for $62,400. Property in her neighborhood is said to be increasing in value at a rate of 7 percent annually. If this is true, what is the current market value of your aunt's real estate?

    1. $65,520   3. $66,768
    2. $66,144   4. $66,971

64. Your home is valued at $104,000. Property in your city is assessed at 70 percent of its value, and the local tax rate is $3.35 per $100. What is the amount of your monthly taxes?

    1. $192.86   3. $290.33
    2. $203.23   4. $331.64

65. In the cost approach, an appraiser makes use of which of the following?

    1. Sales prices of similar properties
    2. The owner's original cost of construction
    3. An estimate of the building's replacement cost
    4. Multiplying the net income by the capitalization rate

66. An appraisal of a church probably would be based on the

    1. market/data approach.
    2. cost approach.
    3. income approach.
    4. capitalization approach.

67. On an FHA loan, the buyer would NOT be required to

    1. pay a 20 percent down payment.
    2. find an approved lender willing to make the loan.
    3. buy a house that meets minimum FHA credit standards.
    4. buy mortgage insurance to protect the lender.

68. Which of the following statements regarding points is true?

    1. Points must be charged to the seller.
    2. One point equals 1 percent of the loan.
    3. Points must be charged to the buyer.
    4. One point equals $1/4$ percent of the loan.

69. X, who works for broker Y on a 50-50 basis, sold a house listed by broker Z for $167,750. The seller agreed to pay a 7 percent commission, but stipulated in the listing that 65 percent was to go to the selling broker. How much commission will X make on this sale (to nearest dollar)?

    1. $2,054
    2. $3,816
    3. $4,110
    4. $7,633

70. The net spendable income from an investment is known as the

    1. budget.
    2. cash flow.
    3. company dollar.
    4. gross income.

71. A broker has calculated the amount of income remaining after deducting all of the firm's commissions from the firm's gross income. The broker has calculated the

    1. budget.
    2. cash flow.
    3. company dollar.
    4. desk cost.

72. A broker has an annual overhead of $200,000, and there are ten desks, each accommodating two salespeople. The broker's desk cost is

    1. $5,000.
    2. $10,000.
    3. $15,000.
    4. $20,000.

73. Encouraging minorities to live in a minority neighborhood is

    1. an acceptable business practice.
    2. blockbusting.
    3. redlining.
    4. steering.

74. A purchase money mortgage and a land contract are similar except for which of the following statements?

    1. The seller is financing the transaction.
    2. The buyer takes possession when the contract is executed.
    3. The buyer gives the seller a down payment.
    4. The buyer has equitable title during the life of the contract.

75. Which of the following is covered by Regulation Z?

   1. A personal property credit transaction for $20,000
   2. A loan with three installments
   3. A real estate purchase agreement.
   4. An agricultural loan for $29,000

76. Which of the following is exempted from the federal fair housing law?

   1. The rental of rooms in an owner-occupied, four-family dwelling
   2. The rental of rooms in an owner-occupied, five-family dwelling
   3. The rental of a single-family home when a broker is used
   4. The lodgings of a private club when the lodgings are operated commercially

77. You purchased a home and neither took possession nor recorded the deed. Which of the following statements best describes your status?

   1. You have given constructive notice to potential buyers of your home.
   2. The deed is not valid between you and the buyer.
   3. You have not given constructive notice to potential buyers of your home.
   4. You have given actual notice to potential buyers of your home.

78. The relationship of the broker to the listing owner who hired him or her is that of

   1. an attorney-in-fact.   3. a trustee.
   2. a strawman.   4. a fiduciary.

79. Which of the following would not be deposited in your trust account?

   1. The commission you earn on a transaction
   2. Earnest money received on a transaction
   3. The down payment for a land contract transaction
   4. An amount sufficient to cover bank service charges on the account

80. All of the following statements correctly describe a limited liability company **EXCEPT**

   1. limited liability companies offer the single-level taxation of a partnership.
   2. limited liability companies may not be directly managed by members.
   3. limited liability companies offer the limited liability of a corporation.
   4. limited liability companies must have at least one member.

81. A real estate agent may NOT legally represent all parties in the same transaction except when

   1. the agent fails to obtain the consent of all parties to the dual agency.
   2. the agent attempts to collect a commission from all parties without the express knowledge and consent of all parties.
   3. the agent has failed to inform all parties that he or she is acting as a dual agent.
   4. the principals are informed of and agree to the agent's actions.

82. You are working as an agent for a prospective buyer. The buyer buys a house listed on the multiple-listing service (MLS) of which you are a member. All of the following statements correctly describe the situation **EXCEPT**

    1. you are a subagent of the listing broker.
    2. you will be entitled to a commission from the buyer.
    3. you could be paid by the seller if the parties agree.
    4. the listing broker is an agent of the seller.

83. Tenancy in common is distinguished by which of the following characteristics?

    1. The co-owners have right of survivorship.
    2. Ownership interests must be equal.
    3. A co-owner cannot will his or her interest in a property.
    4. Each co-owner's interest may be conveyed separately.

84. A plumbing company installed a new furnace and filed a lien for nonpayment immediately on completion. This was most likely a

    1. voluntary lien.   3. novation.
    2. general lien.   4. specific lien.

85. All of the following are examples of functional obsolescence **EXCEPT**

    1. a five bedroom house with one bathroom.
    2. outdated plumbing fixtures.
    3. a roof that leaks.
    4. a poor floor plan.

86. A broker listed and sold a seller's home. The broker earned her commission when

    1. the transaction was closed.
    2. she found a buyer "ready, willing and able" to buy on the terms of the listing.
    3. the buyer's financing contingency was removed from the offer to purchase.
    4. the buyer's check cleared the bank after closing.

87. A salesperson has taken a four-month exclusive-right-to-sell listing on a house. Prior to the expiration of the listing, the salesperson leaves the state and inactivates her license. Which of the following correctly describes the status of the listing?

    1. The listing automatically terminates when the salesperson leaves the state and inactivates her license.
    2. The seller may terminate the listing once the salesperson has left the state.
    3. The broker will have to negotiate with the seller to retain the listing.
    4. The listing will continue as a valid contract between the seller and the broker.

88. A broker was employed to sell a house under an exclusive-right-to-sell listing contract. The listing was dated May 15 and was to expire on November 15 with a commission rate of 7 percent. The seller was declared insane on June 3. The broker presented an offer to purchase to the seller on June 10 from a buyer who had been located by the seller. The offer to purchase was accepted on June 12. Which of the following most accurately describes the status of the broker's right to a commission?

    1. The broker is not entitled to a commission because the seller located the buyer.
    2. The broker is entitled to a commission because the seller accepted an offer to purchase.
    3. The broker is not entitled to a commission because the seller's being declared insane terminates the listing contract.
    4. The broker must split the commission with the seller because the seller located the buyer.

89. All of the following are advantages of an FHA-insured loan **EXCEPT**

    1. low down payment.
    2. buyer protection with FHA insurance.
    3. it enables cash-short buyers to enter the real estate market.
    4. it protects the lender with FHA insurance.

90. Which of the following is NOT a legal requirement of an option?

    1. A purchase price or how it will be determined
    2. Consideration
    3. The date on which the option will expire
    4. The exercise of the option by the optionee

91. A 300-acre farm is divided into house lots. The streets require one-eighth of the whole farm, and there are 280 lots. How many square feet are in each lot?

    1. 38,115
    2. 40,838
    3. 46,671
    4. None of the above

92. The process of reviewing the various approaches to value in order to arrive at a final estimate of market value is called

    1. assemblage.
    2. capitalization.
    3. balance.
    4. reconciliation.

93. A broker and a seller have just signed a listing contract for the sale of the seller's house. All of the following statements correctly describe their situation **EXCEPT**

    1. A fiduciary relationship now exists between the broker and seller.
    2. The broker has become a general agent for the seller.
    3. The broker is an agent and the seller is the principal.
    4. The broker has become a special agent for the seller.

94. The Americans with Disabilities Act (ADA) requires that as of July 26, 1994, certain employers must adopt nondiscriminatory employment procedures and make reasonable accommodations to enable an individual with a disability to perform in his or her employment. Which of the following will be required to comply with ADA?

    1. Employers with 3 or more employees
    2. Employers with 5 or more employees
    3. Employers with 10 or more employees
    4. Employers with 15 or more employees

95. You have just listed a property and the owner has informed you that the roof leaks and the fourth bedroom was added without a building permit being issued. Which of the following best describes the type of disclosure you should make to potential buyers?

    1. You should disclose that the roof leaks.
    2. You do not have to disclose that the bedroom was added without a permit because the project has already been completed.
    3. You do not have to disclose either unless you are instructed to do so by the seller.
    4. You must disclose both the roof leak and the lack of a building permit.

96. Your state views the lender as the owner of mortgaged land. Which of the following theories of mortgage law is reflected by this type of law?

    1. Lien theory   3. Title theory
    2. Equitable redemption   4. Intermediate theory

97. The 1988 amendment to the federal fair housing law expanded the statute of limitations for initiating administrative proceedings from 180 days to

    1. 270 days after the alleged discriminatory housing practice.
    2. one year after the alleged discriminatory housing practice.
    3. two years after the alleged discriminatory housing practice.
    4. three years after the alleged discriminatory housing practice.

98. You have filed a writ of attachment against a business associate's property. Which of the following will hold title to the property subsequent to the writ of attachment being filed?

    1. The court   3. You
    2. A trustee selected by the court 4. Your business associate

99. A broker received three offers on her listing on the same afternoon. One offer was above the list price but involved the seller's holding a land contract, while the second offer was for cash but at the listing price. The third offer also was for cash, but at less than the listing price. How should the broker handle this situation?

    1. The broker should present the offers in the order in which she received them.
    2. The broker should present what she considers to be the best offer first and then continue on to the second and third best offers.
    3. The broker should present the cash offer at list price first.
    4. The broker should present all of the offers at the same time.

100. You lease the 36 apartments in your building for a total monthly rental of $8,000. If this figure represents an 8 percent annual return on your investment, what was the original cost of the property?

1. $100,000
2. $236,000
3. $1,200,000
4. $2,360,000

BROKER EXAMINATION I
ANSWER KEY WITH EXPLANATIONS

NOTE: The information in parentheses at the end of each explanation refers to the part number and outline reference where the material was discussed. For example: (4–VI) = Part 4, outline reference VI.

1. **2.** A leasehold estate, chattels and trade fixtures are classified as personal property. (4–I)

2. **2.** When a person dies intestate, the descendant's real estate and personal property pass to her heirs according to statute. (4–VI)

3. **2.** Rural Development makes and guarantees loans to low-income people in rural areas. FHLMC is a warehousing agency in the secondary mortgage market. FHA insures home mortgages. Farm Service Agency makes and guarantees loans to farmers and ranchers. (10–VII)

4. **4.** The words *as long as* are the key to the creation of a determinable fee, sometimes referred to as a qualified fee, conditional fee or base fee estate. (4–IV)

5. **4.** Under an open listing, if the seller personally sells the property without the aid of any broker, the seller is not obligated to pay the commission. (6–VIII)

6. **4.** The various penalties under the federal fair housing laws are discussed in 7–I.

7. **3.** $80,300 × .08 = $6,424 annual interest

    $6,424 ÷ 12 = $535.333 interest for one month

    $653.00 P&I – $535.333 = $117.67 principal payoff

    $80,300 – $117.67 = $80,182.33 balance after next payment (8)

8. **2.** $804.65 ($121,000 × 6.65) (8)

9. **4.** $804.65 × 360 months = $289,674   Total P&I
                                    –121,000   Loan
                                    $168,674   Total interest   (8)

10. **4.** A conventional mortgage is neither insured nor guaranteed by the government. A down payment generally is higher than with insured and guaranteed loans. (10–VII)

11. **4.** The best way to discover the existence of an encroachment is through a survey. (4–III)

12. **4.** The broker is not entitled to a commission because he had no contractual agreement with the buyer or the seller. (5–I)

13. **3.** The loan amount cannot exceed the DVA appraisal on a DVA loan. The veteran must pay the difference between the appraised value and the purchase price in cash. (10–VII)

14. **4.** Payments on an amortized mortgage include principal and interest. A purchase money mortgage involves seller financing while a graduated payment mortgage has low initial payments that increase over time. (10–IV)

15. **1.** Attachment refers to the act of taking a person's property into legal custody by court or judicial order to hold it available for application to that person's debt to a creditor. An easement is the right to use the land of another for a specific purpose. An appurtenance is a right, privilege or improvement that belongs to and passes with the transfer of the property but is not necessarily a part of the real property. (4–IX)

16. **3.** All listings belong to the broker. June's broker is a dual agent. He is the agent of the seller through the listing and the agent of the buyer through the buyer's broker agreement. This is not illegal as long as all parties to the transaction know about it and agree. (5–I)

17. **4.** The regulation is described in 7–V.

18. **4.** A reverse annuity mortgage becomes due on a specific date, the sale of the property or the death of the borrower. (10–VII)

19. **1.** A graduated lease provides for rent increases at set future dates, while a percentage lease provides for a minimum fixed rent plus a percentage of the business income. Under a net lease, the tenant pays rent plus all or part of the property charges. (4–V)

20. **2.** The vendee (buyer) takes possession when the contract is executed. (6–XII)

21. **4.** Regulation Z requires disclosure of the cost of credit, while RESPA requires disclosure of all settlement costs prior to closing. The Statute of Frauds requires certain contracts to be in writing in order to be enforceable. (10–XII)

22. **4.** The responsibilities of the listing broker to the client are discussed in 5–I.

23. **3.** The dominant tenement owner may terminate the easement right but does not pay the real estate taxes on the servient tenement. The dominant tenement owner may acquire his or her rights under an easement appurtenant by means other than by prescription. (4–III)

24. **2.** The procedure is described in 7–IV.

25. **2.** The different types of buyer brokerage agreements are discussed in 6–VII.

26. **4.** A mortgage is a voluntary act, not involuntary. (10–II)

27. **3.** $70,000 (first investor) + $40,000 (second investor) = $110,000

$200,000 – $110,000 = $90,000, third investor's contribution

$$\frac{\text{part}}{\text{total}} = \text{percent}$$

$90,000 ÷ $200,000 = 0.45, or 45% (8)

28. **4.** The broker is responsible for disclosing physical defects in the house but to disclose that the seller would take less then the list price would be a violation of the broker's fiduciary responsibilites to the seller. (5–I)

29. **3.** The listing contract was between the original owner and the broker. The broker would have the right to a commission from the woman who sold the property if he or she could prove collusion. (5–I)

30. **4.** The principle of *contribution* refers to the added value created by the addition of a specific component to a building. The principle of *increasing and decreasing returns* refers to the amount of added value created by more than one such improvement. (9–III)

31. **3.** Neither *A*'s knowledge of *B*'s making a loan nor the size of such a loan would affect the priority of claims. The court could not rule in favor of *B* if *B* had signed a satisfaction. A subordination clause is a clause in which the mortgagee (*A*) permits a subsequent mortgage (*B*'s loan) to take priority. (10–XII)

32. **3.** $2,380 ÷ 12 months = $198.333 per month

    $198.33 ÷ 30 days = $6.611 per day

    $198.33 × 6 months = $1,189.98

    $6.611 × 29 days = $191.719

    $1,189.98 + $191.719 = $1,381.699 or $1,381.70

    The taxes for the year have not been paid, and when they are, the buyer will be in possession and have to pay the bill. The seller, therefore, must pay (be debited) for the portion of the year that he occupied the property. The buyer receives a credit for the same amount. (8)

33. **1.** $4,100 – $600 salary = $3,500, commission on sales

    $3,500 ÷ 3.5% = $3,500 ÷ 0.035 = $100,000, value of property sold (8)

34. **4.** The broker may serve as an agent of the seller or of any of the buyers. The broker could even represent a buyer and a seller in the same transaction, provided that he or she had the knowledge and consent of all parties involved. (5–I)

35. **3.** A zoning variance for commercial use is economic or locational obsolescence, which would be incurable. (11–II)

36. **4.** (7–V)

37. **4.** What is described in the question could be looked on as "legal" redlining. The lenders refused to loan because of the depressed economic conditions of the neighborhood, not because of the racial or ethnic makeup of the area. (7–I)

38. **4.** Start by adding the desired net $14,000 PLUS existing loan payoff $108,750 and closing costs $3,500 = $126,250, the minimum that the seller must receive

  If the selling price is 100 percent, the commission is 7 percent and the net to seller is 93 percent.

  $126,250 is 93 percent of the selling price.

  Therefore, $126,250 divided by 93% (.93) = selling price of $135,752.69, which is not one of the answer options (8)

39. **4.** The sales comparison approach is considered the most reliable of the three approaches in appraising residential property. (9–IV)

40. **1.** Installment sales under $3,000 are not covered by the imputed interest law. (7–V)

41. **2.** (7–V)

42. **2.** $40,000 gross income – $10,000 expenses = $30,000, net annual income
  $30,000 net annual income ÷ 12% capitalization rate = $30,000 ÷ 0.12 = $250,000, value of real estate (8)

43. **3.** The owners must be husband and wife in tenancy by the entirety. (4–V)

44. **2.** (11–V)

45. **2.** (11–V)

46. **1.** (11–VI)

47. **2.** There is no limitation on the number of shareholders in the corporation, general partnership or limited partnership. (12–I)

48. **3.** The gross rent multiplier (GRM) relates to monthly rental income, not annual.

  $52,000 sale price ÷ $400 monthly rent = 130 gross multiplier (8)

49. **3.** The gross rent and gross income multipliers are used as substitutes for the income approach. Assemblage is joining two or more properties. (9–IV)

50. **1.** (12–I)

51. **4.** (12–VI)

52. **3.** (12–II)

53. **1.** This relationship is described in 5–II.

54. **3.** It is important to distinguish between earning and receiving a commission. (5–I)

55. **4.** The broker must not restrict the buyer's freedom of choice. (7–I)

56. **4.** It is illegal under the federal fair housing law to accept a listing that involves discrimination, such as refusing to sell to members of a protected class. (5–I)

57. **3.** Functional obsolescence is a loss in value due to a deficiency in the floor plan or design of the house. (9–IV)

58. **4.** Real property refers to physical land and appurtenances, including easements, water rights, mineral rights and fixtures. Strawberry bushes are perennial plants and would be considered real property. Percolating water and unexcavated clay also would be considered real property. Personal property refers to anything that can be moved. (4–I)

59. **3.** Disclosing the lowest price that the seller will accept is a violation of the fiduciary relationship. (5–I)

60. **2.** A competitive market analysis is based on the sales comparison approach to value. (9–II)

61. **1.** Double taxation is a primary disadvantage of the corporation form of ownership. (12–I)

62. **3.** $608.52 × 12 = $7,302.24

$7,302.24 ÷ 10% (0.10) = $73,022.40 (8)

63. **3.** $62,400 × 7% (0.07) = $4,368, or $62,400 × 107% (1.07) = $66,768

$62,400 + $4,368 = $66,768 (8)

64. **2.** $104,000 × 70% (0.70) = $72,800, assessed value

Divide by 100 because the tax rate is stated per $100.

$72,800 ÷ 100 = $728

$728 × $3.35 = $2,438.80, annual taxes

Divide by 12 to get monthly taxes.

$2,438.80 ÷ 12 = $203.23 (8)

65. **3.** Sales prices of similar properties are used in the market/data approach. The net income and capitalization rate are used in the income approach. The owner's original cost of construction would be irrelevant, because in the cost approach the appraiser is concerned with the current replacement cost of a structure. (9–IV)

66. **2.** The market/data approach is considered most reliable when appraising a single-family home. The income approach and the capitalization approach are stressed in appraising commercial and industrial properties. (9–IV)

67. **1.** The buyer's down payment on an FHA loan is 3 percent of the first $25,000 and 5 percent of any amount more than $25,000. (10–VII)

68. **2.** One point equals 1 percent of the loan. (10–VII)

69. **2.** $167,750 sales price × 7% commission =

$167,750 × 0.07 = $11,742.50, broker's commission

$5,740 × 65% = $7,632.63 × 0.50 = $3,816, selling salesperson's commission (8)

70. **2.** The budget is the quantified business plan, while company dollars is the amount of income remaining after subtracting all the commissions from the gross income. Gross income is the revenue earned from all the sources in a brokerage firm such as sales and management fees. (12–V)

71. **3.** Budget and company dollar were defined previously. Desk cost is the cost of providing the opportunity for salespeople to conduct their business. (12–V)

72. **2.** $200,000 annual overhead ÷ 20 (10 desks × 2 salespeople each) = $10,000 desk cost (12–VI)

73. **4.** The federal fair housing law was discussed in 7–I.

74. **4.** The vendee in a land contract holds equitable title until the land contract is paid in full, while the mortgagor receives legal title at closing. (6–XII and 10–VII)

75. **1.** The types of agreements not covered by Regulation Z are presented in 7–II.

76. **1.** Rental of rooms in an owner-occupied dwelling of five units or more is not exempted. (7–I)

77. **3.** An unrecorded deed is valid between the parties, but constructive notice must be given to protect against subsequent buyers of the property. (4–VIII)

78. **4.** An attorney-in-fact is a competent, disinterested person authorized by another person to act in his or her place. A strawman is one who buys property for someone else to conceal the identity of the real buyer. A trustee holds property in trust for another to secure the performance of an obligation. (5–I)

79. **1.** A broker may not commingle his own funds with those of his clients in a trust account. (5–I)

80. **2.** Limited liability companies are discussed in 12–I.

81. **4.** Brokers generally are prohibited from representing and collecting compensation from both parties to a transaction unless both parties receive prior knowledge and give mutual consent. (5–I)

82. **1.** In this situation you are the agent of the buyer and the listing broker is the agent of the seller. (5–I)

83. **4.** Answers 1, 2, and 3 are all characteristics of joint tenancy. (4–V)

84. **4.** A voluntary lien is a mortgage lien such as a lien created by an owner who obtains a mortgage loan. A general lien usually affects all the property of a debtor, both real and personal. A specific lien usually is secured by a specific property. (4–III)

85. **3.** A roof that leaks would be an example of physical deterioration. (9–IV)

86. **2.** The broker is entitled to a commission when she is employed by the seller and finds a "ready, willing and able" buyer. (5–I)

87. **4.** The salesperson is an agent of the broker. When the salesperson no longer is employed by the broker, the broker retains any unsold or unexpired listings. The status of the listings remains unchanged. (5–I)

88. **3.** A listing contract terminates on the death or insanity of either party to the contract. (6–VIII)

89. **2.** FHA insurance is provided as protection for the lender. (10–VII)

90. **4.** When an option is given, the optionee gives the optionor consideration, the price is determined and the time is set. The optionee does not have to exercise the option. (6–XI)

91. **2.** 43,560 square feet per acre × 300 acres = 13,068,000 square feet

    13,068,000 square feet × (0.125) = 1,633,500 square feet for streets

    13,068,000 – 1,633,500 = 11,434,500 sq. ft. for lots

    11,434,500 square feet ÷ 280 lots = 40,838 square feet per lot (8)

92. **4.** Reconciliation is the next-to-last step in the appraisal process. (9–V)

93. **2.** The listing agreement is an employment contract. The broker is "employed" to do only one thing and that is to find a "ready, willing and able" buyer. The broker, therefore, is a special agent, not a general agent. (5–I)

94. **4.** The ADA is discussed in 7–II.

95. **4.** The broker is obligated to disclose to the buyer material facts relating to property. (5–I)

96. **3.** Under the lien theory, the borrower is viewed as the owner of mortgaged land. (10–I)

97. **2.** (7–I)

98. **4.** A writ of attachment is a writ filed during a lawsuit that prevents the debtor from transferring the property involved in the suit. (4–IX)

99. **1.** The broker should present the offers in the same sequence as she received them. (6–VII)

100. **3.** $8,000 × 12 = $96,000, annual return

    $96,000 ÷ 8% (0.08) = $1,200,000, original cost of property (8)

BROKER EXAMINATION II

1. You have hauled your heavy farm equipment across the land of your neighbor each day for 20 years without the permission of your neighbor. You may have

    1. an encroachment.
    2. a license.
    3. an easement by prescription.
    4. an easement in gross.

2. The basic reason for choosing among a warranty, a special warranty or a quitclaim deed is to

    1. avoid the need for a habendum clause.
    2. verify the kind of estate the grantee will receive.
    3. explain any restrictions or limitations on the title.
    4. define the covenants by which the grantor is bound.

3. Under their mother's will, a woman and her brother inherited title to a house as tenants in common. The woman married and had title to her share put in joint tenancy with her husband. Her brother is now

    1. a joint tenant with his sister and her husband.
    2. sole owner of the property.
    3. a tenant in common, owning an undivided $1/3$ interest.
    4. a tenant in common, owning an undivided $1/2$ interest.

4. You receive a monthly salary of $900 plus 3.5 percent commission on all your listings that you sell and 3 percent on all of your sales. None of the listings that you took sold last month, but you receive $4,800 salary and commissions. What was the value of the property you sold?

    1. $130,000
    2. $160,000
    3. $111,428
    4. None of the above

5. Your roof overhang has protruded onto a neighbor's adjacent lot for 24 years. A new owner of the lot, after a survey has been ordered, discovers this. In this case, the new neighbor can

    1. do nothing because you have acquired a prescriptive easement after 20 years.
    2. do nothing because you have acquired title to that portion of the land by adverse possession.
    3. have a court order you to remove the overhang.
    4. grant you an easement in gross.

6. Ethically it is appropriate for an appraiser to

    1. have an interest in the property he is appraising.
    2. have a personal interest in the property he is appraising.
    3. have a personal interest in the parties involved in the property he is appraising.
    4. disclose confidential information if given permission by his client.

7. The state needs your farm to build a highway. You have rejected their offer. The state may obtain your property by exercising its right of

   1.   adverse possession.   3.   escheat.
   2.   eminent domain.   4.   police power.

8. Which of the following types of funds would you NOT be able to hold in your trust account?

   1.   Rents on an apartment building you are managing
   2.   Earnest money deposits
   3.   Commissions earned on previous sales
   4.   Security deposits on properties you are managing

9. X owns a life estate and Y holds the future interest in the life estate. When X dies,

   1. X's wife will become the owner under her dower interest.
   2. X's life estate will pass to his heirs according to the terms of his will.
   3. X and Y will hold title as tenants in common.
   4. Y will hold title to the property.

10. A has had an offer to purchase accepted by B. Prior to closing, A will hold

   1.   fee simple title.   3.   legal title.
   2.   defeasible title.   4.   equitable title.

11. A zoning ordinance would not regulate

   1.   land use.   3.   use of the building.
   2.   height of the building.   4.   construction standards.

12. Your property has just gone through a foreclosure sale, but you have six months to buy it back. Your right to reacquire your property is called a(n)

   1.   option.   3.   subordination clause.
   2.   equitable redemption.   4.   statutory redemption.

13. You have pledged your home as security for a mortgage without giving up possession. This is called

   1.   hypothecation.   3.   subordination.
   2.   abstract.   4.   release of mortgage.

14. All of the following statements correctly describe the relationship of a salesperson working for a broker as an employee **EXCEPT**

   1.   The broker may choose to provide fringe benefits.
   2.   The broker may not tell salespeople how to list property.
   3.   The broker may require attendance at sales meetings.
   4.   The broker is required to withhold federal and state income taxes from commissions.

15. The rent on a house is $900 a month, or $10,800 a year; and the house recently sold for $126,000. The gross rent multiplier on the house was

   1.   11.67.   3.   111.7.
   2.   14.   4.   140.

16. A broker has been found guilty of discrimination under the federal fair housing law for the third time in the past seven years. The broker will be subject to a civil penalty not exceeding

    1. $10,000
    2. $25,000
    3. $50,000
    4. $100,000

17. An earthquake tore away some of the land on your farm recently. This is an example of

    1. accession.
    2. accretion.
    3. avulsion.
    4. erosion.

18. All of the following practices constitute discriminatory acts under the federal fair housing law **EXCEPT**

    1. the owner-occupant of a duplex refuses to rent to a family with children.
    2. a lender uses one type of application for whites and another for blacks.
    3. a white broker refers Hispanic prospects only to Hispanic brokers.
    4. a property manager requires a higher security deposit for blacks than for whites.

19. Which of the following statements does NOT correctly describe a building code?

    1. Building codes are enforced by issuing building permits.
    2. In the event of a conflict between a building code and a deed restriction, the building code will prevail.
    3. Building codes specify construction standards that must be met when erecting buildings.
    4. Building inspectors issue certificates of occupancy when the completed structure has been inspected and found satisfactory.

20. If you give your land to your brother for the balance of his life and at his death the land is to go to your sister, his interest or estate is called a

    1. reversion.
    2. curtesy.
    3. base fee.
    4. life estate.

21. All of the following are hazardous substances of concern to real estate professionals **EXCEPT**

    1. radon.
    2. urea-formaldehyde foam insulation (UFFI).
    3. asbestos.
    4. fiberglass.

22. A property manager renting units for an apartment owner is an example of a

    1. special agent.
    2. general agent.
    3. subagent.
    4. dual agent.

23. Which of the following situations would not be prohibited under the federal fair housing law?

    1.   A broker makes a profit by inducing owners to sell because of the prospective entry of minorities into the neighborhood.

    2.   A broker encourages minorities to live in areas of minorities.

    3.   A lender refuses to make mortgage loans in a minority neighborhood.

    4.   A broker refuses to show a house to a potential buyer based on the buyer's sexual orientation.

24. The relationship of trust and confidence that a broker has with a client is a(n)

    1.   escrow relationship.   3.   fiduciary relationship.

    2.   subordination agreement.   4.   trustee relationship.

25. A salesperson may legally accept a bonus from

    1.   a seller for whom she did an excellent job.

    2.   an appreciative buyer.

    3.   a grateful title company.

    4.   a broker/employer.

26. A broker knowingly misled a potential buyer on the boundary lines of a property. The buyer discovered the problem after buying the property. Is the broker guilty of misrepresenting the property?

    1.   Yes, because the broker should have had the property surveyed before commenting on the property boundary lines.

    2.   Yes, because the broker intentionally misled the buyer.

    3.   No, because the broker is not a surveyor.

    4.   No, because the broker did not provide any misrepresentation in writing.

27. You own a defeasible fee estate and sell it on a land contract. Until the land contract has been paid in full, the buyer will hold a(n)

    1.   leasehold estate.   3.   equitable title.

    2.   life estate.   4.   fee simple title.

28. A broker sold a home for $183,000. The broker charged the owner a 7 percent commission and will pay 30 percent of that amount to the listing salesperson and 25 percent to the selling salesperson. What amount of commission will the listing salesperson receive from the sale?

    1. $3,202.50   3. $4,483.50

    2. $3,843   4. $12,810

29. A seller asks a broker to list his home for $105,000. The broker inspects the home and feels that the property is worth $115,000. The broker should

    1.   offer to buy the home for $105,000.

    2.   list the home for $105,000 because she is merely following the instructions of the seller.

    3.   suggest that the seller list the home for $108,000 to allow room for negotiation.

    4.   disclose to the seller that his home is worth $115,000.

30. You have just given an option to buy your house to your friend. Which of the following statements does NOT correctly describe your agreement?

    1. Your friend is the optionee.
    2. Your friend is not obligated to buy your house.
    3. You are the optionor.
    4. You will have to return the fee for the option right to your friend if he chooses not to buy your house.

31. Which of the following facts would not need to be disclosed by a broker?

    1. There is water in the basement.
    2. There is an underground storage tank in the backyard.
    3. There is asbestos wrap on the heating pipes.
    4. The seller has AIDS.

32. A broker was listing a man's house for sale when the man informed him that he was Catholic and could not sell the house to anyone who was not Catholic. The broker should

    1. take the listing but state that he could not promise that he could get a Catholic buyer.
    2. get the request in writing on the listing contract and then attempt to find a Catholic buyer.
    3. take the listing but tell the owner that he would have to check with the state licensing board to make sure it was appropriate.
    4. not take the listing.

33. A broker has entered into a listing contract with a client in which the broker will receive a commission regardless of who sells the property during the term of the listing contract. The broker's listing is a(n)

    1. exclusive-right-to-sell listing.
    2. net listing.
    3. open listing.
    4. exclusive agency listing.

34. Three investors decided to pool their savings and buy an office building for $250,000. If one invested $80,000 and the second contributed $50,000, what percentage of ownership was left for the third investor?

    1. 20%
    2. 32%
    3. 48%
    4. None of the above

35. You own an apartment building that provides you with a gross income of $50,000 a year. Your annual expenses are $12,000. The value of your real estate if you need a 14 percent return on your investment is

    1. $85,714.
    2. $170,928.
    3. $271,429.
    4. $325,143.

36. A buyer's broker has entered into an agreement with a client in which the broker is assured of buyer loyalty relative to any other agents. The buyer may, however, purchase property on his own without the assistance of an agent and thus without any commission due to the buyer's agent. This arrangement is known as a(n)

    1. exclusive agency agreement.
    2. exclusive right agreement.
    3. open agreement.
    4. multiple-listing agreement.

37. *K* owns his home in fee simple. This means that *K* has

    1. a legal life estate.
    2. a personal property interest.
    3. a tenancy by the entirety.
    4. the highest type of interest in real estate.

38. Your home is valued at $143,000. Property in your city is assessed at 80 percent of its value, and the local tax rate is $3.65 per $100. What is the amount of your monthly taxes?

    1. $319.37
    2. $347.96
    3. $352.73
    4. $357.50

39. An owner is unable to make the payments on his mortgage, so the bank forecloses and sells the property. The bank receives less than the loan value. The bank can

    1. sue the borrower for the difference in most states.
    2. sue the broker who sold the home.
    3. do nothing because the home served as collateral for the loan.
    4. do nothing because it is entitled only to the proceeds from the sale of the property.

40. You own a home on a block that is zoned residential; however, there is a retail store on the lot next door to you. The retail store

    1. is an example of down zoning.
    2. is a nonconforming use.
    3. will have to close if you file a complaint with the planning commission.
    4. is a buffer zone.

41. When a broker has an exclusive agency listing

    1. the broker may accept an offer to purchase for the seller.
    2. the seller may sell the property himself without having to pay the broker a commission.
    3. the broker will receive a commission regardless of who sells the property.
    4. only the broker will be allowed to show the property.

42. A doctor built a $400,000 home in a neighborhood of $200,000 homes. This situation reflects the principle of

    1. competition.
    2. conformity.
    3. progression.
    4. regression.

43. You purchased a home with an FHA-insured loan. At closing, the seller was charged the five discount points for the loan. This money will be paid to

    1. the broker.
    2. the lending institution.
    3. the FHA.
    4. you.

44. A short-range business plan is generally a

    1. three-month plan.
    2. six-month plan.
    3. one-year plan.
    4. three-year plan.

45. A federally chartered savings and loan association is regulated by the

    1. Bank Insurance Fund.
    2. Office of Thrift Supervision.
    3. Savings Association Insurance Fund.
    4. U.S. Treasury.

46. You have listed a property. The seller told you that he must net at least $18,000 after all fees and expenses are paid. You estimate the seller's closing cost to be $5,200, and he must pay off an existing loan of $104,600. In addition you are going to charge a 6 percent commission on the sale. What is the least amount that the property can sell for to return the seller's desired net?

    1. $111,277
    2. $130,425
    3. $137,419
    4. None of the above

47. The buyer's broker owes a direct fiduciary responsibility to the

    1. listing broker.
    2. buyer.
    3. seller.
    4. listing salesperson.

48. You are making monthly payments on a straight term mortgage. Your monthly payments include

    1. principal and interest.
    2. interest only with a balloon payment.
    3. principal only with a balloon payment.
    4. principal and interest with a balloon payment.

49. X, who works for broker Y on a 50-50 basis, sold a house listed by broker Z for $192,900. The seller agreed to pay a 6 percent commission but stipulated in the listing that 60 percent was to go to the selling broker. How much commission will X make on this sale (to the nearest dollar)?

    1. $2,083
    2. $3,472
    3. $4,630
    4. $6,944

50. Which of the following responsibilities would a broker NOT owe to a client?

    1. Placing an earnest money payment in his trust account
    2. Procuring a "ready, willing and able" buyer
    3. Presenting all offers promptly to the client
    4. Advising the buyer how to take title to the property

51. A broker listed a house for a client who indicated he was dying of cancer and thus needed to sell as quickly as possible. Can the broker reveal the illness of the client to the prospective buyers?

    1. Yes, because the illness constitutes a material fact to a prospective buyer.
    2. Yes, because the client indicated he wanted to sell as quickly as possible.
    3. No, because disclosure of the illness would compromise the negotiating position of the client.
    4. No, because disclosure of the illness would be a violation of the federal fair housing law.

52. Which of the following agreements would NOT be covered by Regulation Z?

   1. Real estate purchase agreements
   2. Commercial loans
   3. Loans with four or smaller installments
   4. Agricultural loans for amounts of less than $25,000

53. Title of the land and building in a cooperative is held by a

   1. corporation.
   2. general partnership.
   3. homeowners association.
   4. syndicate.

54. You listed a home that was subsequently shown by four cooperating brokers and three buyer's brokers. How many agents were involved in the transactions?

   1. One
   2. Four
   3. Seven
   4. Eight

55. A broker has an accepted offer to purchase on a property and would like to change the language to reflect the desire of the buyer and seller to revise the contract. The broker will accomplish this by means of a(n)

   1. addendum.
   2. amendment.
   3. counteroffer.
   4. recission.

56. The major employer in your city has decided to relocate to another state, resulting in a substantial decline in housing prices. This would be an example of

   1. the principle of regression.
   2. functional obsolescence.
   3. physical deterioration.
   4. economic obsolescence.

57. Which of the following is a physical characteristic of land?

   1. Scarcity
   2. Situs
   3. Immobility
   4. Improvements

58. What is the actual value of your property if the annual taxes are $3,940 and real estate is assessed at 40 percent of actual value? (Figure a level of 35 mills per $1 of assessed value.)

   1. $98,500
   2. $112,571
   3. $281,429
   4. None of the above

59. An easement in gross

   1. benefits the dominant tenement.
   2. has only a dominant tenement.
   3. has only a servient tenement.
   4. has both a dominant and a servient tenement.

60. Ownership is freely transferable in all of the following forms of ownership **EXCEPT**

   1. a sole proprietorship.
   2. a corporation.
   3. an S corporation.
   4. a general partnership.

61. Using the mortgage factor chart on page 87, what is the monthly payment for $129,000 at 8 percent for 30 years?

1. $923.64
2. $946.86
3. $968.79
4. $992.01

62. Using the numbers in question 61, what is the total interest paid over the life of the loan?

1. $209,975.88
2. $210,922.74
3. $211,869.60
4. $212,816.46

63. You and your brother have purchased an apartment building as joint tenants. Which of the following statements does NOT correctly describe your situation?

1. You and your brother hold the right of survivorship.
2. Owners must be related in order to own in joint tenancy.
3. The unities of title, time, interest and possession are required to create a valid joint tenancy.
4. Either you or your brother may partition the land.

64. You and your husband live in a community property state. Which of the following assets owned by you would be considered to be community property?

1. A car given to you after your marriage
2. A duplex that you and your husband purchased after your marriage
3. Stock inherited by your husband after your marriage
4. A house which you owned before you were married

65. A broker has an annual overhead of $300,000, and there are twelve desks, each accommodating two salespeople. The broker's desk cost is

1. $6,250
2. $12,500
3. $18,750
4. $25,000

66. The manager of your brokerage firm doesn't exercise any authority over the organization. Her style is characterized by nonintervention and indifference. This type of management style would be called

1. autocratic.
2. dictatorial.
3. participative.
4. laissez-faire.

67. The personal assistant is generally hired and supervised by

1. a broker.
2. a salesperson.
3. the local board of realtors.
4. the state licensing board.

68. Limited liability companies must have at least

1. 1 member.
2. 10 members.
3. 35 members.
4. 75 members.

69. You have listed a property. The seller told you that he must net at least $26,000 after all fees and expenses are paid. You estimate the seller's closing cost to be $5,000, and he must pay off an existing loan of $119,600. In addition, you are going to charge 6 percent commission on the sale. What is the least amount that the property can sell for to return the seller's desired net?

1. $127,234
2. $154,893
3. $169,825
4. None of the above

70. The Residential Lead-Based Paint Hazard Reduction Act identified procedures for disclosing the presence of lead-based paint in the sale of residential properties built before

1. 1946.
2. 1953.
3. 1964.
4. 1978.

71. A father wants to know how much money his daughter owes on her mortgage loan. The father knows that the interest part of the last monthly payment was $526.49. If his daughter is paying interest at the rate of 8 percent, what was the approximate outstanding balance of the loan before that last payment was made?

1. $70,198.67
2. $78,973.50
3. $90,255.42
4. None of the above

72. A difference between a cooperative and a condominium is that

1. owners are not subject to real estate taxes.
2. a cooperative owner holds fee simple title and a condominium owner hold a proprietary lease.
3. a cooperative owner is not responsible for unpaid real estate taxes of other owners while a condominium owner is.
4. a cooperative owner holds a personal property interest while a condominium owner holds a real property interest.

73. A salesperson lists a home for his broker. Which of the following correctly describes the transaction?

1. The salesperson is the agent of the seller.
2. The broker is the agent of the seller.
3. The salesperson is the subagent of the broker.
4. The broker is the subagent of the seller.

74. The denial of a loan by a lender is a violation of the federal fair housing law if such denial is based on

1. lack of income.
2. familial status.
3. political beliefs.
4. sexual preference.

75. Which of the following would not be a violation of appraisal ethics?

1. Appraising a property you are planning to buy
2. Appraising a property in which you have an equity position
3. Disclosing the value of your appraisal to a third party without permission from your client
4. Advertising your appraisal service in the local newspaper

76. A homeowner with no living heirs died after preparing her will. Upon her death, her closest friend claimed that her house should be disposed of by escheat. Will the property be disposed of by escheat?

    1. Yes, unless the city is planning to take her home through eminent domain.
    2. Yes, because the owner had no living heirs.
    3. No, because residential property is not subject to escheat.
    4. No, unless the will proved to be invalid.

77. All of the following are fiduciary relationships **EXCEPT**

    1. listing broker to seller.
    2. lawyer to client.
    3. mortgagor to mortgagee.
    4. property manager to owner.

78. A married couple owned their home as tenants by the entirety. They then separated, with the husband continuing to live in the house. If the husband decides to sell the home, can he do so without the wife's consent?

    1. Yes, because the wife relinquished her interest when she moved out of the house.
    2. Yes, because under tenancy by the entirety either party may sell the house without the consent of the other party.
    3. No, because the wife holds a dower interest that will not be extinguished upon the sale of the house.
    4. No, because under tenancy by the entirety title may be conveyed only by a deed signed by both parties.

79. A broker listed a home for sale under an exclusive-right-to-sell listing. Another broker cooperated with the listing broker in a cobrokerage. The house was sold, and the commission was split between the listing and selling brokers. Which of the following is NOT true?

    1. The selling broker is a subagent of the seller.
    2. The listing broker is an agent of the seller.
    3. The listing broker's salespeople are subagents of the seller.
    4. Only the seller's agent may receive all or part of the commission paid.

80. Brokers are required to deposit earnest money in a checking (noninterest-bearing) account principally because

    1. this has been the custom in the real estate industry.
    2. they would have to prorate the interest on all deposits.
    3. checking accounts are payable on demand.
    4. savings accounts are insured for less than checking accounts.

81. A salesperson working as an independent contractor

    1. is required to attend sales meetings.
    2. may not be required to follow any set work schedule.
    3. is not responsible for transportation expenses.
    4. may receive fringe benefits if the broker agrees.

82. All of the following statements correctly describe the methods of keeping financial records **EXCEPT**

1.   the cash method records income as it is received.
2.   the accrual method records income when it is earned.
3.   most firms begin operating under the accrual method.
4.   the accrual method records expenses when they are incurred.

83. A broker has met with a customer and declined to work with the person in finding a home. It is legal for the broker to decline the opportunity if the decision is based on the customer's

1.   familial status.   3.   race.
2.   income.   4.   religion.

84. The right of a buyer to rescind a transaction up to midnight of the third business day following the transaction is based on

1.   the secondary mortgage market.   3.   IRS regulations.
2.   RESPA.   4.   Regulation Z.

85. You listed your house with only one licensed broker but reserved the right to sell the property yourself without owing a commission. This relationship is called

1.   a net listing.   3.   an exclusive-agency listing.
2.   an open listing.   4.   an exclusive-right-to-sell listing.

86. A woman owns a four-unit apartment building but does not live there. She is currently advertising for white tenants only. Is her advertising policy legal?

1.   Yes, because the property contains four units.
2.   Yes, because no real estate agent is involved in the marketing of the property.
3.   No, because four-unit properties are not exempted from the Federal Fair Housing Law.
4.   No, because the woman is not living in the apartment building.

87. The civil penalty for a first violation of the Americans with Disabilities Act (ADA) is up to

1. $10,000.   3. $50,000.
2. $25,000.   4. $100,000.

88. You own an apartment building in which one of your tenants subsequent to his lease expiring has continued to live in his unit without a new lease. However, the tenant has continued to pay rent and you have accepted it. This type of tenancy is a(n)

1.   estate for years.   3.   tenancy at will.
2.   estate from year to year.   4.   tenancy at sufferance.

89. The Americans with Disabilities Act became law in

1.   1968.   3.   1990.
2.   1989.   4.   1994.

90. All of the following forms of multiple ownership have the advantage of no double taxation except the

    1. corporation.
    2. general partnership.
    3. limited liability company.
    4. S corporation.

91. Converting information on real estate listings to large print or audio format would be a response to the

    1. the federal fair housing law.
    2. the Americans with Disabilities Act.
    3. Regulation Z.
    4. RESPA.

92. All of the following correctly describe functional obsolescence **EXCEPT**

    1. it generally applies to only the improvements.
    2. it may be curable.
    3. it occurs within the property.
    4. it would be exemplified by a leaky roof.

93. A requirement that all budgeted costs for the planning period be justified each time a new budget is developed is called

    1. the budgeting process.
    2. financial analysis.
    3. a quantified business plan.
    4. zero-base budgeting.

94. Which of the following documents would NOT generally be signed by both parties to a transaction?

    1. Listing contract
    2. Offer to purchase
    3. Option
    4. Warranty deed

95. The Americans with Disabilities Act would NOT require which of the following alterations to be made to public facilities and services?

    1. Attaching grab bars to a rest-room stall
    2. Providing automatic-entry doors
    3. Providing an automatic sprinkler system
    4. Converting real estate listing information to large print or audio format

96. Which of the following statements does NOT correctly describe the protected class of handicap under the federal fair housing law?

    1. The definition of handicap does not include the current illegal use of a controlled substance.
    2. People who have AIDS are protected under the handicap classification.
    3. Persons renting a dwelling are required to permit handicapped persons to make modifications of existing premises at their own expense if these modifications are necessary to afford full enjoyment of the premises.
    4. In a rental property situation a landlord may not allow modification upon an agreement to restore the interior of the premises to the premodification condition.

97. You own a home in which the stove and track lighting have been permanently affixed to the house. The stove and track lighting would now be classified as

   1. estovers.
   2. fixtures.
   3. personal property.
   4. trade fixtures.

98. Which of the following types of depreciation is curable?

   1. Nearness to a meat-packing plant
   2. The major employer in the city goes out of business
   3. Outmoded bathroom fixtures
   4. A school closing

99. A broker has entered into a listing contract with a property owner in which the owner may sell the property herself without owing the broker a commission. In addition, the owner may also list her property simultaneously with other brokers. This is an example of a(n)

   1. exclusive agency listing.
   2. exclusive-right-to-sell listing.
   3. net listing.
   4. open listing.

100. An appraiser is estimating the value of an income property. Using the income capitalization approach, the appraiser will divide the capitalization rate into the

   1. effective gross income.
   2. annual gross income.
   3. annual net income.
   4. annual cash flow after taxes.

BROKER EXAMINATION II
ANSWER KEY WITH EXPLANATIONS

NOTE: The information in parentheses at the end of each explanation refers to the part number and outline reference where the material was discussed. For example: (4–VI) = Part 4, outline reference VI.

1. **3.** An encroachment arises when a building illegally extends beyond the land of its owner. A license may be canceled by the licensor. An easement in gross is the right to use the land of another. (4–III)

2. **4.** The habendum clause follows the granting clause when it is necessary to define the ownership to be enjoyed by the grantee. Any type of deed should explain any restrictions or limitations on the title. (4–VIII)

3. **4.** The sister and her husband jointly own an undivided one-half interest as tenant in common with the brother. (4–V)

4. **1.** $4,800 – $900 salary = $3,900 commission on sales

    $3,900 ÷ 3% = $3,900 ÷ 0.03 = $130,000 value of property sold (8)

5. **1.** An easement by prescription is acquired when the claimant has made use of another's land for up to 20 years, depending on state law. Adverse possession requires exclusive possession of another's land. An easement in gross is not appurtenant to any ownership right in land. The statute of limitations would prevent a court order to remove the overhang. (4–III)

6. **4.** An appraiser has an agency relationship with her client and can disclose confidential information with the permission of her client. (9–VII)

7. **2.** Eminent domain is the right of the government to acquire private property for public use while paying just compensation to the owner. (4–IV)

8. **3.** A broker may not commingle his funds with those of his clients in his trust account. (5–I)

9. **4.** When the life tenant dies, the life estate is terminated. On the death of the life estate owner, full ownership will pass to the owner of the future interest. (4–IV)

10. **4.** After both the buyer and the seller have executed the offer to purchase contract, the buyer acquires equitable title. (6–IX)

11. **4.** Construction standards are regulated by building codes. (11–IV)

12. **4.** Equitable redemption is the process by which the borrower regains her interest is the property prior to public sale. A subordination agreement changes the order of priority of the liens between two creditors. The option was discussed earlier. (10–VI)

13. **1.** Hypothecation is the pledging of property as security for a loan without losing possession of it. Arbitrage, subordination, and release of mortgage were discussed above. (10–XII)

14. **2.** The broker may guide activities and maintain standards of conduct for a salesperson working as an employee. (12–II)

15. **4.** The gross rent multiplier (GRM) relates to monthly rental income, not annual.

$126,000 sale price ÷ $900 monthly rent = 140 gross multiplier (8)

16. **3.** Penalties under the federal fair housing law are discussed in 7–I.

17. **3.** Erosion is the gradual wearing away of land by the action of natural forces. Accession and accretion were discussed above. (4–VI)

18. **1.** Treating people differently because they are members of a protected class is a violation of the federal fair housing laws. There is, however, an exemption covering rentals if the rooms or units are in an owner-occupied, one-family to four-family dwelling. (7–I)

19. **2.** In the event of a conflict between a building code and a deed restriction, the more restrictive of the two will prevail. (11–VI)

20. **4.** Your brother's interest is a life estate because it is limited to your brother's life. A reversion would exist only if the land reverted to you. A base fee may be inherited. Curtesy refers to the life estate of a husband. (4–IV)

21. **4.** (11–V)

22. **2.** A broker employed to sell an owner's home would be a special agent. Cooperating brokers under a multiple-listing service (MLS) would be subagents. Dual agency occurs when a broker represents both the seller and the buyer in a transaction. (5–I)

23. **4.** Sexual orientation is not a protected class under the federal fair housing law. (7–I)

24. **3.** The fiduciary relationship was discussed in 5–I.

25. **4.** A salesperson may accept financial compensation for completing a real estate transaction only from her employing broker. (5–II)

26. **2.** This is clearly a case of intentional misrepresentation. (5–I)

27. **3.** The fact that you own a defeasible fee estate does not affect the vendee's interest of equitable title in the estate. (6–XII)

28. **2.** $183,000 sales price × 7% commission

$183,000 × 0.07 = $12,810 × 0.30 = $3.843 (8)

29. **4.** The broker has a fiduciary responsibility to the seller, which requires that she disclose her fair opinion of value to the principal. (5–I)

30. **4.** The fee for the option right belongs to the owner (optionor) regardless of the outcome of the transaction. (6–XI)

31. **4.** Persons who have AIDS are protected under the federal fair housing law. (7–I)

32. **4.** Religion is a protected class under the federal fair housing law. (7–I)

33. **1.** The exclusive-right-to-sell listing was discussed in 6–VII.

34. **3.** $80,000 (first investor) + $50,000 (second investor) = $130,000

$250,000 – $130,000 = $120,000, third investor's contribution

$$\frac{\text{part}}{\text{total}} = \text{percent}$$

$120,000 ÷ $250,000 = 0.48 or 48% (8)

35. **3.** $50,000 gross income – $12,000 expenses = $38,000 net annual income

$38,000 net annual income ÷ 14% capitalization rate =

$38,000 ÷ 0.14 = $271,429, value of real estate (8)

36. **1.** The various types of buyer agency agreements are discussed in 6–VII.

37. **4.** A fee simple is a real property interest, while a legal life estate is a spouse's estate in all inheritable real estate of the deceased spouse. Tenancy by the entirety is a unit form of ownership in which the owners must be husband and wife. (4–V)

38. **2.** $143,000 × 80% (0.80) = $114,400 assessed value

Divided by 100 because tax rate is stated per $100

$114,400 ÷ 100 = $1,144

$1,144 × $3.65 = $4,175.60 annual taxes

Divide by 12 to get monthly taxes

$4,175.60 ÷ 12 = $347.96

39. **1.** Deficiency judgments may be obtained for any deficiency. (10–VI)

40. **2.** *Down zoning* refers to a situation where the zoning for a parcel of land is changed from a dense to a less-dense usage. The planning commission cannot close the retail store. A nonconforming use generally is removed if it suffers 50 percent or more damage. A buffer zone is a land area that separates one land use from another. (11–II)

41. **2.** The exclusive agency listing was discussed in 6–VII.

42. **4.** The principle of regression states that the value of the better property is affected adversely by the presence of the lesser quality properties. (9–III)

43. **2.** Discount points usually are charged by and paid to the lender when the FHA interest rate is less than the conventional, or market, rate of interest. (10–VII)

44. **3.** Business plans are discussed in 12–III.

45. **2.** Bank deposits are insured by BIF, while savings and loan deposits are insured by SAIF. The U.S. Treasury is the nation's banker and fiscal manager. (10–IX)

46. **4.** Add the desired net, $18,000, plus the existing loan payoff, $104,600, and the closing costs, $5,200. $127,800 is the minimum that the seller must receive.

    If the selling price is 100 percent and the commission is 6 percent, the net to seller is 94 percent.

    $127,800 is 94 percent of the selling price.

    Therefore, $127,800 divided by 94% (.94) equals the selling price of $135,957, which is not one of the options. (8)

47. **2.** Buyer brokerage is discussed in 5–I.

48. **2.** An amortized mortgage includes monthly payment of principal and interest. A partially amortized mortgage includes payment of principal and interest with a balloon payment. (10–IV)

49. **2.** $192,900 sales price × 6% commission =

    $192,900 × 0.06 = $11,574 broker's commission

    $11,574 × 60% = $6,944.40 × .05 = $3,472.20, selling salesperson's commission (8)

50. **4.** A broker may not offer legal advice; only a licensed attorney may do so. (5–I)

51. **3.** The broker owes a fiduciary duty to the principal that includes loyalty. (5–I)

52. **4.** Regulation Z was discussed in 7–III.

53. **1.** Each buyer in a cooperative becomes a shareholder and receives a proprietary lease. (4–V)

54. **2.** The cooperating brokers were subagents of the seller. (5–I)

55. **2.** An amendment changes the language of a contract, while an addendum adds additional terms. (6–XIII)

56. **4.** Functional obsolescence and physical deterioration are losses in value that occur within the property, while economic obsolescence occurs outside the property. The principle of regression was discussed above. (9–IV)

57. **3.** Scarcity, situs and improvements are economic characteristics of land. (4–I)

58. **3.** $3,940 ÷ 0.035 = $112,571 assessed value

$112,571 ÷ 40% = $112,571 ÷ 0.40 = $281,429 market value (8)

59. **3.** An easement in gross does not have a dominant tenement. (4–III)

60. **4.** (12–I)

61. **2.** $946.86 ($129,000 × 7.34) (8)

62. **3.** $946.86 × 360 months = $340,869.60   Total P&I

$129,000.00   Loan

$211,869.60   Total interest (8)

63. **2.** Owners in joint tenancy do not have to be related. (4–V)

64. **2.** Community property is discussed in 4–V.

65. **2.** $300,000 annual overhead ÷ 24 (12 desks × 2 salespeople each) = $12,500 desk cost (12–VI)

66. **4.** Management styles are discussed in 12–IV.

67. **2.** Personal assistants are discussed in 12–IV.

68. **1.** Limited liability companies are discussed in 12–I.

69. **4.** Add the desired net, $26,000, plus the existing loan payoff, $119,600, and the closing costs, $5,000. $150,600 is the minimum that the seller must receive.

If the selling price is 100 percent and the commission is 6 percent, the net to seller is 94 percent.

$150,600 is 94 percent of the selling price.

Therefore, $150,600 divided by 94% (.94) equals the selling price of $160,212.76, which is not one of the options. (8)

70. **4.** The Residential Lead-Based Paint Hazard Reduction Act is discussed in 11–V.

71. **2.** $526.49 × 12 = $6,317.88 annual interest

part ÷ percent = total

$6,317.88 ÷ 8% (0.08) = $78,973.50 (8)

72. **4.** Cooperatives and condominiums are discussed in 4–V.

73. **2.** The broker is the agent of the seller. The salesperson is the agent of the broker and subagent (not agent) of the seller. (5–I)

74. **2.** Familial status was added in 1988. (7–I)

75. **4.** Appraisal ethics are discussed in 9–VII.

76. **4.** Escheat will apply only if the owner dies and leaves no heirs or no will disposing of the real estate or when the property is abandoned. (4–VI)

77. **3.** Mortgagees have a fiduciary relationship with investors who place money in their lending institutions. (5–I)

78. **4.** Tenancy by the entirety is a unit ownership of the property. (4–V)

79. **4.** The cobroker is a subagent of the seller. A broker need not be the seller's agent to receive part of the commission. (5–I)

80. **3.** Brokers are not allowed to earn interest on earnest money deposits. (5–I)

81. **2.** An independent contractor works under limited supervision from the broker. (12–II)

82. **3.** Methods of keeping financial records are discussed in 12–IV.

83. **2.** Familial status, race, and religion are protected classes under the federal fair housing law. (7–I)

84. **4.** Regulation Z is discussed in 7–III.

85. **3.** A net listing is based on the amount of money the seller will receive if the property is sold. In an open listing, the seller retains the right to employ any number of brokers to act as his or her agents. In an exclusive-right-to-sell listing, the seller gives up the right to sell the property himself or herself and thus avoid paying the broker's commission. (6–VII)

86. **4.** The federal fair housing law exempts the rental of units in an owner-occupied one-family to four-family dwelling. (7–I)

87. **3.** The ADA is discussed in 7–II.

88. **2.** A periodic estate is a lease for an indefinite period of time without a specific expiration date; notice must be given to terminate. (4–V)

89. **3.** The ADA is discussed in 7–II.

90. **1.** Double taxation is a disadvantage of a corporation. (12–I)

91. **2.** This is an example of the type of alteration that might be made to public facilities and services. (7–II)

92. **4.** Physical deterioration would reflect loss in value because of wear and tear, for example, a leaky roof. (9–IV)

93. **4.** The budgeting process is discussed in 12–VI.

94. **4.** The grantee does not sign a warranty deed. (4–VIII)

95. **3.** (7–II)

96. **4.** (7–I)

97. **2.** Fixtures are classified as real property. (4–I)

98. **3.** The other answers are examples of locational obsolescence. (9–III)

99. **4.** The open listing is least beneficial to the broker. (6–VII)

100. **3.** The formula for the capitalization rate is discussed in 9–IV.

GLOSSARY

abandonment The voluntary and permanent cessation of use or enjoyment with no intention to resume or reclaim one's possession or interest. May pertain to an easement of a property.

abstract of title A condensed version of the history of a title to a particular parcel of real estate as recorded in the county clerk's records; consists of a summary of the original grant and all subsequent conveyances and encumbrances affecting the property.

abutting The joining, reaching or touching of adjoining land. Abutting parcels of land have a common boundary.

accelerated depreciation A method of calculating for tax purposes the depreciation of income property at a faster rate than would be achieved using the straight-line method. Note that any depreciation taken in excess of what would be claimed using the straight-line rate is subject to **recapture** as ordinary income to the extent of the gain resulting from the sale. *See also STRAIGHT-LINE METHOD.*

acceleration clause A provision in a written mortgage, note, bond or conditional sales contract that in the event of default, the whole amount of the principal and the interest may be declared due and payable at once.

accretion An increase or addition to land by the deposit of sand or soil washed up naturally from a river, lake or sea.

accrued depreciation The actual depreciation that has occurred to a property at any given date; the difference between the cost of replacement new (as of the date of the appraisal) and the present appraised value.

acknowledgment A declaration made by a person to a notary public or other public official authorized to take acknowledgments that an instrument was executed by him or her as a free and voluntary act.

actual eviction The result of legal action originated by a lessor, by which a defaulted tenant is physically ousted from the rented property pursuant to a court order. *See also EVICTION.*

actual notice Express information or fact; that which is known; actual knowledge.

administrator The party appointed by the county court to settle the estate of a deceased person who died without leaving a will.

ad valorem tax A tax levied according to value; generally used to refer to real estate tax. Also called **general tax.**

adverse possession The actual, visible, hostile, notorious, exclusive and continuous possession of another's land under a claim to title. Possession for a statutory period may be a means of acquiring title.

affidavit A written statement signed and sworn to before a person authorized to administer an oath.

agent   One who represents or has the power to act for another person (called the principal). The authorization may be express, implied or apparent. A fiduciary relationship is created under the **law of agency** when a property owner, as the principal, executes a listing agreement or management contract authorizing a licensed real estate broker to be her or his agent.

agreement of sale   A written agreement by which the purchaser agrees to buy certain real estate and the seller agrees to sell, on the terms and conditions set forth in the agreement.

air lot   A designated airspace over a piece of land. Air lots, like surface property, may be transferred.

air rights   The right to use the open space above a property, generally allowing the surface to be used for another purpose.

alienation   The act of transferring property to another. Alienation may be voluntary, such as by gift or sale, or involuntary, such as through eminent domain or adverse possession.

alienation clause (due-on-sale clause)   The clause in a mortgage or deed of trust that states that the balance of the secured debt becomes immediately due and payable at the mortgagee's option if the title is transferred or the property is sold. In effect, this clause prevents the mortgagor from assigning the debt without the mortgagee's approval.

alluvion   The actual soil increase resulting from accretion.

amenities   The tangible and intangible features that increase the value or desirability of real estate.

Americans with Disabilities Act (ADA)   A federal law, effective in 1992, designed to elimnate discrimination against individuals with disabilities.

amortization   The liquidation of a financial burden by installment payments, which include principal and interest.

amortized loan   A loan in which the principal and interest are payable in monthly or other periodic installments over the term of the loan.

antitrust laws   The laws designed to preserve the free enterprise of the open marketplace by making illegal certain private conspiracies and combinations formed to minimize competition. Violation of antitrust laws in the real estate business generally involves either **price fixing** (brokers conspiring to set fixed compensation rates) or allocation of customers or markets (brokers agreeing to limit their trades or dealings to certain areas or properties).

appraisal   An estimate of the quantity, quality or value of something. The process through which conclusions about property value are obtained; also refers to the report that sets forth the process of estimation and conclusion of value.

appraised value   An estimate of a property's present worth.

appreciation   An increase in the worth or value of a property, due to economic or related causes, which may prove to be either temporary or permanent; opposite of depreciation.

appurtenant   Belonging to; incident to; annexed to. For example, a garage is appurtenant to a house, and the common interest in the common elements of a condominium is appurtenant to each apartment. Appurtenances pass with the land when the property is transferred.

arbitration   A means of settling a controversy between two parties through the medium of an impartial third party whose decision on the controversy (if agreed upon) will be final and binding.

assessment   The imposition of a tax, charge or levy, usually according to established rates.

assignment   The transfer in writing of rights or interest in a bond, mortgage, lease or other instrument.

assumed name statute (fictitious name statute)   The law, in effect in most states, that stipulates that no person shall conduct a business under any name other than his or her own individual name, unless such person files the desired name with the county clerk in each county where the business is conducted. In the case of brokers and salespeople, statement of such filing should be submitted to the state's real estate commission.

assumption of mortgage   The transfer of title to property to a grantee, by which the grantee assumes liability for payment of an existing note secured by a mortgage against the property. Should the mortgage be foreclosed and the property sold for a lesser amount than that due, the grantee/purchaser who has assumed and agreed to pay the debt secured by the mortgage is personally liable for the deficiency. Before a seller may be relieved of liability under the existing mortgage, the lender must accept the transfer of liability for payment of the note.

attachment   The method by which a debtor's property is placed in the custody of the law and held as security, pending the outcome of a creditor's suit.

attorney-in-fact   The holder of a power of attorney.

attorney's opinion of title   An instrument written and signed by the attorney who examines the title, stating her or his opinion as to whether a seller may convey good title.

automatic extension   A clause in a listing agreement that states that the agreement will continue automatically for a certain time period after its expiration date. In many states, use of this clause is discouraged or prohibited.

avulsion   A sudden tearing away of land by the action of natural forces.

balloon payment   The final payment of a mortgage loan that is considerably larger than the required periodic payments because the loan amount was not fully amortized.

bargain and sale deed   A deed that carries with it no warranties against liens or other encumbrances but that does imply the grantor has the right to convey title. Note that the grantor may add warranties to the deed at his or her discretion.

base fee   A determinable fee estate that may be inherited.

base line   One of a set of imaginary lines running east and west and crossing a principal meridian at a definite point. Base lines are used by surveyors for reference in locating and describing land under the rectangular survey system (or government survey method) of property description.

benchmark   A permanent reference mark or point established for use by surveyors when measuring differences in elevation.

beneficiary   1. The person for whom a trust operates or in whose behalf the income from a trust estate is drawn. 2. A lender who lends money on real estate and takes back a note and deed of trust from the borrower.

bequest   A provision in a will providing for the distribution of personal property.

bilateral contract   A contract in which each party promises to perform an act in exchange for the other party's promise to perform.

bill of sale   A written instrument given to pass title to personal property.

binder   An agreement that may accompany an earnest money deposit for the purchase of real property as evidence of the purchaser's good faith and intent to complete the transaction.

blanket mortgage   A mortgage that covers more than one parcel of real estate and provides for each parcel's partial release from the mortgage lien on repayment of a definite portion of the debt.

blockbusting   The illegal practice of inducing homeowners to sell their properties by making representations regarding the entry or prospective entry of minority persons into the neighborhood.

blue-sky laws The common name for state and federal laws that regulate the registration and sale of investment securities.

boycotting Two or more businesses conspire against other businesses to reduce competition.

branch office A secondary place of business apart from the principal or main office from which real estate business is conducted. A branch office generally must be run by a licensed real estate broker, broker salesperson or associate broker working on behalf of the broker operating the principal office.

breach of contract The failure, without legal excuse, of one of the parties to a contract to perform according to the contract.

broker One who buys and sells for another for a commission. *See also REAL ESTATE BROKER.*

brokerage The business of buying and selling for another for a commission.

broker/salesperson A person who has passed the broker's licensing examination but is licensed to work only on behalf of a licensed broker and who may be allowed to manage an office. In many states, known as (licensed as) associate broker or broker/associate.

budget loan A loan in which the monthly payments made by the borrower cover not only interest and a payment on the principal but also $1/12$ of such expenses as taxes, insurance, assessments, private mortgage insurance premiums and similar charges.

buffer zone A strip of land that separates one land use from another.

building code An ordinance specifying minimum standards of construction of buildings for the protection of public safety and health.

building line A line fixed at a certain distance from the front and/or sides of a lot beyond which no structure can project; a setback line used to ensure a degree of uniformity in the appearance of buildings and unobstructed light, air and view.

building restrictions The limitations on the size or type of property improvements established by zoning acts or by deed or lease restrictions. Building restrictions are considered encumbrances, and violations render the title unmarketable.

bundle of legal rights The theory that land ownership involves ownership of all legal rights to the land, such as possession, control within the law and enjoyment, rather than ownership of the land itself.

business plan a three-year to five-year blueprint for an organizational or individual real estate practitioner.

canvassing The practice of making telephone calls or visiting from door to door to seek prospective buyers or sellers; in the real estate business, generally associated with acquired listings in a given area.

capacity of parties The legal ability of persons to enter into a valid contract. Most persons have full capacity to contract and are said to be **competent parties.**

capital gain Profit earned from the sale of an asset.

capital investment The initial capital and the long-term expenditures made to establish and maintain a business or investment property.

capitalization The process of converting into present value (or obtaining the present worth of) a series of anticipated future periodic installments of net income. In real estate appraisal, it usually takes the form of discounting. The formula is expressed as

$$\frac{\text{income}}{\text{rate}} = \text{value}$$

capitalization rate The rate of return a property will produce on the owner's investment.

cash flow The net spendable income from an investment, determined by deducting all operating and fixed expenses from the gross income. If expenses exceed income, a negative cash flow is the result.

casualty insurance A type of insurance policy that protects a property owner or other person from loss or injury sustained as a result of theft, vandalism or similar occurrences.

caveat emptor A Latin phrase meaning "Let the buyer beware."

certificate of sale The document generally given to a purchaser at a tax foreclosure sale. A certificate of sale does not convey title; generally, it is an instrument certifying that the holder may receive title to the property after the redemption period has passed and that the holder paid the property taxes for that interim period.

certificate of title The statement of opinion on the status of the title to a parcel of real property, based on an examination of specified public records.

chain of title The succession of conveyances from some accepted starting point by which the present holder of real property derives her or his title.

chattels Personal property.

city planning commission A local governmental organization designed to direct and control the development of land within a municipality.

cloud on title A claim or encumbrance that may affect the title to land.

codicil A testamentary disposition subsequent to a will that alters, explains, adds to or confirms the will, but does not revoke it.

coinsurance clause A clause in insurance policies covering real property that requires the policyholder to maintain fire insurance coverage generally equal to at least 80 percent of the property's actual replacement cost.

collateral Something of value given or pledged to a lender as a security for a debt or obligation.

commercial property A classification of real estate that includes income-producing property such as office buildings, restaurants, shopping centers, hotels and stores.

commingled property Property of a married couple that is so mixed or commingled that it is difficult to determine whether it is separate or community property. Commingled property becomes community property.

commingling The illegal act of a real estate broker who mixes the money of other people with that of his or her own; brokers are required by law to maintain a separate trust account for other parties' funds held temporarily by the broker.

commission The payment made to a broker for services rendered, such as in the sale or purchase of real property; usually a percentage of the selling price of the property.

common elements The parts of a property that are necessary or convenient to the existence, maintenance and safety of a condominium or that are normally in common use by all of the condominium residents. All condominium owners have an undivided ownership interest in the common elements.

common law A body of law based on custom, usage and court decisions.

community property A system of property ownership based on the theory that each spouse has an equal interest in the property acquired by the efforts of either spouse during marriage.

comparables The properties listed in an appraisal report that are substantially equivalent to the subject property.

competent parties Persons who are recognized by law as being able to contract with others; usually those of legal age and sound mind. *See also CAPACITY OF PARTIES.*

composite depreciation A method of determining the depreciation of a multibuilding property using the average rate at which all the buildings are depreciating.

condemnation   A judicial or administrative proceeding or process to exercise the power of **eminent domain.**

condominium   The absolute ownership of an apartment or a unit, generally in a multiunit building, based on a legal description of the airspace the unit actually occupies, plus an undivided interest in the ownership of the common elements, which are owned together with the other condominium unit owners. The entire tract of real estate included in a condominium development is called a *parcel* or *development parcel.* One apartment or space in a condominium or a part of a property intended for independent use and having lawful access to the public way is called a unit. Ownership of one unit also includes a definite undivided interest in the common elements.

conformity   *See PRINCIPLE OF CONFORMITY.*

consideration   Something of value that induces one to enter into a contract. Consideration may be "valuable" (money or commodity) or "good" (love and affection). Also, an act of forbearance, or the promise thereof, given by one party in exchange for something from the other. Forbearance is a promise *not* to do something.

constructive eviction   1. Acts by the landlord that so materially disturb or impair the tenant's enjoyment of the leased premises that the tenant is effectively forced to move out and terminate the lease without liability for any further rent. 2. A purchaser's inability to obtain clear title.

constructive notice   Notice given to the world by recorded documents. All persons are charged with knowledge of such documents and their contents, whether or not they have actually examined them. Possession of property also is considered constructive notice that the person in possession has an interest in the property.

contract   An agreement entered into by two or more legally competent parties by the terms of which one or more of the parties, for a consideration, undertakes to do or to refrain from doing some legal act or acts. A contract may be either **unilateral,** where only one party is bound to act, or **bilateral,** where all parties to the instrument are legally bound to act as prescribed.

contract for deed   A contract for the sale of real estate under which the sale price is paid in periodic installments by the purchaser, who is in possession and holds equitable title although actual title is retained by the seller until final payment. Also called an **installment contract** or **land contract.**

contract for exchange of real estate   A contract for sale of real estate in which the consideration is paid wholly or partly in property.

conventional loan   A loan that is not insured or guaranteed by a government agency.

conveyance   A written instrument that evidences transfer of some interest in real property from one person to another.

cooperative   A residential multiunit building whose title is held by a trust or corporation that is owned by and operated for the benefit of persons living within the building. These persons are the beneficial owners of the trust or the shareholders of the corporation, each having a proprietary lease.

corporation   An entity or organization created by operation of law whose rights of doing business are essentially the same as those of an individual. The entity has continuous existence until dissolved according to legal procedures.

correction lines   The provisions in the rectangular survey system (government survey method) made to compensate for the curvature of the earth's surface. Every fourth township line (at 24-mile intervals) is used as a correction line on which the intervals between the north and south range lines are remeasured and corrected to a full six miles.

cost approach   The process of estimating the value of a property by adding the appraiser's estimate of the reproduction or replacement cost of the building, less depreciation, to the estimated land value.

counseling The business of providing people with expert advice on a subject, based on the counselor's extensive, expert knowledge of the subject.

counteroffer A new offer made as a reply to an offer received, having the effect of rejecting the original offer. The original offer cannot be accepted thereafter unless revived by the offeror's repeating it.

cul-de-sac A dead-end street that widens sufficiently at the end to permit an automobile to make a U-turn.

curtesy A life estate, usually a fractional interest, given by some states to the surviving husband in real estate owned by his deceased wife. Most states have abolished curtesy.

cycle A recurring sequence of events that regularly follow one another, generally within a fixed interval of time.

datum A horizontal plane from which heights and depths are measured.

dba Doing business as.

debenture A note or bond given as evidence of debt and issued without security.

debt Something owed to another; an obligation to pay or return something.

declining balance method An accounting method of calculating depreciation for tax purposes designed to provide large deductions in the early years of ownership. *See also ACCELERATED DEPRECIATION.*

decreasing returns *See DIMINISHING RETURNS.*

deed A written instrument that when executed and delivered conveys title to or an interest in real estate.

deed of reconveyance The instrument used to reconvey title to a trustor under a deed of trust once the debt has been satisfied.

deed of trust An instrument used to create a mortgage lien by which the mortgagor conveys her or his title to a trustee, who holds it as security for the benefit of the note holder (the lender); also called a **trust deed.**

deed restrictions The clauses in a deed limiting the future uses of the property. Deed restrictions may impose a variety of limitations and conditions, such as limiting the density of buildings, dictating the types of structures that can be erected and preventing buildings from being used for specific purposes or from being used at all.

default The nonperformance of a duty, whether arising under a contract or otherwise; failure to meet an obligation when due.

defeasance clause A clause used in leases or mortgages that cancels a specified right on the occurrence of a certain condition, such as cancellation of a mortgage on repayment of the mortgage loan.

deficiency judgment A personal judgment levied against the mortgagor when a foreclosure sale does not produce sufficient funds to pay the mortgage debt in full.

delinquent taxes Unpaid taxes that are past due.

delivery The legal act of transferring ownership. Documents such as deeds and mortgages must be delivered and accepted to be valid.

delivery in escrow Delivery of a deed to a third person until the performance of some act or condition by one of the parties.

demand The willingness of persons to buy available goods at a given price; often coupled with **supply.**

density zoning The zoning ordinances that restrict the average maximum number of houses per acre that may be built within a particular area, generally a subdivision.

depreciation 1. In appraisal, a loss of value in property due to all causes, including physical deterioration, functional obsolescence and economic obsolescence. 2. In real estate investment, an expense deduction for tax purposes taken over the period of ownership of the income property.

descent   The hereditary succession of an heir to the property of a relative who dies intestate.

determinable fee estate   A fee simple estate in which the property automatically reverts to the grantor on the occurrence of a specified event or condition.

devise   A transfer of real estate by will or last testament. The donor is the devisor and the recipient is the devisee.

diminishing returns   The principle that applies when a given parcel of land reaches its maximum percentage return on investment and further expenditures for improving the property yield a decreasing return.

discount points   An added loan fee charged by a lender to make the yield on a lower-than-market-value loan competitive with higher-interest loans. *See also POINT.*

discount rate   The rate of interest a commercial bank must pay when it borrows from its federal reserve bank. Consequently, the discount rate is the rate of interest the banking system carries within its own framework. Member banks may take certain promissory notes that they have received from customers and sell them to their district federal reserve bank for less than face value. With the funds received, the banks can make further loans. Changes in the discount rate may cause banks and other lenders to reexamine credit policies and conditions.

dispossess   To oust from land by legal process.

dominant tenement   A property that includes in its ownership the appurtenant right to use an easement over another's property for a specific purpose.

dower   The legal right or interest recognized in some states that a wife acquires in the property her husband held or acquired during their marriage. During the lifetime of the husband, the right is only a possibility of an interest; on his death it can become an interest in land.

duress   The use of unlawful constraint that forces action or inaction against a person's will.

DVA loan   A mortgage loan on approved property made to a qualified veteran by an authorized lender and guaranteed by the Department of Veterans Affairs to limit possible loss by the lender. Also called a **GI-guaranteed mortgage.**

earnest money deposit   An amount of money deposited by a buyer under the terms of a contract.

easement   A right to use the land of another for a specific purpose, such as for a right-of-way or utilities; an incorporeal interest in land. An easement appurtenant passes with the land when conveyed.

easement by necessity   An easement allowed by law as necessary for the full enjoyment of a parcel of real estate; for example, a right of ingress and egress over a grantor's land.

easement by prescription   An easement acquired by continuous, open, uninterrupted, exclusive and adverse use of the property for the period of time prescribed by state law.

easement in gross   An easement that is not created for the benefit of any land owned by the owner of the easement but that attaches personally to the easement owner. For example, the right to an easement granted by *A* to *B* to use a portion of *A*'s property for the rest of *B*'s life would be an easement in gross.

economic life   The period of time over which an improved property will earn an income adequate to justify its continued existence.

economic obsolescence   The impairment of desirability or useful life arising from factors external to the property, such as economic forces or environmental changes, that affect supply-demand relationships in the market. Loss in the use and value of a property arising from the factors of economic obsolescence is to be distinguished from loss in value from physical deterioration and functional obsolescence, both of which are inherent in the property. Also referred to as locational obsolescence or environmental obsolescence.

emblements Growing crops that are produced annually through the tenant's own care and labor and that she or he is entitled to take away after the tenancy is ended. Emblements are regarded as personal property even prior to harvest, so if the landlord terminates the lease, the tenant still may reenter the land and remove such crops. If the tenant terminates the tenancy voluntarily, however, he or she generally is not entitled to the emblements.

eminent domain The right of a government or municipal quasi-public body to acquire property for public use through a court action called **condemnation,** in which the court determines that the use is a public use and determines the price or compensation to be paid to the owner.

employee status The status of one who works as a direct employee of an employer. An employer is obligated to withhold income taxes and Social Security taxes from the compensation of his or her employees. *See also INDEPENDENT CONTRACTOR.*

employment contract A document evidencing formal employment between the employer and the employee or between the principal and the agent. In the real estate business, this generally takes the form of a listing or management agreement.

encroachment A fixture or structure, such as a wall or fence, that invades a portion of a property belonging to another.

encumbrance Any lien—such as a mortgage, tax or judgment lien; easement; restriction on the use of the land; or an outstanding dower right—that may diminish the value of the property.

endorsement The act of writing one's name, either with or without additional words, on a negotiable instrument or on a paper attached to such instrument.

equalization The raising or lowering of assessed values for tax purposes in a particular county or taxing district to make them equal to assessments in other counties or districts.

equitable title The interest held by a vendee under a contract for deed or an installment contract; the equitable right to obtain absolute ownership to property when legal title is held in another's name.

equity The interest or value that an owner has in a property over and above any mortgage indebtedness.

erosion The gradual wearing away of land by water, wind and general weather conditions; the diminishing of property caused by the elements.

escheat The reversion of property to the state in the event its owner dies without leaving a will and has no heirs to whom the property may pass by lawful descent.

escrow The closing of a transaction through a third party called an escrow agent, or *escrowee,* who receives certain funds and documents to be delivered on the performance of certain conditions in the escrow agreement.

estate for years An interest for a certain, exact period of time in property leased for a specified consideration.

estate in land The degree, quantity, nature and extent of interest that a person has in real property.

estate in severalty An estate owned by one person.

estoppel certificate A legal instrument executed by a mortgagor showing the amount of the unpaid balance due on a mortgage and stating that the mortgagor has no defenses or offsets against the mortgagee at the time of execution of the certificate. Also called a *certificate of no defense.*

estovers Legally allowed necessities such as the right of a tenant to use timber on leased property to support a minimum need for fuel or repairs.

ethical   Conforming to professional standards of conduct.

et ux   The Latin abbreviation for *et uxor,* meaning "and wife."

eviction   A legal process to oust a person from possession of real estate.

evidence of title   A proof of ownership of property, which is commonly a certificate of title, a title insurance policy, an abstract of title with lawyer's opinion or a Torrens registration certificate. *See also TORRENS SYSTEM.*

exchange   A transaction in which all or part of the consideration for the purchase of real property is the transfer of like-kind property (that is, real estate for real estate).

exclusive-agency listing   A listing contract under which the owner appoints a real estate broker as his or her exclusive agent for a designated period of time to sell the property on the owner's stated terms for a commission. The owner, however, reserves the right to sell without paying anyone a commission by selling to a prospect who has not been introduced or claimed by the broker.

exclusive-right-to-sell listing   A listing contract under which the owner appoints a real estate broker as his or her exclusive agent for a designated period of time to sell the property on the owner's stated terms and agrees to pay the broker a commission when the property is sold, whether by the broker, the owner or another broker.

executed contract   A contract in which all parties have fulfilled their promises and thus performed the contract.

execution   The signing and delivery of an instrument. Also, a legal order directing an official to enforce a judgment against the property of a debtor.

executor   The male person designated in a will to handle the state of the deceased. The probate court must approve any sale of property by the executor. A female is called the *executrix.*

executory contract   A contract under which something remains to be done by one or more of the parties.

expenses   The short-term costs that are deducted from an investment property's income, such as minor repairs, regular maintenance and renting costs.

expressed contract   An oral or written contract in which the parties state its terms and express their intentions in words.

Fair Housing Act of 1968   The term for Title VIII of the Civil Rights Act of 1968 as amended, which prohibits discrimination based on race, color, sex, religion, national origin, handicaps and familial status in the sale and rental of residential property.

Federal Home Loan Mortgage Corporation (FHLMC)   A federally chartered corporation created to provide a secondary mortgage market for conventional loans (Freddie Mac).

Federal Housing Administration (FHA)   A federal administrative body created by the National Housing Act in 1934 to encourage improvement in housing standards and conditions, to provide an adequate home-financing system through the insurance of housing mortgages and credit, and to exert a stabilizing influence on the mortgage market.

federal income tax   An annual tax based on income, including monies derived from the lease, use or operation of real estate.

Federal National Mortgage Association (FNMA)   "Fannie Mae" is the popular name for this federally chartered corporation, which creates a secondary market for existing mortgages. FNMA does not loan money directly, but rather buys DVA, FHA and conventional loans.

fee simple estate   The maximum possible estate or right of ownership of real property continuing forever. Sometimes called a *fee* or *fee simple absolute.*

FHA appraisal   An FHA evaluation of a property as security for a loan. Includes the study of the physical characteristics of the property and surroundings, and the location of the property.

FHA loan   A loan insured by the FHA and made by an approved lender in accordance with FHA regulations.

fiduciary relationship   A relationship of trust and confidence, as between trustee and beneficiary, attorney and client, principal and agent.

financing statement   *See UNIFORM COMMERCIAL CODE.*

first mortgage   A mortgage that creates a superior voluntary lien on the property mortgaged relative to other charges or encumbrances against the property.

fiscal policy   The government's policy in regard to taxation and spending programs. The balance between these two areas determines the amount of money the government will withdraw or feed into the economy in an attempt to counter economic peaks and slumps.

fixture   An article that was once personal property but has been so affixed to real estate that it has become real property.

forcible entry and detainer   A summary proceeding for restoring to possession of land one who is wrongfully kept out or has been wrongfully deprived of the possession.

foreclosure   A legal procedure by which property used as security for a debt is sold to satisfy the debt in the event of default in payment of the mortgage note or default of other terms in the mortgage document. The foreclosure procedure brings the rights of all parties to a conclusion and passes the title in the mortgaged property either to the holder of the mortgage or to a third party who may purchase the realty at the foreclosure sale, free of all encumbrances affecting the property subsequent to the mortgage.

foreign acknowledgment   An acknowledgment taken outside of the state in which the land lies.

franchise   A private contractual agreement to run a business using a designated trade name and operating procedures.

fraud   A misstatement of a material fact made with intent to deceive or made with reckless disregard of the truth and that actually does deceive.

freehold estate   An estate in land in which ownership is for an indeterminate length of time, in contrast to a **leasehold estate.**

functional obsolescence   The impairment of functional capacity or efficiency. Functional obsolescence reflects the loss in value brought about by factors that affect the property, such as overcapacity, inadequacy or changes in the art. The inability of a structure to perform adequately the function for which it currently is employed.

future interest   A person's present right to an interest in real property that will not result in possession or enjoyment until some time in the future, such as a **reversion** or right of reentry.

gap   A defect in the chain of title of a particular parcel of real estate; a missing document or conveyance that raises doubt as to the present ownership of the land.

general contractor   A construction specialist who enters into a formal construction contract with a landowner or master lessee to construct a real estate building or project. The general contractor often contracts with several **subcontractors** specializing in various aspects of the building process to perform individual jobs.

general lien   A lien on all real and personal property owned by a debtor.

general partnership   *See PARTNERSHIP.*

general tax   *See AD VALOREM TAX.*

general warranty deed   A deed that states that the title conveyed therein is good from the sovereignty of the soil to the grantee therein and that no one else can successfully claim the property. This type of deed contains several specific warranties sometimes referred to as the English Covenants of Title.

GI-guaranteed mortgage   *See DVA LOAN.*

government lots   Fractional sections in the rectangular survey system (government survey method) that are less than one full quarter-section in area.

Government National Mortgage Association (GNMA)   "Ginnie Mae," a federal agency and division of HUD that operates special assistance aspects of federally aided housing programs and participates in the secondary market through its mortgage-backed securities pools.

graduated lease   Lease that provides for rent increases at set future dates.

graduated payment mortgage   A mortgage loan for which the initial payments are low but increase over the life of the loan.

grant   The act of conveying or transferring title to real property.

grant deed   A type of deed that includes three basic warranties: (1) the owner warrants that she or he has the right to convey the property; (2) the owner warrants that the property is not encumbered other than with those encumbrances listed in the deed; and (3) the owner promises to convey any after-acquired title to the property. Grant deeds are popular in states that rely heavily on title insurance.

grantee   A person to whom real estate is conveyed; the buyer.

grantor   A person who conveys real estate by deed; the seller.

gross lease   A lease or property under which a landlord pays all property charges regularly incurred through ownership, such as repairs, taxes, insurance and operating expenses. Most residential leases are gross leases.

gross national product   The total value of all goods and services produced in the United States in a year.

gross rent multiplier   A figure used as a multiplier of the gross monthly rental income of a property to produce an estimate of the property's value.

ground lease   A lease of land only, on which the tenant usually owns a building or is required to build her or his own building as specified in the lease. Such leases are usually long-term net leases; a tenant's rights and obligations continue until the lease expires or is terminated through default.

guaranteed sale plan   An agreement between the broker and the seller that if the seller's real property is not sold before a certain date, the broker will purchase it for a specified price.

guardian   One who guards or cares for another person's rights and properties. A guardian has legal custody of the affairs of a minor or a person incapable of taking care of his or her own interests, called a *ward*.

habendum clause   The deed clause beginning "to have and to hold," which defines or limits the extent of ownership in the estate granted by the deed.

heir   One who might inherit or succeed to an interest in land under the state law of descent when the owner dies without leaving a valid will.

hereditaments   Every kind of inheritable property, including personal, real corporeal and incorporeal.

highest and best use   The possible use of land that will produce the greatest net income and thus develop the highest land value.

holdover tenancy   A tenancy by which a lessee retains possession of leased property after her or his lease has expired and the landlord, by continuing to accept rent from the tenant, agrees to the tenant's continued occupancy as defined by state law.

holographic will   A will that is written, dated and signed in the handwriting of the maker.

homeowner's insurance policy A standardized package insurance policy that covers a residential real estate owner against financial loss from fire, theft, public liability and other common risks.

homeowner's warranty program An insurance program offered to buyers by some brokerages, warranting the property against certain defects for a specified period of time.

homestead The land and the improvements thereon designated by the owner as his or her homestead and, therefore, protected by state law, either in whole or in part, from forced sale by certain creditors of the owner.

HUD The Department of Housing and Urban Development; regulates FHA and GNMA.

hypothecation The pledge of property as security of a loan in which the borrower maintains possession of the property while it is pledged as security.

implied contract A contract under which the agreement of the parties is demonstrated by their acts and conduct.

implied grant A method of creating as easement. One party may be using another's property for the benefit of both parties, for example, a sewer on a property that serves two or more properties.

improvement 1. Improvements *on* land: any structure, usually privately owned, erected on a site to enhance the value of the property; for example, buildings, fences and driveways. 2. Improvements *to* land: usually a publicly owned structure, such as a curb, sidewalk or sewer.

inchoate right Incomplete right, such as a wife's dower interest in her husband's property during his life.

income approach The process of estimating the value of an income-producing property by capitalization of the annual net income expected to be produced by the property during its remaining useful life.

incorporeal right A nonpossessory right in real estate; for example, an **easement** or right-of-way.

increasing returns The principle that applies when increased expenditures for improvements to a given parcel of land yield an increasing percentage return on investment.

independent contractor One who is retained to perform a certain act but who is subject to the control and direction of another only as to the end result, and not as to how he or she performs the act. Unlike an employee, an independent contractor pays all of his or her expenses, pays his or her income and Social Security taxes and receives no employee benefits. Many real estate salespeople are independent contractors.

index lease Lease that allows the rent to be increased or decreased periodically, based on changes in a selected economic index, such as the Consumer Price Index.

industrial property All land and buildings used or suited for use in the production, storage or distribution of tangible goods.

installment contract See CONTRACT FOR DEED.

installment sale A method of reporting gain received from the sale of real estate when the sale price is paid in two or more installments over two or more years. If the sale meets certain requirements, a taxpayer can spread recognition of the reportable gain over more than one year, which may result in tax savings.

insurable title A title to land that a title company will insure.

insurance The indemnification against loss from a specific hazard or peril through a contract (called a policy) and for a consideration (called a premium).

interest A charge made by a lender for the use of money.

interim financing   A short-term loan usually made during the construction phase of a building project, often referred to as a *construction loan.*

intestate   The condition of a property owner who dies without leaving a will. Title to such property passes to his or her heirs as provided in the state law of descent.

invalid   Having no force or effect.

invalidate   To render null and void.

investment   Money directed toward the purchase, improvement and development of an asset in expectation of income or profits. A good financial investment has the following characteristics: safety, regularity of yield, marketability, acceptable denominations, valuable collateral, acceptable duration, required attention and potential appreciation.

joint tenancy   The ownership of real estate by two or more parties who have been named in one conveyance as joint tenants. On the death of a joint tenant, her or his interest passes to the surviving joint tenant or tenants by the right of survivorship.

joint venture   The joining of two or more people to conduct a specific business enterprise. A joint venture is *similar* to a partnership in that it must be created by agreement between the parties to share in the losses and profits of the venture. It is *unlike* a partnership in that the venture is for one specific project only, rather than for a continuing business relationship.

judgment   The official and authentic decision of a court on the respective rights and claims of the parties to an action or suit. When a judgment is entered and recorded with the county recorder, it usually becomes a general lien on the property of the defendant for a ten-year period.

judgment clause   A provision that may be included in notes, leases and contracts by which the debtor, lessee or obligor authorizes any attorney to go into court to confess a judgment against him or her for a default in payment. Also called a *cognovit.*

laches   An equitable doctrine used by the courts to bar a legal claim or prevent the assertion of a right because of undue delay, negligence or failure to assert the claim or right.

land   The earth's surface extending downward to the center of the earth and upward infinitely into space.

land contract   *See CONTRACT FOR DEED.*

law of agency   *See AGENT.*

lawyer's opinion of title   *See ATTORNEY'S OPINION OF TITLE.*

lease   A contract between a landlord (the lessor) and a tenant (the lessee) transferring the right to exclusive possession and use of the landlord's real property to the lessee for a specified period of time and for a stated consideration (rent). By state law, leases for longer than a certain period of time (generally one year) must be in writing to be enforceable.

leasehold estate   A tenant's right to occupy real estate during the term of a lease, generally considered to be a personal property interest.

legacy   A disposition of money or personal property by will.

legal description   A description of a specific parcel of real estate sufficient for an independent surveyor to locate and identify it. The most common forms of legal description are **rectangular survey, metes and bounds** and subdivision **lot and block (plat).**

legality of object   An element that must be present in a valid contract. All contracts that have for their object an act that violates the laws of the United States or the laws of a state to which the parties are subject are illegal, invalid and not recognized by the courts.

lessee   The tenant who leases a property.

lessor   One who leases property to a tenant.

leverage   The use of borrowed money to finance the bulk of an investment.

levy   To assess, seize or collect. To levy a tax is to assess a property and set the rate of taxation. To levy an execution is to seize officially the property of a person to satisfy an obligation.

license   1. A privilege or right granted to a person by a state to operate as a real estate broker or salesperson. 2. The revocable permission for a temporary use of land—a personal right that cannot be sold.

lien   A right given by law to certain creditors to have their debt paid out of the property of a defaulting debtor, usually by means of a court sale.

life estate   An interest in real or personal property that is limited in duration to the lifetime of its owner or some other designated person.

life tenant   A person in possession of a life estate.

liquidity   The ability to sell an asset and convert it into cash at a price close to its true value.

lis pendens   A public notice that a lawsuit affecting title to or possession, use and enjoyment of a parcel of real estate has been filed in either a state or federal court.

listing agreement   A contract between a landowner (as principal) and a licensed real estate broker (as agent) by which the broker is employed as agent to sell real estate on the owner's terms within a given time, for which service the landowner agrees to pay a commission.

listing broker   The broker in a multiple-listing situation from whose office a listing agreement is initiated, as opposed to the **selling broker,** from whose office negotiations leading to a sale are initiated. The listing broker and the selling broker may, of course, be the same person. *See also MULTIPLE LISTING.*

littoral rights   1. A landowner's claim to use water in large lakes and oceans adjacent to her or his property. 2. The ownership rights to land bordering these bodies of water up to the high-water mark.

lot and block description   A description of real property that identifies a parcel of land by reference to lot and block numbers within a subdivision, as identified on a subdivided **plat** duly recorded in the county recorder's office.

management agreement   A contract between the owner of income property and a management firm or individual property manager outlining the scope of the manager's authority.

marginal lease   A lease agreement that barely covers the costs of operation for the property.

marginal real estate   Land that barely covers the costs of operation.

marketable title   A good or clear salable title reasonably free from risk of litigation over possible defects; also called a *merchantable title.*

market/data approach   A method of appraising or evaluating real property based on the proposition that an informed purchaser would pay no more for a property than the cost to him or her of acquiring an existing property with the same utility. This approach is applicable when an active market provides sufficient quantities of reliable data that can be verified from authoritative sources. The approach is relatively unreliable in an inactive market or in estimating the value of properties for which no real comparable sales data are available. It is also questionable when sales data cannot be verified with principals to the transaction. Also referred to as the *market comparison* or *direct sales comparison approach.*

market price   The actual selling price of a property.

market value   The most profitable price a property will bring in a competitive and open market under all conditions requisite to a fair sale. The price at which a buyer would buy and a seller would sell, each acting prudently and knowledgeably, and assuming the price is not affected by undue stimulus.

mechanic's lien A statutory lien created in favor of contractors, laborers and materialmen or material suppliers who have performed work or furnished materials in improving real property.

metes-and-bounds description A legal description of a parcel of land that begins at a well-marked point and follows the boundaries, using direction and distances around the tract, back to the **point of beginning.**

mill One-tenth of one cent. Some states use a mill rate to compute real estate taxes; for example, a rate of 52 mills would be 5.2 cents tax for each dollar of assessed valuation of a property.

millage rate A property tax rate obtained by dividing the total assessed value of all the property in the tax district into the total amount of revenue needed by the taxing district. This millage rate then is applied to the assessed value of each property in the district to determine individual taxes.

misrepresentation To represent falsely; to give an untrue idea of a property. May be accomplished by omission or concealment of a material fact.

monetary policy The government regulation of the amount of money in circulation through such institutions as the Federal Reserve Board.

money judgment A court judgment ordering payment of money rather than specific performance of a certain action. *See also JUDGMENT.*

money market Those institutions, such as banks, savings-and-loan associations and life insurance companies, who supply money and credit to borrowers.

month-to-month tenancy A periodic tenancy—the tenant rents for one period at a time. In the absence of a rental agreement (oral or written), a tenancy generally is considered to be from month to month.

monument A fixed natural or artificial object used to establish real estate boundaries for a metes-and-bounds description.

mortgage A conditional transfer or pledge of real estate as security for a loan. Also, the document creating a **mortgage lien.**

mortgage lien A lien or charge on a mortgagor's property that secures the underlying debt obligations.

mortgagor One who, having all or part of title to property, pledges that property as security for a debt; the borrower.

multiple listing An exclusive listing (generally, an exclusive right to sell) with the additional authority and obligation on the part of the listing broker to distribute the listing to other brokers in the multiple-listing organization.

municipal ordinances The laws, regulations and codes enacted by the governing body of a municipality.

mutual rescission The act of putting an end to a contract by mutual agreement of the parties.

negligence Carelessness and inattentiveness resulting in violation of trust. Failure to do what is required.

net income The gross income of the property minus the operating expenses (not including debt service).

net lease A lease requiring the tenant to pay not only rent but also costs incurred in maintaining the property, including taxes, insurance, utilities and repairs.

nonconforming use A use of property that is permitted to continue after a zoning ordinance prohibiting it has been established for the area.

nonhomogeneity A lack of uniformity; dissimilarity. Because no two parcels of land are exactly alike, real estate is said to be nonhomogeneous or heterogeneous.

notarize   To certify or attest to a document, as by a **notary public.**

notary public   A public official authorized to certify and attest to documents, take affidavits, take acknowledgments, administer oaths and perform other such acts.

note   An instrument of credit given to attest a debt.

novation   Acceptance by parties to an agreement to replace an old debtor with a new one. A novation releases liability.

offer and acceptance   The two components of a valid contract; a "meeting of the minds."

officer's deed   A deed by sheriffs, trustees, guardians, etc.

one hundred percent commission plan   A salesperson compensation plan by which the salesperson pays his or her broker a monthly service charge to cover the costs of office expenses and receives 100 percent of the commissions from the sales that he or she negotiates.

open-end mortgage   A mortgage loan expandable by increments up to a maximum dollar amount, all of which is secured by the same original mortgage.

open listing   A listing contract under which the broker's commission is contingent on the broker's producing a **"ready, willing and able" buyer** before the property is sold by the seller or another broker; the principal (owner) reserves the right to list the property with other brokers.

option   The right to purchase property within a definite time at a specified price. No obligation to purchase exists, but the seller is obligated to sell if the option holder exercises the right to purchase.

optionee   The party that receives and holds an option.

optionor   The party that grants or gives an option.

ownership   The exclusive right to hold, possess or control, and dispose of a tangible or intangible thing. Ownerships may be held by a person, corporation or governmental entity.

package mortgage   A method of financing in which the loan that finances the purchase of a home also finances the purchase of certain items of personal property, such as a washer, dryer, refrigerator, stove and other specified appliances.

parol evidence rule   Law that states that no prior or contemporary oral or extraneously written agreement can change the terms of a contract.

partial eviction   A case in which the landlord's negligence deprives the tenant of the use of all or part of the premises.

participation financing   A mortgage in which the lender participates in the income of the mortgaged venture beyond a fixed return, or receives a yield on the loan in addition to the straight interest rate.

partition   The division of cotenants' interests in real property when the parties do not all voluntarily agree to terminate the co-ownership; takes place through court procedures.

partnership   An association of two or more individuals who carry on a continuing business for profit as co-owners. Under the law, a partnership is regarded as a group of individuals rather than as a single entity. A **general partnership** is a typical form of joint venture in which each general partner shares in the administration, profits and losses of the operation. A limited partnership is a business arrangement by which the operation is administered by one or more general partners and funded by limited or silent partners, who are by law responsible for losses only to the extent of their investment.

party wall   A wall that is located on or at a boundary line between two adjoining parcels for the use of the owners of both properties.

payee   The party that receives payment.

payor   The party that makes payment to another.

percentage lease A lease commonly used for retail property in which the rental is based on the tenant's gross sales at the premises; often stipulates a base monthly rental plus a percentage of any gross sales above a certain amount.

performance bond A binding agreement, often accompanied by surety and usually posted by one who is to perform work for another, that assures that a project or undertaking will be completed as per the agreement or contract.

periodic estate An interest in leased property that continues from period to period—week to week, month to month or year to year.

personal assistant An individual working for a broker or salesperson who handles non-sales-related aspects of real estate transactions.

personal property Items, called **chattels,** that do not fit into the definition of real property; movable objects.

physical deterioration A reduction in utility resulting from an impairment of physical condition. For purposes of appraisal analysis, it is most common and convenient to divide physical deterioration into curable and incurable components.

plat A map of a town, section or subdivision indicating the location and boundaries of individual properties.

plat book A record of recorded subdivisions of land.

point A unit of measurement used for various loan charges; one point equals 1 percent of the amount of the loan. *See also DISCOUNT POINTS.*

point of beginning The starting point of the survey situated in one corner of the parcel in a metes-and-bounds legal description. All **metes-and-bounds descriptions** must follow the boundaries of the parcel back to the point of beginning.

police power The government's right to impose laws, statutes and ordinances to protect the public health, safety and welfare, including zoning ordinances and building codes.

power of attorney A written instrument authorizing a person (the attorney-in-fact) to act on behalf of the maker to the extent indicated in the instrument.

premises The specific section of a deed that states the names of the parties, recital of consideration, operative words of conveyance, legal property description and appurtenance provisions.

prepayment clause In a mortgage, the statement of the terms on which the mortgagor may pay the entire or stated amount of the mortgage principal at some time prior to the due date.

prepayment penalty A charge imposed on a borrower by a lender for early payment of the loan principal to compensate the lender for interest and other charges that would otherwise be lost.

price fixing *See ANTITRUST LAWS.*

primary mortgage market *See SECONDARY MORTGAGE MARKET.*

principal 1. A sum lent or employed as a fund or investment, as distinguished from its income or profits. 2. The original amount (as in a loan) of the total due and payable at a certain date. 3. A main party to a transaction—the person for whom the agent works.

principal meridian One of 35 north and south survey lines established and defined as part of the rectangular survey system (government survey method).

principle of conformity The appraisal theory stating that buildings that are similar in design, construction and age to other buildings in the area have a higher value than they would have in a neighborhood of dissimilar buildings.

priority The order of position or time. The priority of liens generally is determined by the chronological order in which the lien documents are recorded; tax liens, however, have priority, even over previously recorded liens.

probate The formal judicial proceeding to prove or confirm the validity of a will or proof of heirship and to settle the affairs of the deceased.

procuring cause The effort that brings about the desired result. Under an open listing, the broker who is the procuring cause of the sale receives the commission.

property management The operation of the property of another for compensation. Includes marketing space; advertising and rental activities; collection, recording and remitting rents; maintenance of the property; tenant relations; hiring employees; keeping proper accounts; and rendering periodic reports to the owner.

property tax Taxes levied by the government against either real or personal property. The right to tax real property in the United States rests exclusively with the states, not with the federal government.

proration The proportional division or distribution of expenses of property ownership between two or more parties. Closing statement prorations generally include taxes, rents, insurance, interest charges and assessments.

prospectus A printed advertisement, usually in pamphlet form, presenting a new development, subdivision, business venture or stock issue.

public utility easement A right granted by a property owner to a public utility company to erect and maintain poles, wires and conduits on, across or under her or his land for telephone, electric power, gas, water or sewer installation.

pur autre vie A Latin term meaning "for the life of another." A life estate pur autre vie is a life estate measured by the life of a person other than the grantee. Also spelled per autrie vie.

purchase-money mortgage A note secured by a mortgage or deed of trust given by a buyer, as a mortgagor, to a seller, as a mortgagee, as part of the purchase price of the real estate.

qualification The act of determining the prospect's needs, abilities and urgency to buy and then matching these with available properties.

quitclaim deed A conveyance by which the grantor transfers whatever interest he or she has in the real estate without warranties or obligations.

range A strip of land six miles wide, extending north and south and numbered east and west according to its distance from the principal meridians in the rectangular survey system (government survey method) of land description.

"ready, willing and able" buyer One who is prepared to buy property on the seller's terms and is ready to take positive steps to consummate the transaction.

real estate Land; a portion of the earth's surface extending downward to the center of the earth and upward infinitely into space, including all things permanently attached thereto, whether by nature or by man.

real estate broker Any person, partnership, association or corporation that sells (or offers to sell), buys (or offers to buy) or negotiates the purchase, sale or exchange of real estate, or that leases (or offers to lease) or rents (or offers to rent) any real estate or the improvements thereon for others and for a compensation or valuable consideration. A real estate broker may not conduct business without a real estate broker's license.

Real Estate Settlement Procedures Act (RESPA) The federal law ensuring that the buyer and seller in a real estate transaction have knowledge of all the settlement costs when the purchase of a one-family to four-family residential dwelling is financed by a federally related mortgage loan. Federally related loans include those made by savings-and-loan associations, insured by the FHA or DVA, administered by HUD, or intended to be sold by the lenders to an agency. Prohibits kickbacks.

reality of consent An element of all valid contracts. Offer and acceptance in a contract usually are taken to mean that reality of consent also is present. This is not the case, however, if any of the following are present: mistake, misrepresentation, fraud, undue influence or duress.

real property Real property consists of land, anything affixed to it so as to be regarded as a permanent part of the land, that which is appurtenant to the land and that which is immovable by law, including all rights and interests.

REALTOR® A registered trademark term reserved for the sole use of active members of local REALTOR® boards affiliated with the National Association of REALTORS®.

recapture See *ACCELERATED DEPRECIATION.*

receiver The court-appointed custodian of property involved in litigation, pending final disposition of the matter before the court.

reconciliation The final step in the appraisal process in which the appraiser reconciles the estimates of value received from the market/data, cost and income approaches to arrive at a final estimate of market value for the subject property.

recording The act of entering or recording documents affecting or conveying interests in real estate in the recorder's office established in each county. Until recorded, a deed or mortgage generally is not effective against subsequent purchases or mortgage liens.

recovery fund A fund established in some states from real estate license funds to cover claims of aggrieved parties who have suffered monetary damage through the actions of a real estate licensee.

rectangular survey system A system established in 1785 by the federal government, which provides for surveying and describing land by reference to principal meridians and base lines.

redemption period A period of time established by state law during which a property owner has the right to redeem her or his real estate from a foreclosure or tax sale by paying the sales price, interest and costs. Many states do not have mortgage redemption laws.

redlining The illegal practice of denying loans or restricting their number for certain areas of a community.

Regulation Z A regulation of the Federal Reserve Board designed to ensure that borrowers and customers in need of consumer credit are given meaningful information with respect to the cost of credit.

release To relinquish an interest in or claim to a parcel of property.

relocation service An organization that aids a person in selling a property in one area and buying another property in another area.

remainder The remnant of an estate that has been conveyed, to take effect and be enjoyed after the termination of a prior estate, such as when an owner conveys a life estate to one party and the remainder to another.

renegotiable rate mortgage A mortgage loan that is granted for a term of 3 to 5 years and secured by a long-term mortgage of up to 30 years with the interest rate being renegotiated or adjusted each period.

rent A fixed, periodic payment made by a tenant of a property to the owner for possession and use, usually by prior agreement of the parties.

rent schedule A statement of proposed rental rates, determined by the owner or the property manager or both, based on a building's estimated expenses, market supply and demand, and the owner's long-range goals for the property.

replacement cost The cost of construction at current prices of a building having utility equivalent to the building being appraised but built with modern materials and according to current standards, design and layout.

reproduction cost The cost of construction at current prices of an exact duplicate or replica using the same materials, construction standards, design, layout and quality of workmanship and embodying all the deficiencies, superadequacies and obsolescences of the subject building.

rescission The termination of a contract by mutual agreement of the parties.

reservation in a deed   The creation by a deed to property of a new right in favor of the grantor. Usually involves an **easement,** a **life estate** or a mineral interest.

restriction   A limitation on the use of real property, generally originated by the owner or subdivider in a deed.

reverse annuity mortgage   A mortgage loan that allows the owner to receive periodic payments based on the equity in the home.

reversion   The remnant of an estate that the grantor holds after he or she has granted a life estate to another person; the estate will return or revert to the grantor. Also called a *reverter.*

reversionary right   An owner's right to regain possession of leased property on termination of the lease agreement.

rezoning   The process involved in changing the existing zoning of a property or area.

right of first refusal   A person's right to have the first opportunity to either lease or purchase real property.

right of survivorship   *See JOINT TENANCY.*

riparian rights   An owner's rights in land that borders flowing water such as a stream or river. These rights include access to and use of the water.

Rural Development   A federal agency of the U.S. Department of Agriculture that channels credit to farmers and rural residents and communities; formerly known as the Farm Service Agency and Farmer's Home Administration (FmHA).

sale and leaseback   A transaction in which an owner sells her or his improved property and, as part of the same transaction, signs a long-term lease to remain in possession of the premises.

sales contract   A contract containing the complete terms of the agreement between buyer and seller for the sale of a particular parcel or parcels of real estate.

salesperson   A person who performs real estate activities while employed by or associated with a licensed real estate broker.

satisfaction   A document acknowledging the payment of a debt.

secondary mortgage market   A market for the purchase and sale of existing mortgages, designed to provide greater liquidity for mortgages; also called the secondary money market. Mortgages are originated in the *primary mortgage market.*

section   A portion of a township under the rectangular survey system (government survey method). A township is divided into 36 sections numbered 1 to 36. A section is a square with mile-long sides and an area of one square mile, or 640 acres.

self-proving will   A will in which the witnesses give their testimony at the time of signing. This testimony is preserved in a notarized affidavit to eliminate the problem of finding the witnesses at the maker's death and to assist in the probating procedure.

selling broker   *See LISTING BROKER.*

separate property   The real property owned by a husband or wife prior to their marriage.

servient tenement   The land on which an easement exists in favor of an adjacent property (called a *dominant estate* or *tenement*) also called a *servient estate.*

setback   The amount of space local zoning regulations require between a lot line and a building line.

severalty   The ownership of real property by one person only, also called **sole ownership.**

situs   The personal preference of people for one area over another, not necessarily based on objective facts and knowledge.

sole ownership   *See SEVERALTY.*

sovereignty of the soil   The beginning of the record of ownership of land by conveyance from the sovereign or the state.

special assessment A tax or levy customarily imposed against only those specific parcels of real estate that will benefit from a proposed public improvement such as a street or sewer.

special warranty deed A deed in which the grantor warrants or guarantees the title only against defects arising during the period of his or her tenure and ownership of the property and not against defects existing before that time, generally using the language, "by, through, or under the grantor but not otherwise."

specific lien A lien affecting or attaching only to a certain, specific parcel of land or piece of property.

specific performance suit A legal action brought in a court of equity in special cases to compel a party to carry out the terms of a contract. The basis for an equity court's jurisdiction in breach of a real estate contract is the fact that land is unique, and mere legal damages would not adequately compensate the buyer for the seller's breach.

sponsoring broker A duly licensed real estate broker who employs a salesperson. Under law, the broker is responsible for the acts of her or his salespeople.

squatter's rights Those rights acquired through adverse possession. By "squatting" on land for a certain statutory period under prescribed conditions, one may acquire title by limitations. If an **easement** only is acquired, instead of the title to the land itself, one has title by prescription, or **easement by prescription.**

statute of frauds The part of a state law that requires certain instruments such as deeds, real estate sales contracts and certain leases to be in writing to be legally enforceable.

statute of limitations That law pertaining to the period of time within which certain actions must be brought to court.

statutory lien A lien imposed on property by statute, for example, a tax lien, in contrast to a voluntary lien, which an owner places on his or her own real estate, for example, a mortgage lien.

steering The illegal practice of channeling home seekers to particular areas or avoiding specific areas, either to maintain or to change the character of an area, or to create a speculative situation.

straight-line method A method of calculating depreciation for tax purposes computed by dividing the adjusted basis of a property less its estimated salvage value by the estimated number of years of remaining useful life.

subcontractor *See GENERAL CONTRACTOR.*

subdivision A tract of land divided by the owner, known as the subdivider, into blocks, building lots and streets according to a recorded subdivision plat that must comply with local ordinances and regulations.

subletting The leasing of premises by a lessee to a third party for part of the lessee's remaining term. *See also ASSIGNMENT.*

subordination A relegation to a lesser position, usually in respect to a right or security.

subordination agreement An agreement that changes the order of priority of liens between two creditors.

subrogation The substitution of one creditor for another, with the substituted person succeeding to the legal rights and claims of the original claimant. Subrogation is used by title insurers to acquire the right to sue from the injured party to recover any claims they have paid.

substitution An appraisal principle stating that the maximum value of a property tends to be set by the cost of purchasing an equally desirable and valuable substitute property, assuming that no costly delay is encountered in making the substitution.

suit for possession A court suit initiated by a landlord to evict a tenant from leased premises after the tenant has breached one of the terms of the lease or has held possession of the property after the lease's expiration.

suit for specific performance   A legal action brought by either a buyer or a seller to enforce performance of the terms of a contract.

suit (bill) to quiet title   A legal action intended to establish or settle the title to a particular property, especially when there is a cloud on the title.

summation appraisal   An approach under which value equals estimated land value plus reproduction costs of any improvements after depreciation has been subtracted.

supply   The amount of goods available in the market to be sold at a given price. The term often is coupled with **demand.**

surety bond   An agreement by an insurance or bonding company to be responsible for certain possible defaults, debts or obligations contracted for by an insured party; in essence, a policy insuring one's personal and/or financial integrity. In the real estate business, a surety bond generally is used to ensure that a particular project will be completed at a certain date or that a contract will be performed as stated.

survey   The process by which boundaries are measured and land areas are determined; the on-site measurement of lot lines, dimensions and positions of buildings on a lot, including the determination of any existing **encroachments** or **easements.**

syndicate   A combination of two or more persons or firms to accomplish a joint venture of mutual interest. Syndicates dissolve when the specific purpose for which they were created has been accomplished.

taxation   The process by which a government or municipal quasi-public body raises monies to fund its operation.

tax lien   A charge against property created by the operation of law. Tax liens and assessments take priority over all other liens.

tax rate   The rate at which real property is taxed in a tax district or county. For example, in a certain county, real property may be taxed at a rate of 56 mills (or 0.056) per dollar of assessed valuation.

tax sale   A court-ordered sale of real property to raise money to cover delinquent taxes.

tenancy at sufferance   The tenancy of a lessee who lawfully comes into possession of a landlord's real estate but who continues to occupy the premises improperly after her or his lease rights have expired.

tenancy at will   An estate that gives the lessee the right to possession until the estate is terminated by either party; the term of this estate is indefinite.

tenancy by the entirety   The joint ownership, recognized in some states, of property acquired by husband and wife during marriage. On the death of one spouse, the survivor becomes the owner of the property.

tenancy in common   A form of co-ownership by which each owner holds an undivided interest in real property as if he or she were the sole owner. Each individual has the right to partition. Unlike a joint tenancy, there is no right of survivorship between tenants in common, and owners may have unequal interests.

tenant   One who holds or possesses lands or tenements by any kind of right of title.

tenement   Everything that may be occupied under a lease by a tenant.

termination (lease)   The cancellation of a lease by the action of either party. A lease may be terminated by expiration of the term; surrender and acceptance; constructive eviction by lessor; or option when provided in the lease for breach of covenants.

termination (listing)   The cancellation of a broker-principal employment contract. A listing may be terminated by death or insanity of either party, expiration of listing period, mutual agreement, sufficient written notice or the completion of performance under the agreement.

testate   Having made and left a valid will.

testator   A male will maker.

testatrix   A female will maker.

time is of the essence   A phrase in a contract that requires the performance of a certain act within a stated period of time.

title insurance   Insurance designed to indemnify the holder for loss sustained by reason of defects in a title, up to and including the policy limits.

Torrens system   A method of evidencing title by registration with the proper public authority, generally called the registrar. Named for its founder, Sir Robert Torrens.

township   The principal unit of the rectangular survey system (government survey method). A township is a square with six-mile sides and an area of 36 square miles.

township lines   The lines running at six-mile intervals parallel to the base lines in the rectangular survey system (government survey method).

trade fixtures   The articles installed by a tenant under the terms of a lease and removable by the tenant before the lease expires.

trust   A fiduciary arrangement by which property is conveyed to a person or institution, called a **trustee,** and held and administered on behalf of another person, called a **beneficiary.**

trust deed   An instrument used to create a mortgage lien by which the mortgagor conveys his or her title to a trustee, who holds it as security for the benefit of the note holder (the lender); also called a **deed of trust.**

trustee   One who as agent for others handles money or holds title to their land.

trustee's deed   A deed executed by a trustee conveying land held in a trust.

undivided interest   *See TENANCY IN COMMON.*

unearned increment   An increase in the value of a property caused by increased population, development and demand for which the owner is not responsible.

Uniform Commercial Code   A codification of commercial law, adopted in most states, that attempts to make uniform laws relating to commercial transactions, including chattel mortgages and bulk transfers. Security interests in chattels are created by an instrument known as a security agreement. Article 6 of the code regulates bulk transfers, that is, the sale of a business as a whole, including all fixtures, chattels and merchandise.

unilateral contract   A one-sided contract by which one party makes a promise to induce a second party to do something. The second party is not legally bound to perform; if the second party does comply, however, the first party is obligated to keep the promise.

unity of ownership   The four unities traditionally needed to create a joint tenancy—unity of title, unity of time, unity of interest, unity of possession.

urban renewal   The acquisition of run-down city areas for purposes of redevelopment.

useful life   In real estate investment, the number of years a property will be useful to the investors.

usury   The practice of charging more than the rate of interest allowed by law.

valid contract   A contract that complies with all the essential elements of a contract and is binding and enforceable on all parties to it.

valid lease   An enforceable lease that has the following essential parts: lessor and lessee with contractual capacity, offer and acceptance, legality of object, description of the premises, consideration, signatures and delivery. Leases for more than one year also must be in writing.

value   The present worth of future benefits arising from the ownership of real property. To have value, a property must have utility, scarcity, effective demand and transferability.

variable rate mortgage   A mortgage loan that contains an interest rate provision related to a selected index. Under this provision, the interest rate may be adjusted annually either up or down.

Pass your exam...the <u>first</u> time

 1. Questions & Answers to Help You Pass the Real Estate Exam, 5th Edition

by John W. Reilly and Paige Bovee Vitousek
This best-selling exam guide is perfect for students preparing for today's more rigorous licensing exams--including ASI, AMP, PSI and state-developed and administered exams.
• more than 1,700 practice questions with the answers fully explained and clarified
• identifies commonly confused terms, called "false friends," to help students choose correct terms on the actual exam

Softcover, 316 pages, 8 1/2 x 11"   *Order #1970-0405*

2. ExamGuide Software

3.5" IBM-compatible disks
Order #1516-0301

 3. Real Estate Exam Guide (ASI), 4th Edition

by William H. Pivar
Chances for testing success are dramatically increased because of numerous practice questions for all the real estate topics covered on the ASI exam. So authoritative, it's like holding up a mirror to the actual ASI sales and broker exams.
• more than 650 current, ASI-style practice questions that pinpoint areas for additional review
• four 80-question sample exams weighted like the ASI exam

Softcover, 272 pages, 8 1/2 x 11"   *Order #1970-0604*

4. Real Estate Exam Guide Software: Designed for ASI Sales and Broker Exams

3.5" IBM-compatible disks
Order #1516-2401

 5. Guide to Passing the PSI Real Estate Exam, 2nd Edition

by Lawrence Sager
This up-to-the-minute, national PSI preparatory exam guide provides the edge students need to pass this challenging exam.
• more than 400 practice questions pinpoint areas that require additional review
• parallels the actual exam in topic content and question format
• answer keys for the sample exams provide rationales as well as correct answer choices

Softcover, 240 pages, 8 1/2 x 11"   *Order #1970-0902*

6. Guide to Passing the PSI Real Estate Exam Software

3.5" IBM-compatible disks
Order #1516-1301

 7. Guide to Passing the AMP Real Estate Exam

by Joyce Bea Sterling
The first-ever exam preparation tool geared specifically to the AMP exam!
• key point reviews at the end of each chapter for additional reinforcement
• answer keys that offer a brief explanation of each correct answer, helping students understand rationales.
• chapter-ending sections that highlight state or local practices
• two 100-question practice exams

Softcover, 256 pages, 8 1/2 x 11"   *Order #1970-1101*

State Specific Exam Guides also available!

 8. Key Point Review Audio Tapes for Modern Real Estate Practice

Working in tandem with Modern Real Estate Practice, the tapes illustrate complex topics and help students review and reinforce all crucial points.
• course and exam review
• a perfect "refresher" for students
• make-up materials

Set of 2 audiocassette tapes
Order #1516-0101

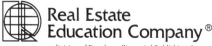 **Real Estate Education Company** ®
a division of Dearborn Financial Publishing, Inc.

155 North Wacker Drive
Chicago, Illinois 60606-1719 • 1-800-437-9002

See the order form on back for a complete listing of all exam prep materials (including state specific titles).

Real Estate Exam Study Tools Order Form

To order, fax this form to 312-836-1146 or call 1-800-437-9002

	Order Number		Product Format	Qty.	Price each	Total Amount
1.	1970-0405	Questions & Answers To Help You Pass the Real Estate Exam, 5th Edition	*Print*	_____	$24.95	_____
2.	1516-0301	Exam Guide Software-3 1/2" IBM-Compatible Disks	*Software*	_____	$39.95	_____
3.	1970-0604	Real Estate Exam Guide: ASI, 4th Edition	*Print*	_____	$24.95	_____
4.	1516-2401	Real Estate Software for ASI Sales and Broker Exams-3 1/2" IBM-Comp Disk	*Software*	_____	$39.95	_____
5.	1970-0902	Guide to Passing the PSI Real Estate Exam, 2nd Edition	*Print*	_____	$24.95	_____
6.	1516-1301	Guide to Passing the PSI Real Estate Exam Software-3 1/2" IBM-Comp Disk	*Software*	_____	$35.95	_____
7.	1970-1101	**NEW!** Guide to Passing the AMP Real Estate Exam	*Print*	_____	$24.95	_____
8.	1516-0101	Key Point Review Audio Tapes for Modern Real Estate Practice	*Audio*	_____	$25.95	_____
9.	1610-0705	Real Estate Math, 5th Edition	*Print*	_____	$18.95	_____
10.	1512-1006	Mastering Real Estate Mathematics, 6th Edition	*Print*	_____	$25.95	_____
11.	1519-1201	Mastering Real Estate Mathematics Video	*Video*	_____	$28.95	_____
12.	1517-0801	Real Estate Math. SuccessMaster Tutorial Software-Windows Based Disks	*Software*	_____	$39.95	_____
13.	1510-0213	Modern Real Estate Practice Study Guide	*Print*	_____	$15.95	_____
14.	1518-0101	Modern Real Estate Practice in **Illinois** Keypoint Review Audios	*Audio*	_____	$26.95	_____
15.	1518-0801	Modern Real Estate Practice in **New York** Keypoint Review Audios	*Audio*	_____	$27.00	_____
16.	1518-0501	Modern Real Estate Practice in **North Carolina** Keypoint Review Audios	*Audio*	_____	$27.00	_____
17.	1518-0701	Modern Real Estate Practice in **Pennsylvania** Keypoint Review Audios	*Audio*	_____	$24.95	_____
18.	1518-0901	Modern RE Practice in **Texas** Keypoint Review Audios	*Audio*	_____	$24.95	_____
19.	1518-0301	**California** Real Estate Audio Exam Guide	*Audio*	_____	$27.00	_____
20.	1970-0703	**California** Real Estate Exam Guide, 3rd Edition	*Print*	_____	$29.95	_____
21.	1516-1003	**California** Real Estate Exam Prep Software	*Software*	_____	$39.95	_____
22.	1519-1101	**California** Real Estate Video Exam Guide	*Video*	_____	$34.95	_____
23.	1610-1019	**Florida** Keypoint Review Audio Tapes for Salespersons	*Audio*	_____	$29.95	_____
24.	1610-1101	**Florida** Keypoint Review Audio Tapes for Brokers	*Audio*	_____	$34.95	_____
25.	1610-0319	**Florida** Real Estate Exam Guide, 19th Edition	*Print*	_____	$19.95	_____
26.	1970-0305	H/T Prepare for the Texas Real Estate Exam, 5th Edition	*Print*	_____	$24.95	_____
27.	1556-1202	Questions & Answers To Help You Pass the RE Appraisal Exam, 2nd Ed.	*Print*	_____	$34.95	_____
28.	1556-1301	Exam Guide for the Residential Appraisal Certification Exam	*Print*	_____	$39.95	_____
29.	1517-0101	SuccessMaster National Edition	*Software*	_____	$149.95	_____
30.	1517-0801	SuccessMaster Math Tutor	*Software*	_____	$39.95	_____

To order your software on 5.25" floppy disks, please call 1-800-437-9002

Please add applicable sales tax for the following states: CA, FL, IL, NY.

Subtotal _____
Tax _____
Shipping/Handling **$7.00**
Total _____

Please indicate form of payment:

☐ Check ☐ Credit card

☐ VISA ☐ MasterCard ☐ American Express

Card # _____

Exp. Date: ____ / ____ Signature _____
MO. YR.

Ship to:

Name _____

Company _____

Street Address _____

City _____ State _____ Zip _____

Daytime Telephone ( ) _____

Please quote source code number 707301

RISK-FREE, 100% MONEY-BACK GUARANTEE
If you are not satisfied for any reason, simply return any of the products you have ordered within 30 days in good condition for a full refund. Software products can not be returned if opened.

Real Estate Education Company®
a division of Dearborn Financial Publishing, Inc.
155 North Wacker Drive
Chicago, Illinois 60606-1719 • 1-800-437-9002

Order by FAX:
1-312-836-1146

Order by Phone:
1-800-437-9002

Pass your exam...the <u>first</u> time

Real Estate Exam Study Tools Order Form

To order, fax this form to 312-836-1146 or call 1-800-437-9002

	Order Number		Product Format	Qty.	Price each	Total Amount
1.	1970-0405	Questions & Answers To Help You Pass the Real Estate Exam, 5th Edition........	*Print*	_____	$ 24.95	_____
2.	1516-0301	Exam Guide Software-3 1/2" IBM-Compatible Disks...	*Software*	_____	$ 39.95	_____
3.	1970-0605	Real Estate Exam Guide: ASI, 5th Edition..	*Print*	_____	$ 24.95	_____
4.	1516-2401	Real Estate Software for ASI Sales and Broker Exams-3 1/2" IBM-Comp Disk....	*Software*	_____	$ 39.95	_____
5.	1970-0903	Guide to Passing the PSI Real Estate Exam, 3rd Edition....................................	*Print*	_____	$ 24.95	_____
6.	1516-1301	Guide to Passing the PSI Real Estate Exam Software-3 1/2" IBM-Comp Disk....	*Software*	_____	$ 35.95	_____
7.	1970-1101	Guide to Passing the AMP Real Estate Exam..	*Print*	_____	$ 24.95	_____
8.	1965-1032	Realty Bluebook, 32nd Edition..	*Print*	_____	$ 20.95	_____
9.	1516-0101	Key Point Review Audio Tapes for Modern Real Estate Practice........................	*Audio*	_____	$ 25.95	_____
10.	1610-0705	Real Estate Math, 5th Edition..	*Print*	_____	$ 18.95	_____
11.	1512-1006	Mastering Real Estate Mathematics, 6th Edition..	*Print*	_____	$ 25.95	_____
12.	1519-1201	Mastering Real Estate Mathematics Video...	*Video*	_____	$ 28.95	_____
13.	1517-0801	Real Estate Math SuccessMaster Tutorial Software-Windows Based Disks.......	*Software*	_____	$ 39.95	_____
14.	1510-0213	Modern Real Estate Practice Study Guide...	*Print*	_____	$ 15.95	_____
15.	1518-0801	Modern Real Estate Practice in **New York** Keypoint Review Audios...................	*Audio*	_____	$ 27.00	_____
16.	1518-0501	Modern Real Estate Practice in **North Carolina** Keypoint Review Audios...........	*Audio*	_____	$ 27.00	_____
17.	1518-0701	Modern Real Estate Practice in **Pennsylvania** Keypoint Review Audios.............	*Audio*	_____	$ 27.00	_____
18.	1518-0901	Modern Real Estate Practice in **Texas** Keypoint Review Audios.........................	*Audio*	_____	$ 27.00	_____
19.	1518-0301	**California** Real Estate Audio Exam Guide...	*Audio*	_____	$ 27.00	_____
20.	1970-0703	**California** Real Estate Exam Guide, 3rd Edition..	*Print*	_____	$ 29.95	_____
21.	1516-1003	**California** Real Estate Exam Prep Software...	*Software*	_____	$ 39.95	_____
22.	1519-1101	**California** Real Estate Video Exam Guide...	*Video*	_____	$ 34.95	_____
23.	1610-1020	**Florida** Keypoint Review Audio Tapes for Salespersons.................................	*Audio*	_____	$ 29.95	_____
24.	1610-1101	**Florida** Keypoint Review Audio Tapes for Brokers...	*Audio*	_____	$ 29.95	_____
25.	1610-0321	**Florida** Real Estate Exam Manual, 21st Edition..	*Audio*	_____	$ 29.95	_____
26.	1961-0104	Language of Real Estate..	*Print*	_____	$ 29.95	_____
27.	1556-1202	Questions & Answers To Help You Pass the RE Appraisal Exam, 2nd Ed..........	*Print*	_____	$ 34.95	_____
28.	1556-1301	Exam Guide for the Residential Appraisal Certification Exam............................	*Print*	_____	$ 39.95	_____
29.	1517-0101	SuccessMaster National Edition...	*Software*	_____	$149.95	_____
30.	1517-0801	SuccessMaster Math Tutor...	*Software*	_____	$ 39.95	_____

To order your software on 5.25" floppy disks, please call 1-800-437-9002

Please indicate form of payment:

☐ Check   ☐ Credit card

☐ **VISA**   ☐ **MasterCard**   ☐ **AMERICAN EXPRESS**

Card # _____

Exp. Date: ____ / ____ Signature_____
     MO.   YR.

Ship to:

Name _____

Company _____

Street Address _____

City_____State_____Zip_____

Daytime Telephone (___) _____

Please add applicable sales tax for the following states: CA, FL, IL, NY.

Subtotal	_____
Tax	_____
Shipping/Handling	$7.00
Total	_____

Source Code 707301

RISK-FREE, 100% MONEY-BACK GUARANTEE

If you are not satisfied for any reason, simply return any of the products you have ordered within 30 days in good condition for a full refund. Software products can not be returned if opened.

 Order by FAX:
1-312-836-1146

 Order by Phone:
1-800-437-9002

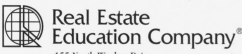 **Real Estate Education Company**®

155 North Wacker Drive
Chicago, Illinois 60606-1719 • 1-800-437-9002